Gender, Identity and Educational Leadership

Also Available From Bloomsbury

Sociology, Gender and Educational Aspirations: Girls and Their Ambitions, Carol Fuller
Evidence Informed Leadership in Education, Alison Taysum

Gender, Identity and Educational Leadership

Kay Fuller

Bloomsbury Academic
An imprint of Bloomsbury Publishing Plc

B L O O M S B U R Y
LONDON • NEW DELHI • NEW YORK • SYDNEY

Bloomsbury Academic
An imprint of Bloomsbury Publishing Plc

50 Bedford Square
London
WC1B 3DP
UK

1385 Broadway
New York
NY 10018
USA

www.bloomsbury.com

BLOOMSBURY and the Diana logo are trademarks of Bloomsbury Publishing Plc

First published 2013
Paperback edition first published 2015

British Library Cataloguing-in-Publication Data
A catalogue record for this book is available from the British Library.

ISBN: HB: 978-1-4411-6607-4
PB: 978-1-4742-3462-7
ePDF: 978-1-4411-1841-7
ePUB: 978-1-4411-3375-5

Library of Congress Cataloging-in-Publication Data
Congress Cataloging-in-Publication Data
Fuller, Kay (College teacher)
Gender, identity, and educational leadership/Kay Fuller.
pages cm
Includes bibliographical references and index.
ISBN 978-1-4411-6607-4 (hardback) – ISBN 978-1-4411-1841-7 (epdf) –
ISBN 978-1-4411-3375-5 (epub) 1. School management and organization–
Social aspects–Great Britain. 2. Educational leadership–Sex differences–Great Britain.
3. Multicultural education–Great Britain. 4. Group identity–Great Britain. I. Title.
LB2901.F87 2013
371.20941–dc23
2013020295

Typeset by Newgen Knowledge Works (P) Ltd., Chennai, India

To Mum and Dad – my first teachers –
they taught me to walk and talk;
to read and write; to love life and face death
To Lynn – for leading me through school

Contents

Tables

Acknowledgements

I am particularly grateful to the 18 headteachers who gave me an insight into their life stories and their headships. I am also grateful to the headteacher, teacher and non-teaching colleagues with whom I have worked in schools.

I am also grateful to Professor Helen Gunter, Professor Peter Ribbins, Dr Des Rutherford and Dr Christopher Rhodes for their teaching and continuing dialogue.

I would like to thank Dr Marianne Coleman whose research inspired me early in this project; also for her very helpful comments on an earlier version of Chapter 2. I am grateful to Professor Hywel Thomas for reviewing an earlier version of Chapter 3; also for ongoing dialogue about education and leadership. I am deeply grateful to Professor Christine Skelton for her insights into gender theory and continued support and guidance; also for her comments on an earlier version of Chapter 4. Thanks are also due to Professor David Gillborn for his thoughts on an earlier version of Chapter 6.

I am particularly grateful to my colleague Sheila Jackson for all her practical support and encouragement during the completion of this book. So too I am grateful to Professor Emma Smith for her educational leadership and personal support.

I have very much valued the ongoing informal dialogue with Professor Graham Butt, Dr Stephanie Prestage and Dr Nick Peim. Other colleagues too numerous to mention have also provided considerable support and conversation.

1

Context and Rationale

Aims

Gender, Identity and Educational Leadership has three main aims. First, this book provides new data about the distribution of women secondary school headteachers in local authorities across the United Kingdom. Women's under-representation as educational leaders has been well documented during the last 25 years. Secondly, it gives an insight into how far 18 women *and* men engaged in a (pro)feminist leadership discourse. Feminist scholars have linked educational leadership with concerns for social justice. Thirdly, it examines how far the headteachers' values, life roles, personal and professional experiences impacted on headteachers' recognition of differences with respect to gender, social class and ethnicity. Headteachers' recognition of diversity among the school population is likely to impact on the distribution of resources as well as status in the field of education. Unless individual and group interests are recognized there is unlikely to be representation in the leadership discourse.

Rationale

Gender has largely referred to women in the discourse about educational leadership. A number of books discuss men teachers and masculinities (Drudy et al., 2005; Haywood and Mac an Ghaill, 2003; Sargent, 2001; Thornton and Bricheno, 2006) but none of these consider the debates around gender and approaches to leadership. Instead, in the books on leadership the emphasis has been on a search for differences between women and men as school leaders (Coleman, 2002) or women's ways of leading (Grogan and Shakeshaft, 2011). Such an approach might perpetuate a view of women and men as binary opposites; and of gender as the physical embodiment of particular ways of being. It might also perpetuate stereotypes about women and men in the workplace in positions of power in the lives of the children and young people, as well as staff and wider communities.

A book is needed that draws on post-structural gender theory recognizing women and men take on multiple femininities and masculinities. Their gender performances are intersected by social class, 'race' and ethnicity, and sexuality (Connell, 2005). Their personal histories and the contexts in which they find themselves also impact on gender and leadership performances. Teachers and headteachers need to engage with post-structural gender theory to ensure that the school population is not viewed as distinct homogeneous groups defined by biological sex: women and men as staff; girls and boys as pupils. The research on which the book is based is presented through a conceptual framework that incorporates gender theory and feminist and values-led critical leadership theory.

Gender theories

A focus in Chapter 2 – *Gender and Educational Leadership* – on the under-representation of women in secondary school headship and on the fluidity of gendered leadership performance draws on seemingly contradictory gender theories. Concern about unequal opportunities for women aspiring to headship is located in feminist theories of equality and difference. The examination of fluid and complex performances of gendered leadership unconnected with the body draws on post-structural gender theory. It rejects essentialist notions of gender. Francis (2010) has used Bakhtin's (1981) literary and linguistic concepts of monoglossia and heteroglossia to reconceptualize this discursive struggle.

Gender and leadership

Second-wave feminism – Theories of equality and difference

The existing literature has largely focused on women's experiences of becoming headteachers and 'doing' headship. Management and leadership theory based on men's experiences was critiqued for its exclusion of women (Blackmore, 1989; Shakeshaft, 1987). The assumption was that men did leadership and management. Women's invisibility in the field prior to the late 1980s led to a burgeoning literature concerned with their experiences. Two main themes emerged that are linked to the questions of '*who* does leadership?' and '*how* is leadership done?' First, women's under-representation in educational leadership across the Western and developing world could be located in feminist theory of equality that argued women should not be excluded from the field because of their sex. Women are equally capable as men. However, in arguing women's socio-cultural roles have developed differently to men's in their taking greater responsibility for domestic arrangements including childcare, it can also be located in feminist theory of difference. Women's needs might be different to men's regarding career progression. Scott (1988) summarized the argument:

> Those who argue that sexual difference ought to be an irrelevant consideration in schools, employment, the courts, and the legislature are put in the equality category. Those who insist that appeals on behalf of women ought to be made in terms of the needs, interests, and characteristics common to women as a group are placed in the difference category. (p. 38)

Secondly, women's ways of doing headship should be valued equally with men's (Grogan and Shakeshaft, 2011; Shakeshaft, 1987). Indeed, educational leadership itself has been reconceptualized in a feminist critique and reconstruction of power that is used to empower rather than to control (Blackmore, 1989). A feminist construction of leadership need not be exclusive to women (Hall, 1999). The idea that men might do (pro)feminist leadership draws on post-structural theories of gender. The construction and performance of gender (and leadership) are influenced by context and circumstance (Butler, 1990, 2004).

A feminist reconstruction of leadership

Blackmore (1989) rejected a traditional masculinist construct of leadership to propose a feminist reconstruction of leadership that was 'both educative and conducive to democratic process, and, one would hope, consistent with education' (p. 93). It was based on a counter-discourse that challenged the dominant discourse promoting individualism, hierarchical relationships, bureaucratic rationality and abstract moral principles. Its key elements included:

- a view of power as multidimensional and multidirectional,
- leadership practised in different contexts by different people not merely equated to formal roles,
- leadership to empower rather than to control others,
- a relational view of morality in which moral practice is rational within given contexts and social and political relations and not according to abstract moral laws or principles,

- leadership concerned with communitarian and collective activities and values (adapted from Blackmore, 1989, p. 93).

Values-led Educational Leadership is the focus of Chapter 3. The influence of feminist scholarship on critical leadership studies has been recognized (Grace, 2000). However, feminist leadership is not exclusive to women. Hall (1999) proposed that feminist school leadership might be exercised by both women and men in the interest of social justice, 'if a feminist leader is defined as someone who is committed to identifying all kinds of injustice in education and working towards eradicating them, then men as well as women are just as likely to be feminist leaders' (p. 158). Her thinking resonated with post-structural gender theory that rejected the connection between gender and biological sex. The rejection of a universal womanhood or manhood meant masculinist leadership was not exclusive to men either. Women engaged in leadership practices designed to control and direct others (Reay and Ball, 2000).

The intersection of gender with social class, 'race' and ethnicity, disability and sexuality recognized multiple masculinities and femininities,

> black as well as white, working-class as well as middle-class. This is welcome, but it risks another kind of over-simplification. It is easy in this framework to think there is a black masculinity or a working-class masculinity. (Connell, 2005, p. 76)

Social categories need scrutiny but so do the power relations between them,

> we have to unpack the milieux of class and race and scrutinise the gender relations operating within them. There are after all gay black men and effeminate factory hands, not to mention middle class rapists and cross dressing bourgeois. (Connell, 2005, p. 76)

A social justice discourse requires the recognition of differences. Mac an Ghaill (1994) explored multiple masculinities among school pupils and staff to identify (pro)feminist as well as managerial masculinities among staff. There was a shift towards intersectionality,

> Recognizing that identity politics takes place at the site where categories intersect thus seems more fruitful than challenging the possibility of talking about categories at all. Through an awareness of intersectionality, we can better acknowledge and ground the differences among us and negotiate the means by which these differences will find expression in constructing group politics. (Crenshaw, 1991, p. 1299)

What has traditionally been ascribed as 'feminine' and 'masculine' has also been deconstructed. The complexity of gender construction or interpretation by others (including researchers) must be noted. One headteacher's colleagues constructed gendered leadership to reveal their understanding of a shifting performance of gendered educational leadership in relation to their existing narratives of gender construction (Fuller, 2010).

Gender monoglossia and heteroglossia

Like other education feminists, I am drawn to multiple, seemingly incompatible, feminist gender theories. I see both sides of the 'equality-versus-difference' debate (Scott, 1988, p. 38). I see gender as a complex and fluid performance that challenges the notion of embodied gender or sex but I remain interested in women's under-representation in leadership. It *is* an 'impossible choice' (Scott, 1988, p. 43). Attracted to multiple discourses, I have found myself rocking back and forth between them, hence the 'intellectual sea-sickness' (Raphael Reed, 2001). Alternately in stasis I might be drawn wholly into neither, hence the potential for paralysis (Francis, 1999). Francis (2010) has identified a way to conceptualize the complexity and fluidity of multiple gender performances as they are done by women/girls and men/boys as they are biologically sexed. It is possible to draw on multiple gender theories to explore what it means to be a woman or man doing gendered headship in a profession led predominantly by men. Francis (2010) used Bakhtin's linguistic and literary concepts of monoglossia and heteroglossia. Her retheorization describes my own discursive struggle.

Bakhtin (1981) described the struggle between opposing discourses as the natural state in a dialogic interaction. An individual is either drawn towards the monoglossic discourse of the dominant social group or is pushed away from it to the heteroglossic possibilities that form counter-discourses. Education feminist theorists might draw on multiple discourses of feminist theories of equality and difference as well as post-structuralist feminist discourse. It is possible to draw on older discourses to engage in new ones.

> . . . The importance of struggling with another's discourse, its influence in the history of an individual's coming to ideological consciousness, is enormous. One's own discourse and one's own voice, although born of another or dynamically stimulated by another, will sooner or later begin to liberate themselves from the authority of the other's discourse. (Bakhtin, 1981, p. 79)

Gender monoglossia enables the description of traditionally ascribed 'feminine' behaviours or speech enacted by those identified as women/girls. It enables the description of traditionally ascribed 'masculine' behaviours or speech enacted by men/boys. Gender heteroglossia describes the transgression by women/girls in doing 'masculine' behaviours; or by men/boys doing 'feminine' behaviours (Francis, 2010). Women's and men's enactments of 'masculinities' might be recognized where they exercise power to control others in masculinist approaches to leadership for example. So too, might men's and women's enactments of 'femininities' where they are nurturers of children and staff in a feminist approach to leadership. There is a nuanced mixture of compliance with, and subversion of, gender monoglossia as the researcher or reader perceives it. Francis (2010) gives the example of a girl (biologically embodied) adopting a socio-culturally expected appearance in wearing long hair as gender monoglossia. The girl's subversions of it as gender heteroglossia are her interest in maths, physical education and playing football and disinterest in anything 'blonde', 'prom queen' or 'pretty and fluffy' (Francis, 2010, p. 484).

The monoglossia associated with educational leadership ascribed as 'masculinist' (Blackmore, 1989) might also be linked with 'masculinized' education policy discourse that speaks of a market, competition and 'performativity' (Lingard and Douglas, 1999, p. 62). Alternatively, the heteroglossia of feminist, values-led and critical leadership discourses disrupts that. Headteachers' efforts to work with people to empower them might be constructed as resistance of a highly regulated, performance and audit culture (Strain, 2009). As might making space for personal values (Gold et al., 2003; Moore et al., 2002; Stevenson, 2007) even though that might be limited (Hatcher, 2005; Wright, 2003). How headteachers do leadership might be influenced by *who* they are. Their social identities as they are gendered, classed and 'raced' might impact on leadership performance and discourse. In the next section I outline Bourdieu's thinking tools used throughout the discussion of headteachers' leadership discourse.

Social theory

Our identities as they are gendered, classed and 'raced' impact on our status in families, education and the workplace. Our status impacts on our access to various forms of capital. Vincent (2003) notes:

> Our understanding of who we are, the others with whom we identify and those with whom we do not, how the social groupings to which we belong are

perceived, these factors are now understood to be key in understanding and interrogating the concept of social justice. Education, because of its crucial role in the production and reproduction of particular identities and social positionings, is a particularly fruitful site in which to consider the playing out, or the performance, of social justice and identity issues. (p. 2)

Feminist educational leadership discourse is concerned with social justice. Headteachers who recognize multiple gendered, classed and 'raced' identities among the school population might engage with distributive, cultural and associational forms of justice (Cribb and Gewirtz, 2003). In this section I explain how I use aspects of Bourdieu's social theory to think about headteachers' recognition of differences.

Bourdieu's thinking tools

Bourdieu's social theory has been used widely to theorize about education from a variety of perspectives including educational policy (Blackmore, 2010a; Thomson, 2005); knowledge production (Gunter, 2002, 2003, 2006a); school leadership (see Lingard and Christie, 2003; Thomson, 2010); parental involvement (Reay, 2000); gender (McLeod, 2005); social class (Reay, 1995); and race (McKnight and Chandler, 2012). Critiques of Bourdieu's work relate to his misrecognition of gender theory (McLeod, 2005) and race theory (Hanchard, 2003) as well as his negotiation of the structure–agency opposition (see Lovell, 2007). However, academics use his ideas as a set of thinking tools (Blackmore, 2010a; Reay, 2004). In this book I use the tools of 'habitus', 'field', 'forms of capital', 'misrecognition' and 'symbolic violence' to think about women's achievement of headship; the values on which women and men based their headship; and headteachers' recognition of differences among the school population, and the implications thereof. An explanation of what is meant by each follows.

Habitus

We must acknowledge our own, and others', 'prejudices' and 'situatedness' before engaging in meaningful dialogue (Shields and Edwards, 2005, p. 72). Situatedness is likened to Bourdieu's concept of 'habitus', it influences 'significantly how a text or another person are understood' (Shields and Edwards, 2005, p. 72). Bourdieu (2005) defines habitus as 'systems of durable, transposable dispositions' (p. 72). It provides a 'guiding map' that enables a social actor 'to adjust to the world of choices even as it remains as an unconscious activity within the mind of the social actor' (McKnight and Chandler, 2012, p. 83). Reay (1995) identifies four main aspects:

- *habitus as embodiment* (demonstrated in standing, speaking and walking as well as feeling and thinking);
- *habitus and agency* (there is a dialectic interaction between a habitus and a field, the external circumstances in which an individual finds herself; there is choice though it might be limited);
- *compilation of individual and collective trajectories* (the notion of where the habitus of individuals in the same group converges to form a collective understanding);
- *the complex interplay between past and present* (the habitus formed by early childhood is constantly modified to form layers of socialisation).

There is a sense of individual habitus formed as part of our dialectic interaction with the collective habitus enacted in a number of social fields. That might be seen as a gender, social class or ethnic habitus. The intersection of major sociological categories might help define situatedness but other factors include: 'geographical location, family structures, immediate economic circumstances, the historical events that immediately precede and surround a person – global, national, provincial, local, personal – and all the meanings that these factors hold for us' (Shields and Edwards, 2005, p. 73).

Blackmore (2010a) refers to a working-class or 'teacherly habitus' that consists of 'that practical common sense or intuitive way of knowing that mediates subjective experience and objective structures, leading to particular ways of doing, thinking, moving and speaking or dispositions' (p. 102). A gendered, classed and ethnic *head*teacherly habitus is developed through the socialization processes of interacting with family, educational and professional fields. Factors such as gender, social class, ethnicity, sexuality and disability sit alongside specific life experiences relating to family, education, faith communities, relationships and professional experiences to impact on a headteacherly habitus. Headteachers may have experienced particular moments of vulnerability in being 'beside oneself' of being 'undone' by passion, grief or rage (Butler, 2004, p. 19). Butler (2004) sees the value of reflecting on such life experiences.

> [I]f we stay with the sense of loss, are we left feeling only passive and powerless, as some fear? Or are we, rather, returned to a sense of human vulnerability, to our collective responsibility for the physical lives of one another? (Butler, 2004, p. 23)

Of course that depends on our opportunity and capacity to reflect. The debilitating impact of some experiences should not be underestimated. Grundy (1993) referred to the therapeutical discourse analogy suggested by Habermas (1974) as a means to understanding enlightenment. An internal dialogic struggle between competing discourses might result in the exercise of personal agency in embracing the heteroglossia of a pluralist society. Self-knowledge through self-reflection might be emancipatory in enabling headteachers to connect with an idea of infinitely varied forms of situatedness or habitus. So doing, their understanding of what obstructs the progress of one person more or less than another might deepen.

Field

I have referred to the interaction between habitus and field. Bourdieu (1985) describes the construction of a social space of active properties as a 'field of forces, i.e., as a set of objective power relations that impose themselves on all who enter the field and that are irreducible to the intentions of the individual agents or even to the direct interactions among the agents' (p. 724). The active properties are the different kinds of power or capital extant in the field as economic, cultural or social capital. The position of the agent in the social space is 'defined by the positions he [*sic*] occupies in the different fields, that is, in the distribution of the powers that are active within each of them' (Bourdieu, 1985, p. 724). Thus the field is multidimensional. As well as economic, cultural and social capital, there can be symbolic capital as 'prestige, reputation, renown' (p, 724). In this book, I refer to the social fields of family, education and faith communities that influence headteachers' formation of habitus and acquisition of values. The professional fields of teaching and educational leadership also inform their headteacherly habitus. Their recognition of differences among school staff and pupils also relate to the field of education. Bourdieu and Passeron (2000) argue social inequalities are reproduced in the field of education. Feminist gender theorists have critiqued Bourdieu's concept of field for removing agency (McLeod, 2005). Others see it as a way to reconcile structure and agency (Reay, 1995). McLeod (2005) sees the possibility of continuity and change in gender habitus as individuals cross and re-cross different fields.

Forms of capital

Three forms of capital available in a given field are identified as economic, cultural and social capital (Bourdieu, 1986). Economic capital can be converted into money. Cultural capital might be converted into economic capital. It also exists in other states: embodied as 'long-lasting dispositions of the mind and body' (Bourdieu, 1986, p. 47); objectified as books and access to computers and the internet; or institutionalized as educational qualifications. Social capital in the form of social connections might be converted into economic capital. However, it also impacts on the development of long-lasting dispositions as well as access to power and influence. Cultural capital in its institutionalized state is a possible explanation for the 'unequal scholastic achievement of children originating from the different social classes by relating academic success i.e., the specific profits which children from the different classes and class fractions can obtain in the academic market, to the distribution of cultural capital between the classes and class fractions' (Bourdieu, 1986, p. 47). It is of particular interest here. Headteachers are responsible for the education of children in a system that sets great store on educational qualifications as the measure of children's success and school effectiveness. Their professional success or failure is measured by the acquisition by children of cultural capital in the form of General Certificates of Secondary Education (GCSEs), A level and other qualifications that lead to further and higher education, employment and training. Their status in the field of educational leadership might afford them additional capital in the form of resources or autonomy. The academization of the school system has promised headteachers greater autonomy with regard to curriculum decisions for example. However, with regard to pupils' school experiences, external inequalities are exacerbated by the sorting arrangements of schools in an ordering of 'academic identities' (Ball, 2010). The differences between children identified as 'ability' differences obscure access to resources. This has been identified as misrecognition (Ball, 2010). Headteachers' access to, acquisition of and professional distribution of forms of capital is used to consider social class in Chapter 5.

Misrecognition

Recognition, non-recognition and misrecognition impact on our identities. Taylor (1994) argues, 'our identity is partly shaped by recognition or its absence, often by the misrecognition of others, and so a person or group of people can suffer real damage, real distortion, if the people or society around them mirror back to them a confining or demeaning or contemptible picture of themselves' (p. 25). Misrecognition is not just disrespectful, it can impose 'a grievous wound' (Taylor, 1994, p. 26). In rethinking recognition, Fraser (2000) reconceptualizes misrecognition as status subordination. Reciprocal recognition that acknowledges a need for status equality might result in 'a politics aimed at overcoming subordination by establishing the misrecognized party as a full member of society, capable of participating on a par with the rest' (Fraser, 2000, p. 113). For some an unburdening of 'excessive constructed distinctiveness' is needed; for others 'underacknowledged distinctiveness' may need to be taken into account (Fraser, 2000, p. 115). A non-identitarian politics relocates misrecognition in the institutional matrix and political economy to prioritize the redistribution of resources (Fraser, 2000). Fraser reconceptualizes a three-dimensional approach to social justice as redistribution, recognition and representation (Fraser, 2007). She argues for participatory parity in the public arena. Similarly, Cribb and Gewirtz (2003) distinguish between distributive, cultural and associational justice. Distributive justice is concerned with resources. Cultural justice is concerned with domination by one group over another, non-recognition and disrespect. Associational justice links with participatory parity in dialogue and decision-making.

Bourdieu's notion of misrecognition describes how social actors forget that what they regard as natural and obvious is arbitrary and contested, 'the historical arbitrariness of the historical institution which becomes forgotten as such by trying to ground itself in mythic reason, . . . or, more routinely, by becoming naturalized and so acquiring a recognition rooted in misrecognition' (2000, p. 94). Misrecognition of the reproduction of inequalities in schools might occur through headteachers' non-recognition or misrecognition of groups who share characteristics in common such as gender, social class and ethnicity. It might occur through misrecognition of what is required by groups to achieve educational outcomes as they are measured by the current system. It might lead to maldistribution of material resources as well as under-representation in the public sphere. More particularly it might occur in the uncritical adoption of educational policy and the uncritical perpetuation of existing organizational practices. This concept enables examination of what is recognized and why as well as what is not recognized and hidden. More importantly it enables examination of what headteachers might forget to question.

Symbolic violence

Symbolic violence occurs as the combined impact of misrecognition and lack of access to power and capital that occurs in a particular field.

> Every power to exert symbolic violence, i.e. every power which manages to impose meanings and to impose them as legitimate by concealing the power

relations which are the basis of its force, adds its own specifically symbolic force to those power relations. (Bourdieu and Passeron, 2000, p. 4)

Those who are dominated adhere to the power of the field or institution as it is exerted through rational communication (Bourdieu, 2000). They are forced to acquiesce to the 'arbitrariness of rationalized force' (Bourdieu, 2000, p. 83). Inequalities are reproduced through the institutions of schools, for example, and dominant gender, social class and ethnicity discourses. Headteachers may have experienced symbolic violence as women and men, from particular social class and ethnic backgrounds. Alternately they may have witnessed symbolic violence in the fields of family, education and the workplace.

Recognition, non-recognition and misrecognition

I have referred to the importance of recognition. Throughout this book I present and discuss headteachers' recognition of differences. Headteachers' accounts of life experiences in the formation of a headteacherly habitus are examples of *self-recognition*. Their construction of differences among the school population is discussed as *recognizing staff differences* and *recognizing pupils' differences*. Where headteachers did not recognize differences it is described as *non-recognition*. *Misrecognition* is identified where headteachers might have forgotten to question or test the reasoning behind particular ways of working. Each chapter is framed using these terms to discuss 'Gendered Leadership' (Chapter 2); 'Values-led Leadership' (Chapter 3); 'Gender' (Chapter 4); 'Social Class' (Chapter 5); and 'Ethnicity' (Chapter 6).

Policy context

The current National Curriculum (QCA, 2007) makes a commitment to promoting equal opportunities and enabling pupils to challenge discrimination and stereotyping. The most recent teacher standards require teachers to 'stretch and challenge pupils of all backgrounds, abilities and dispositions' (DfE, 2011, p. 6). They refer specifically to the Equality Act (HM Government, 2010a) and the Prevent Strategy (HM Government, 2011) to define what is meant by not undermining 'fundamental British values' including 'democracy, the rule of law, individual liberty and mutual respect and tolerance of different faiths and beliefs' (DfE, 2011, p. 4). The Prevent Strategy is specifically anti-terrorist. However, the Equality Act (HM Government, 2010a) is a recent piece of UK legislation that outlines nine characteristics 'protected' from discrimination in education, the workplace and elsewhere. These characteristics are age, disability, gender reassignment, marriage and civil partnership, pregnancy and maternity, race, religion or belief, sex and sexual orientation. There is a public sector duty for local authorities to give 'due regard to the desirability of exercising [its functions] in a way that is designed to reduce the inequalities of outcome which result from socio-economic disadvantage' (HM Government, 2010a, Part 1, 1.1). This legislation follows on from historic legislation such as the Race Relations Acts (1965, 1976), the Equal Pay Act (1970), the Sex Discrimination Act (1975), the Disability Discrimination Act (1995) and the Employment Equalities Regulations (Sexual Orientation, 2003; Religion or Belief, 2003; Age, 2006). Following the death of Stephen Lawrence, MacPherson (1999) identified a role for education and schools in preventing institutional racism. Schools should value cultural diversity through the school curriculum and prevent racism. Schools were advised to record all racist incidents; report and publish all recorded incidents; publish annually the numbers and self-defined ethnic identity of pupils excluded from school. School inspections should examine the implementation of such strategies. The Coalition government has also made a commitment to tackling homophobic bullying in schools (HM Government, 2010b).

Why headteachers' recognition of differences matters

At the time this research took place government educational policies included Every Child Matters (DfES, 2003a) and Personalizing Learning (DfES, 2004a). The first focused largely on children's welfare, the second on their learning. Each used the rhetoric of child-centred education. Simultaneously, the teaching workforce was being remodelled (DfES, 2003b). Headteachers were concerned with policy initiatives that impacted on school operational management and organization as well as pedagogical practice in a socially inclusive and welfarist framework. New Labour educational policy has been widely critiqued (see, for example, the December 2008 issue of *Oxford Review of Education*). There was concern too for the impact of gender, social class and ethnic background on educational achievement. Research findings were shared regarding gender (DCSF, 2009a–c); social class (DCSF, 2009d) and ethnicity (DfES, 2005). By contrast, current localist educational policy that decentralizes/recentralizes education is unlikely to reconcile the tension between autonomy and the equity agenda that

New Labour tried to promote (Lupton, 2011). It is precisely because schools are being removed from the processes of local democratic accountability as part of local authorities that we should be interested in headteachers' recognition of diversity among the school workforce and pupil population.

The research project

The research project comprised three stages. First was a statistical survey of the distribution of women secondary school headteachers across England and Wales in 2005 (Fuller, 2009). Those findings have been updated in 2010 for this book and now include Scotland and Northern Ireland. The survey contextualizes the second and third stages of research. The second stage followed Coleman (2002) to ascertain women's and men's experiences of becoming and being headteachers. A high proportion of headteachers claimed they were aware of individual differences (Coleman, 2002; Fuller, 2009). The third stage used semi-structured face-to-face interviews with 18 secondary school headteachers (nine women and nine men) in a single English urban local authority to investigate headteachers' construction of individual differences among the pupil and staff populations. The findings of the third stage are reported here.

Headteachers provided detailed responses to questions about the life experiences that influenced their management and leadership; the life roles that influenced their headship; and how their personal values influenced headship. They were asked to identify the individual differences between pupils in the school and how the curriculum catered for individual needs. Headteachers also identified the individual differences between staff working in the school and how they catered for their individual needs. Finally, they were asked to cite further examples of how their awareness of individual differences informed headship. These were conversations with a purpose (Ribbins, 2007). Semi-structured interviews lasted for between one and two hours. They were recorded and transcribed. Transcripts were coded using Nvivo 8 to identify headteachers' discourse of difference in relation to themselves, the staff and pupils. They were re-coded specifically with regard to gender, social class and ethnicity. Headteachers provided biographical detail that may be sensitive. They gave full written and informed consent to my use of data. However, their participation in this qualitative research relied on my trustworthiness in reporting the findings anonymously. All the headteachers have been given pseudonyms. At the time of writing 13 no longer work in the same schools.

Schools have not been identified. Occasionally, where relevant, types of school have been referred to as comprehensive, selective, independent; mixed or single sex; faith; and schools for 11–16- or 11–18-year-olds. There are occasions where identifying the sex of a headteacher is sufficient. There is also clearly a benefit of making the link or noting the gap between headteachers' personal histories and their engagement with particular leadership discourses. Just as there is a benefit in linking or noting the gaps. I have provided some case studies to demonstrate such links in Chapters 2 and 7. In Chapters 4–6 I have identified distinct headteacher groups as *gender aware* or *unaware*; *class aware* or *unaware*; and *ethnicity aware* or *unaware* to consider the connections and gaps between formative personal and professional experiences and headteacherly habitus.

I have taken a narrative approach that provides a less sanitized construction of leadership and management than that of much of the literature (Cowie and Crawford, 2009). Narrative accounts are context bound, in other words the same process might yield different results at a different time. Interviews took place during the middle term of the New Labour government between 2003 and 2005. Consequently, headteachers revealed the pressing concerns of that time. I have used headteachers' words to enable nuanced meanings to surface throughout my discussion. There is a sense of lived reality. As such it is located in the humanistic knowledge province in its concern with 'gathering and theorizing from the experiences and biographies of those who are leaders and managers and those who are managed and led' (Gunter and Ribbins, 2003, p. 133). However, it is also located in the critical province in its concern 'to reveal and emancipate practitioners from injustice and oppression of established power structures' (Gunter and Ribbins, 2003, p. 133).

The limitations of a small sample size and the self-reported accounts of headteachers must be acknowledged. I am mindful that these interview responses only provide a glimpse. Headteachers do not necessarily convey accurate portraits of their leadership practice (Gronn, 2007). I refer to leadership discourse because these are self-reports; headteachers talked about practice. So doing they located their thoughts and feelings in broader discourses. To consider leadership practice I would need to engage in an ethnographic study that enabled observations over a period of time and access to the views of others. It is important to note that my gender, social class and ethnic identities might impact on the interpretation of headteachers' constructions of difference. My professional experiences might impact on my interpretation of headteachers' educational leadership discourse. There follow some brief biographical details about the researcher.

The researcher

I am a single, White, middle-class woman working in higher education. I construct my family origins as manual working class. My family's educational aspirations and free higher education enabled me to study for an English degree after completing A levels. Following graduation I worked in retail management. My understanding of gender theories has enabled me to retrospectively recognize the glass ceiling I hit in retail management. At the time I constructed my desire for a career change as motivated by being frustrated with the business world and wanting to do something beneficial for others. I studied for a Postgraduate Certificate in Education (PGCE) and entered teaching as a mature student. A successful secondary school teaching career led to taking on posts in middle and senior school leadership. I have deconstructed my frustrations in senior school leadership as resistance of a system I disliked. I moved into higher education to lead the Initial Teacher Education course for secondary English teachers. I have continued my research into gender and educational leadership. Throughout my school teaching career I engaged with further study by taking higher degrees largely in educational leadership and management. My education has given me the social mobility some headteachers describe in this research. I have come to value the labyrinthine path my various careers have taken and the insights that has given me.

The authority

This research took place in a large urban authority in England. Headteachers were working in 18 schools in wards described in Table 1.1. Schools were geographically located in the city centre, to the east, south, west and north of the centre inner ring and in the outer ring. Details are given in Table 1.1 of the proportion of the population in relation to the average for the city for ethnicity and worklessness and unemployment. It is possible to see that some schools were located in wards where the majority of the population was Black and global majority/Black and minority ethnicity (BGM/BME) or White; where the majority of the population were either in or out of work. I aim to give a flavour of the demographic context. Estimates show that in 2009 63.3 per cent of the population were White British with 2.1 per cent being White Irish and 2.6 per cent being White Other. The next largest group was Asian or Asian British – Pakistani (9.7%) followed by Asian or Asian British – Indian (5.8%) and Black Caribbean (4%). The total proportion of BGM people was 32 per cent.

Table 1.1 Sample of schools by ward including descriptions of population by BME background and in relation to worklessness and unemployment

Ward	No. of schools	Geographical location	Proportion of population of BME backgrounds in relation to authority average	Proportion of worklessness/ unemployment in relation to authority average
A	1	Central	Higher	Well above
B	1	Inner ring	Significantly above	Above
C	1	Outer ring	Below	Average worklessness but higher unemployment
D	1	Outer ring	Below	Above
E	1	Outer ring	Below	Below
F	1	Inner ring	Similar	Below
G	2	Inner ring	Slightly above	Similar
H	3	Outer ring	Below	Below
I	1	Outer ring	Below	Below
J	1	Outer ring	Below	Worklessness higher but unemployment below
K	2	Outer ring	Above	Well above
L	1	Outer ring	Lower	Below
M	1	Outer ring	Higher	Worklessness below but unemployment similar
N	1	Outer ring	Below	Well below

The schools

Headteachers worked in a range of schools as community comprehensive, selective and independent schools; mixed and single-sex schools; 11–16 and 11–18 schools; special; and faith schools. School size ranged from less than 500 pupils on roll to almost 1,500. Table 1.2 gives school-level data regarding type of school, sex and age of pupils, number on roll, the ethnic mix, proportion of pupils eligible for free school meals (FSM), pupils with special educational needs (SEN) and pupils with English as an additional language (EAL). The information was taken from Ofsted inspection reports where available. This table reflects inconsistencies in the language used in the reporting of pupil population data by Ofsted.

School type	Sex and age	Number of pupils on roll	Ethnic mix	Proportion of pupils eligible for FSM	Pupils with SEN
Faith comprehensive	Mixed 11–16	500–1,000	58% BME	Well above average	No data
Faith comprehensive	Mixed 11–16	Less than 500	75% Pakistani	High proportion	Increasing nu
Community comprehensive	Mixed 11–18	1,000–1,500	87% White British with White Irish, Indian, other Asian heritages, Black British Caribbean as well as Mixed heritage students	Broad mix	Below averag
Community comprehensive	Mixed 11–18	1,000–1,500	Predominantly White with BME proportion lower than national average	Very substantially above average	Average prio attainment below nati average
Community comprehensive	Mixed 11–18	1,000–1,500	40%	40%	6%
Comprehensive	Boys 11–16	500–1,000	Predominantly White with large Pakistani group	Well above average	Above avera learning d
Selective independent	Girls 11–18	500–1,000	No data	No data	No data
Selective independent	Boys 11–18	500–1,000	No data	No data	No data
Community comprehensive	Mixed 11–18 with 60% boys	1,000–1,500	Majority White with Black Caribbean	Above average	Below avera

munity nprehensive	Mixed 11–18	500–1,000	76% White British	High well above average	High proportion
al school	Mixed 11–19	Below 500	White British background with other significant ME groups: Asian British-Pakistani, Asian British Indian, Black British Caribbean	No data	Moderate learning difficulties but increasing numbers with complex difficultie
al school	Mixed 11–19	Below 500	No data	No data	All
munity prehensive	Mixed 11–16	500–1,000	Two-thirds ME with White other the highest proportion	Very high	Above average
ive	Boys 11–18	500–1,000	85% BME with Pakistani and Indian largest groups	52%	Attainment high
ive	Girls 11–18	500–1,000	One-third White British; one-third Asian and Asian British	Below average, socio-economically advantaged in general	Some dyslexia but n registered SEN
munity rehensive	Mixed 11–16	500–1,000	54% ME; 28% Asian; 15% Black African Caribbean; 11% other groups; 46% White	28%	30%
munity rehensive	Girls 11–18	500–1,000	Multicultural school; three-fourths Indian or Pakistani background; one-fifth Afro-Caribbean; fewer than 4% White British	50%	50% with low readi levels on arrival
ive	Girls 11–18	500–1,000	Majority White British, sizeable proportion of Asian Indian; small numbers from each of a very large number of ME groups	Socio-economically well above average	Very high proportic of physical, social, emotional or behavioural difficul

Table 1.3 Headteachers by sex and school type

School type	Women	Men
Comprehensive	5	6
Selective	3	2
Special	1	1
11–16	2	3
11–18	7	6
Mixed	5	6
Single sex	4	3
Faith	0	2

The headteachers

Women and men were working in the full range of schools. Table 1.3 shows how many women and men in the sample were leading each type of school. Throughout I refer to 'women'/'female' and 'men'/'male' simply to identify the biological sex of headteachers, staff or pupils. My use of the terms 'feminist'/'feminine'/'femininity' and 'masculinist'/'masculine'/'masculinity' denote gender performance and are not linked to biological sex.

Structure of the book

This book comprises seven chapters. Following this introductory chapter, Chapter 2 (*Gender and Educational Leadership*) comprises two distinct parts. In the first, it reports the distribution of women secondary school headteachers by local authority in England, Wales, Scotland and Northern Ireland in 2010. There are nuanced variations between local authorities. There is limited access to headship for BGM/BME women and men and lack of information about headteachers' social class origins. The second part uses Blackmore's (1989) feminist reconstruction of leadership and literature about women's leadership to examine headteachers' accounts of leadership. Links and gaps are identified between headteacherly habitus (informed by personal and professional experiences) and gendered leadership discourse. Chapter 3 takes forward the notion of *Values-led Leadership* to examine headteachers' values formation and their handling of values conflicts with staff, and pupils and families.

Chapters 4–6 are concerned with headteachers' recognition of differences among the school population. Chapter 4 (*What Diversity Means to Headteachers:*

Gender) uses headteachers' accounts of personal and professional experiences to identify two distinct groups of headteachers as *gender aware* or *gender unaware*. By this, I simply mean the former group recounted experiences demonstrating experience or awareness of unequal gender relations. Included are headteachers who experienced the symbolic violence of direct sex discrimination and headteachers who witnessed unequal gender relations in the fields of family, education and/or the workplace. The second group might also be aware of unequal gender relations but did not recount any examples. In other words, unequal gender relations did not pervade their life history accounts. The findings regarding headteachers' recognition of gender differences among pupils and staff are presented by headteacher group.

Chapter 5 (*What Diversity Means to Headteachers: Social Class*) is concerned with similar groups of headteachers as either *class aware* or *class unaware*. Again unequal social class relations did not pervade the latter group's biographical accounts. Headteachers' recognition of differences with regard to social class is presented as two separate groups. The connections and gaps between headteacherly habitus and headteachers' recognition of unequal social class relations are revealed. In Chapter 6 (*What Diversity Means to Headteachers: Ethnicity*), I identify a group as *ethnically aware* and the remaining headteachers as *ethnically unaware*. Again I look for the connections and gaps between habitus and recognition of differences with regard to ethnicity. The book ends with a chapter that looks at the implications of the research in identifying nine misrecognitions about

- the reasons for women's under-representation in headship,
- connections between biological sex and gendered leadership,
- shared understandings of transrational values,
- group desires, interests and needs,
- the impact of an equality discourse,
- gender relations among pupils,
- engagement with parents across differences,
- the impact of curriculum choices and grouping arrangements,
- endemic racism.

It encourages head/teachers to reflect on their own experiences and constructions of difference.

2

Gender and Educational Leadership

Introduction

There is a considerable mismatch between the proportion of women in the English teaching workforce and those reaching headship. About 61.5 per cent of the secondary school teaching workforce is women but women comprise only 36 per cent of headteachers (DfE, 2012). In 2008, the National College for School Leadership (NCSL, 2008) reported an 'all time high' of women secondary headteachers at 36 per cent. That increase was partly explained by removing the Welsh authorities from the data and there has been no further increase (see Fuller, 2009). There remains concern about the career progression of women in the United Kingdom (see McNamara et al., 2008, 2010). In Chapter 1, I provided an overview of gender theories relating to educational leadership. Concern for women's under-representation is located in feminist theories of equality and difference (Blackmore, 1989; Shakeshaft, 1987).

Post-structural gender theories conceptualize gender as performance that is unfixed to biological sex (Butler, 1990). Thus a feminist reconstruction of leadership that uses power to empower rather than to control (Blackmore, 1989) is not exclusive to women (Hall, 1999). So too the notion of multiple femininities and masculinities as they intersect or interact with social class, ethnicity and sexuality rejects the notion of a universal woman/manhood (Connell, 2005). Yet experiences of sex discrimination against some women and girls make concern with women's career progress and the education of girls a continued priority. This engagement with seemingly contradictory gender theories has been conceptualized as gender monoglossia and heteroglossia (Francis, 2010). It makes possible a discussion about women and men's (as they are biologically sexed) leadership of schools staffed by women and men and populated by girls and boys while recognizing gender performance is not fixed to the body.

In this chapter I address three broad areas found in the literature. First, there is discussion of women's under-representation. I update findings about the distribution of women secondary headteachers across the United Kingdom. Secondly, the notion of androgynous educational management and leadership style (a concept used to explain the lack of differences between women and men 'doing' headship) is re-examined to illustrate the fluidity of gender performance. Thirdly, I link Blackmore's (1989) feminist reconstruction of leadership with Grogan and Shakeshaft's (2011) five approaches that 'characterize women's educational leadership' (p. 2) and Gray's (1993) 'gender paradigms' to analyse headteachers' leadership discourse. I refer specifically to two headteachers who engage with feminist leadership discourse and two who do not. Finally, there is a summary of key points as advice and guidance for teachers and aspiring headteachers.

Under-representation of women

The under-representation of women in educational leadership has been reported across the Western world in the United States (Shakeshaft, 1987), Australia (Blackmore, 1999), Europe (Wilson, 1997) and the United Kingdom (Adler et al., 1993; Coleman, 2002; Edwards and Lyons, 1994; Fuller, 2009; Hall, 1996; McLay and Brown, 2000; McNamara et al., 2008, 2010; Ouston, 1993; Ozga, 1993). Concern for women's equal access to management and leadership posts is located in feminist theories of equality and difference (see Chapter 1). This book focuses specifically on secondary school headship, however women are under-represented in each phase from primary school (see Thornton and Bricheno, 2000) through secondary school to further (see Shain, 2000) and higher education (see, for example, Brooks and McKinnon, 2001). Research in the United Kingdom has included women from various sectors and school phases (Adler et al., 1993; Grace, 1995; Hall, 1996; Jirasinghe and Lyons, 1996; Ouston, 1993; Ozga, 1993). However, there is relatively little writing that focuses on women secondary school headteachers in England (Cliffe, 2011; Coleman, 1996a,b, 2000, 2001; Edwards and Lyons, 1994; Gray, 1989, 1993; Moreau et al., 2007, 2008; Reay and Ball, 2000; Smith, 2011). Other than this research (Fuller, 2009, 2012) only Coleman's gender-focused research has included women *and* men (2002, 2003a,b, 2005a,b). Increasing the visibility of women leaders in educational research carried out largely by women researchers is located in feminist theory of equality. Women seek equal access to social power by demonstrating they are equally able as men.

Reasons for women's under-representation comprise a complex range of interacting factors as: (1) socialization and stereotyping; (2) internal barriers; and (3) macro (societal), meso (organizational) and micro (personal) level culture and tradition factors (Cubillo and Brown, 2003). In England, women's disproportionate responsibility for childcare and domestic arrangements, alongside direct and indirect discrimination during the selection process and among workplace peers (Coleman, 2002, 2005a; Fuller, 2009; Ozga, 1993; Ribbins and Marland, 1994) works at all three levels. Women are socialized into taking greater responsibility for home and family fulfilling the stereotype in so doing. They consequently perpetuate cultural barriers. As headteachers and homemakers/mothers/carers they undertake multiple roles 'striking a balance' (Coleman, 2002, p. 149) between career and family. Women headteachers were more likely to be single and have fewer children than men (Coleman, 2002; Fuller, 2009) suggesting many choose not to perform multiple roles. While reasons for women's under-representation may vary nationally, there are regional variations that need further investigation within the United Kingdom (see Tables 2.1 and A1–A5).

Regional variations

Women are under-represented in secondary school headship in England, Wales, Scotland and Northern Ireland as demonstrated by comparisons between the proportion of women in teaching and headship posts (see Table 2.1).

Table 2.1 Comparison between the proportion of women teachers and headteachers in the United Kingdom

	England (%)	Wales (%)	Scotland (%)	Northern Ireland (%)
Proportion of secondary school women teachers in 2005 (McNamara et al., 2008)	58	33	59	63
Proportion of women state secondary school headteachers in 2005 (Fuller, 2009)	29.9	17.2	No data	No data
Proportion of women state secondary school headteachers in 2010 (collated from www.schoolswebdirectory.co.uk)	35.5	26.5	27	29.8

There has been speculation about regional variations (Edwards and Lyons, 1994) with recent investigations revealing similar variations continue to exist (Coleman, 2005a; Fuller, 2009, and see Tables A1–A5: Distribution of women secondary school headteachers by local authority in England, Wales, Scotland and Northern Ireland).

Research in the north-east revealed the male domination of school headship (Grace, 1995). Women were accommodated in a largely 'enduring culture of male leadership' (Grace, 1995, p. 190). While there has been improvement in some authorities, inconsistencies remain. The proximity to London has been advantageous for women.

> The London effect is apparent, with Birmingham being the only other large city with a relatively large number of female secondary heads. . . . The presence of more female heads therefore does not appear to be a distinctly urban phenomenon but does seem to be regionally biased. (Coleman, 2005a, p. 9)

Women were better represented in regions surrounding London confirming the 'ILEA effect' that equal opportunity policies were 'pursued with . . . exceptional commitment and resources' (Edwards and Lyons, 1994, p. 8). Believing they could succeed women perpetuated a cycle of success and succession. Role models and mentors were available. Lack of role models and mentors has been cited as a barrier (Coleman, 2002; Edwards and Lyons, 1994). In areas where there are few women headteachers they are lost or never existed.

There has been a long tradition of liberal education for girls in Birmingham (Watts, 1998) that may have contributed to women's success there. The literature cites women who identified influential role models in single-sex schools (Ozga, 1993); as well as those denying they had a positive impact (Ribbins and Marland, 1994). The inherent conservatism of the north-east (Grace, 1995) might prevail in areas such as Wales, preventing women from aspiring not only to headship but from entering teaching at all, though that appears to be improving (McNamara et al., 2008). There may still be a need for further equal opportunities training for school governing bodies whose members comprise selection panels (Coleman, 2005a; Edwards and Lyons, 1994; Grace, 1995).

Regional variations have also been identified in the international literature. Women have been represented in school principalship in greater proportions in South Australia where 'gender equity has been pursued for a long period and in a committed fashion' (Lingard and Douglas, 1999, p. 85); and in Jewish secular public high schools (Addi-Raccah, 2006). However, it remains the case that women are under-represented in school leadership worldwide (see Sobehart, 2009).

The distribution of women secondary school headteachers (UK)

Table 2.1 demonstrated the gap between the proportion of women teachers and headteachers. Tables A1–A5 list the distribution of women by local authority in England, Wales, Scotland and Northern Ireland.

Recognizing women headteachers

Table 2.2 lists 27 authorities in England where 50 per cent or more secondary headteachers were women in 2010. Women make up 61.5 per cent of the English secondary teaching workforce (DfE, 2012); 33 per cent in Wales, 59 per cent in Scotland and 63 per cent in Northern Ireland (McNamara et al., 2008). In just six English local authorities the proportion of women matches or exceeds the overall proportion of women in the teaching workforce. Two are London boroughs – Richmond-Upon-Thames and Waltham Forest; two are in non-metropolitan districts in south – Luton and Southampton; two are in metropolitan districts in the north-west – Knowsley and Stockport. Table 2.2 also shows the change between 2005 and 2010. In some cases there have been considerable increases or decreases.

There were fewer women than men in the secondary teaching workforce in Wales in 2005. Thus women are proportionately represented in headship in seven authorities where there are 33 per cent or more women headteachers. In Denbighshire and Monmouth over 50 per cent of headteachers were women. Again there was considerable change in some authorities between 2005 and 2010 (see Table 2.3).

In Scotland, there was a similar proportion of women in the teaching workforce to England (see Table 2.1). In two authorities, 50 per cent of headteachers were women (see Table 2.4).

Not recognizing women as headteachers

Of Northern Ireland's five education authorities there were none where the proportion of women headteachers matched that in the teaching workforce (see Table A5). In Belfast, 42.9 per cent of headteachers were women. Elsewhere the proportion of women ranged from 31.8 per cent in the western Education and Library Board (ELB) to as few as 23.5 per cent in the southern ELB. In Scotland,

Table 2.2 Local authorities in England where 50 per cent or more secondary headteachers are women

Local authority	Size of authority (no. of schools)	Proportion of women, 2005 (%)	Proportion of women, 2010 (%)	Difference (%)
Blackpool	8	37.5	50.0	12.5
Enfield	18	50	50.0	0.0
Hackney	10	87.5	50.0	-37.5
Hammersmith and Fulham	8	25	50.0	25.0
Harrow	10	45.5	50.0	4.5
Hounslow	14	50	50.0	0.0
Islington	10	33.3	50.0	16.7
Leicester	20	43.8	50.0	6.2
North Lincolnshire	12	35.7	50.0	14.3
Solihull	14	46.2	50.0	3.8
Southwark	10	57.1	50.0	-7.1
East Sussex	27	37	51.9	14.9
Newham	15	66.7	53.3	-13.4
Oldham	15	13.3	53.3	40.0
Bath and North East Somerset	13	46.2	53.8	7.6
Bristol	18	33.3	55.6	22.3
Poole	9	37.5	55.6	18.1
Lewisham	14	53.8	57.1	3.3
Reading	7	42.9	57.1	14.2
Camden	10	55.6	60.0	4.4
Kingston-Upon-Thames	10	30	60.0	30.0
Richmond-Upon-Thames	8	50	62.5	12.5
Stockport	14	21.4	64.3	42.9
Southampton	12	50	66.7	16.7
Waltham Forest	17	58.8	70.6	11.8
Knowsley	9	45.5	77.8	32.3
Luton	12	66.7	83.3	16.6

there were no women headteachers at all in three authorities. There were fewer than 20 per cent in seven other urban and rural authorities (see Table A4). Similarly, in Wales there were no women in Ceredigion and 20 per cent or fewer women headteachers in a further nine urban and rural authorities (see Table A3).

Table 2.3 Local authorities in Wales where 33 per cent or more secondary headteachers are women

Local authority	Size of authority (no. of schools)	Proportion of women, 2005 (%)	Proportion of women, 2010 (%)	Difference (%)
Denbighshire	8	50	75	25
Pembrokeshire	8	25	50	25
Monmouth	5	50	40	10
Rhondda Cynon Taff	19	21.1	36.8	15.7
Caerphily	16	31.3	35.7	4.4
Powys	14	15.4	35.7	20.3
Wrexham	9	22.2	33.3	11.1

Table 2.4 Local authorities in Scotland where 50 per cent or more secondary headteachers are women

Local authority	Size of authority (no. of schools)	Proportion of women, 2005	Proportion of women, 2010 (%)	Difference
Orkney Islands	4	No data	50	No data
Perth and Kinross	10	No data	50	No data

In England, fewer than 20 per cent of headteachers were women in three London boroughs; and in five authorities in the English metropolitan districts. There were no women in two authorities in the English non-metropolitan districts. There were 20 per cent or fewer women in eight further urban and rural authorities (see Tables A1 and A2). There is no simple interpretation of these data. Qualitative research is needed at authority and school levels to establish the reasons for such inconsistencies.

Women's absence from headship constitutes their non-recognition at many levels. They are not given voice in public arenas at local, regional and national levels (Cribb and Gewirtz, 2003; Fraser, 2007). Their absence is likely to lead to women teachers' non-recognition as potential leaders. That some women believe they exercise agency in their career choices might demonstrate their underestimation of the impact of structural barriers (Moreau et al., 2007; Smith, 2011). While I do not suggest women are 'passive dupes' (Smith, 2011, p. 22) there is possible misrecognition of the reasons for under-representation by women themselves, headteachers and others. Long-held assumptions may need to be challenged. The gender regimes of schools and senior leadership teams need further investigation at authority and school levels (McNamara et al., 2010). National training programmes such as the National Professional Qualification for Headship (NPQH) and Leading from the Middle (LftM) have provided opportunities for women to network in person and online (McNamara et al., 2008). Even so these leadership development programmes 'carefully ignored' (Coleman and Fitzgerald, 2008, p. 129) gender issues such as work/life balance and women's career progression disadvantages due to family responsibilities, ethnicity and other equity issues. Women already aspiring to educational leadership access such programmes; some women's aspirations are blocked long before that.

Misrecognition of women's achievement of headship

In Chapter 1, I explained Bourdieu's notion of misrecognition and the subsequent symbolic violence that occurs when the reasons for a given situation remain forgotten or uncontested. I do not doubt that historical and structural barriers to women's advancement remain in place. However, my analysis of the distribution of women headteachers by authority only enables a nuanced understanding of *where* in the United Kingdom women have achieved headship against the odds (Coleman, 2001). There are points to be made about the misrecognition of women's achievement of leadership regarding *which* women succeed. First, there is little research into women's achievement of headship with regard to their ethnicity, social class origins, sexuality and disability. A statistical analysis of the distribution of women misrecognizes the importance of the intersections of gender with BGM/BME heritage (Crenshaw, 1991). The proportions of BME women (and men) who achieved headship remain 'worryingly low' (McNamara et al., 2008, p. iii). Indeed 3.1 per cent of secondary school headteachers were from BME backgrounds compared with 8.6 per cent of classroom teachers (DfE, 2012). About 4.4 per cent of women secondary headteachers and 2.6 per cent of men were from BME backgrounds compared with 8.4 and 8.8 per cent of classroom teachers (DfE, 2012). Government data breaks down ethnic groups further. Lumby with Coleman (2007) notes there has been little attention paid to the ethnicity of staff. Three studies (Bush et al., 2006; McKenley and Gordon, 2002; McNamara et al., 2009) are concerned with the ethnicity of educational leaders. The themes of barriers to promotion and appointment, the experience of being a Black manager and leader, affirmative action, specially designed training and development for BME leaders and generic leadership development relating to ethnicity and diversity have emerged (Lumby with Coleman, 2007). A further study investigates the career progression of leaders in London (Coleman and Campbell-Stevens, 2010). Two programmes for BGM/BME leaders, Investing in Diversity (Campbell-Stevens, 2009; Coleman and Campbell-Stephens, 2010; Johnson and Campbell-Stevens, 2010, 2013) and Equal Access to Promotion (Ogunbawo, 2012) have been reported (see Chapter 6 for further discussion). There is little known about headteachers' social class origins. As members of a graduate profession, headteachers have acquired cultural capital associated with being middle class. However questions remain about the proportion of headteachers who may be first generation graduates who achieved social mobility (see Chapter 5 for further discussion). There is a heteronormative approach in the literature that reports the experiences of women balancing careers with the demands of relationships and motherhood that reports relationships in terms of marital status. A gap remains in the literature with regard to lesbian and gay, bisexual, transgendered and questioning (LGBTQ) headteachers' experiences of becoming and being headteachers. Lumby with Coleman (2007) notes compared to sex, ethnicity and disability there is uncertainty about recording sensitive areas such as sexual orientation and religion for monitoring purposes.

Secondly, there may be underestimation of the impact of structures and overestimation of the exercise of women teachers' agency (Moreau et al., 2007; Smith, 2011). Bourdieu's notions of habitus and field have been critiqued by feminists for leaving too little space for reflexivity and human agency, for collapsing habitus into the social field of its production (see Lovell, 2007; McLeod, 2005). However, Reay (2004) sees such criticism as ironic when the rationale for their development was an 'an attempt to transcend dualisms of agency-structure, objective-subjective and the micro-macro' (p. 432). Nevertheless, an individual's access to particular forms of capital in the social fields of family and education will variously impact on their career progression (see Chapter 5 for further discussion). Neither Reay (2004) nor McLeod (2005) see habitus and field as wholly restrictive. Each sees the possibilities of continuity and change, perhaps women teachers have seen it in a similar way (Moreau et al., 2007; Smith, 2011).

Thirdly, there is a danger that recent educational policy designed to divorce schools from local authorities through academization may result in less monitoring of equality and diversity issues in the recruitment and promotion of staff as well as pupil attainment. The loss of 'centralism' might take the equity agenda backwards for staff as well as pupils (Lupton, 2011; Raffo, 2011). While the discourse around gendered educational leadership has shifted to a conceptualization of *how* educational leadership is done, there is still a debate to be had about *who* is doing it. Further exploration is needed of the reasons for regional differences in order to replicate or develop successful initiatives in areas where there remain unequal opportunities for women. In the section that follows I move from the consideration of *who* does leadership to explore *how* leadership is done.

Approaches to leadership

Research taking an essentialist approach, suggesting leadership differences might be based on biological sex found few differences between women and men (Coleman, 2002; Fuller, 2009; Jirasinghe and Lyons, 1996). Women and men drew on a range of gendered attributes and qualities from both 'gender paradigms' and was referred to as androgynous (Coleman, 2002; Gray, 1989, 1993; Hall, 1996). By contrast, Grogan and Shakeshaft (2011) report five approaches that characterize women's educational leadership as:

> leadership for learning,
> leadership for social justice,
> relational leadership,
> spiritual leadership,
> balanced leadership. (p. 2)

The authors acknowledge not *all* women value such approaches and that many men also value them.

Androgynous educational management and leadership style

An androgynous educational management and leadership style was identified among women and men (Coleman, 2002). Gray's (1989, 1993) 'gender paradigms' were used to investigate the differences between women's and men's leadership styles (Coleman, 2002; Collard, 2001; Fuller, 2009) even though the gender paradigms were never intended to be 'exact paradigms for gender difference' (Gray, 1993, p. 112). Two types of school were the primary school seen as 'caring, nurturing, creative, intuitive, aware of individual differences, non-competitive, tolerant, subjective, informal etc.' (Gray, 1989, p. 41); and the secondary school was 'highly regulated, conformist, normative, competitive, evaluative, disciplined, objective, formal, rule bound etc.' (Gray, 1989, p. 41). The descriptors were constructed as 'feminine' and 'masculine' and used to determine the self-reported gendered styles of headteachers (Coleman, 2002; Fuller, 2009). The consistency in findings was in their 'cut(ting) across the two paradigms' (Coleman, 1996b, p. 166). Women were 'androgynous leaders able to select from a wide range of qualities' (Coleman, 1996b, p. 173). Men also selected qualities from both gender paradigms (Coleman, 2002). Further research within a single large local authority confirmed similar findings among women and men (Fuller, 2009).

Women could be just as controlling as men in their direction, organization, instruction and supervision of others (Jirasinghe and Lyons, 1996). A balance of both 'masculine' and 'feminine' attributes might be what was required in headship (Gray, 1993; Jirasinghe and Lyons, 1996). Hall (1996) argued 'for a view of school leadership and management that draws on the behaviours that are exclusive property of neither men nor women' (p. 3). Women were 'hard and soft, tough and loving, controlling and caring' (Hall, 1996, p. 135). They might prefer to use power to empower but when that failed 'they reverted to, reluctantly and relatively rarely, to a less preferred but more directive use of power' (Hall, 1996, p. 162). Hall (1997) claimed describing 'management as masculine is to create obstacles to women's promotion, implying it is antipathetic to the qualities that draw people in to teaching and, in its association with managerialism, possibly immoral' (p. 320). Headteachers challenged management as masculine by achieving headship and in their behaviour in post. Women 'dismantl(ed) and then recreat(ed) images of headship, as they ma(de) sense of their new roles and forge(d) their personal and professional identities in a new context' (Hall, 1997, p. 322) drawing on a range of feminine and masculine attributes to achieve their goals.

Regan's (1990) metaphor of a double helix, that was inclusive, encompassing and legitimizing the 'double set of qualities' of the 'either/or' and 'both/and' (p. 568) ways of managing within herself described the contradictions in leadership style that colleagues pointed out. She documented 'her own experience of recognizing and valuing complication and contradiction and subjectivity' (Adler et al., 1993, p. 128). Here was the complexity of gendered behaviour within one individual. It is akin to the notion of contextualized gender performance described in post-structural gender theory (Butler, 1990). Narrative accounts of contradictory leadership approaches suggest women exercised similarly flexible and fluid styles. The combination of 'friendly support (that) is a prerequisite, but also a certain amount of ruthlessness, or selfishness, or single mindedness' (Ozga, 1993, p. 55) sums up other accounts (Adler et al., 1993; Hustler et al., 1995; Ribbins and Marland, 1994). Such research demonstrates the fluidity of gender performance depending on circumstances and context that resonates with post-structural gender theory though it stems from an altogether different approach (see Fuller, 2010).

Masculinity and educational leadership

In Chapter 1, I noted lack of research into masculinities and school leadership. However, masculinity studies have focused on the interaction between gender and class, ethnicity and sexuality in work and unpaid work (see Cockburn, 1985; Collinson, 1992; Connell, 2005; Haywood and Mac an Ghaill, 2003; Jackson and Scott, 2002; McLean et al., 1997; Roper, 1994; Russell, 1999; Tolson, 1977; Whitehead and Barrett, 2001; Willis, 1979). Multiple masculinities were enacted in schools by 'Macho Lads' 'surviv[ing]' against authoritarianism' through 'fighting, fucking and football' (Mac an Ghaill, 1994, p. 56); 'Academic Achievers', on 'ladders of social mobility'; 'New Enterprisers' 'making something of (their) li(ves)'; and 'Real Englishmen' 'looking for real experiences' as the 'arbiters of culture' (Mac an Ghaill, 1994, p. 64). Teachers were gendered groups of 'Professionals', 'Old Collectivists' and 'New Entrepreneurs', led by a male headteacher as leading New Entrepreneur. The 'Professionals' represented a 'specific mode of masculinity, with a vocabulary that emphasized authority, discipline and control' (Mac an Ghaill, 1994, p. 19). The 'Old Collectivists' were supporters of comprehensive education and student-centred pedagogy. They were concerned with pastoral care and increasing access for girls and Black students. Anti-sexist, multicultural initiatives represented a 'specific occupational version of masculinity . . . in this conventional "feminine" sector of secondary schools, that was informed by an engagement with feminist ideas' (Mac an Ghaill, 1994, p. 20). 'New Entrepreneurs' were managerial. They marketed school as a commodity, were heads of vocational subjects and relatively new to the profession. Lingard and Douglas (1999) refer to new forms of entreprencurial masculinity as opposed to older paternalistic masculinity.

In an exploration of managers and masculinity in further education, Whitehead (2001) found men were unable to talk about links between their management and their gender. Man was 'the invisible gendered subject' (Whitehead, 2001, p. 77). He concludes, 'for many men adoption of (pro)feminism is complex, fraught and potentially threatening to their ontological security given the decentering of men and masculinity inherent in feminist discourse' (2001, p. 79). Where some women may have repositioned themselves, men were unlikely to de-centre themselves. Thus masculinist/managerial discourses continue to speak to 'a maleist view of the world' (p. 79). While men remain invisible gendered subjects,

> equal opportunities will remain largely rhetoric, confined to the margins in practice and gathering dust as policy documents. For most men managers' inability to see their own gender as a factor in inequality enables them to continue to regard equal opportunities as language from the 'other'; a gender-invisible state which, paradoxically, possibly permits them to 'believe' in their personal commitment to equal opportunities, while at the same time regarding it as 'women's problem'. (Whitehead, 2001, p. 79)

Feminist leadership

In Chapter 1, I also referred to Blackmore's (1989) feminist reconstruction of leadership. It is worth recapping its key elements in relation to other literature.

A view of power as multidimensional and multidirectional; leadership practised in different contexts by different people not merely equated to formal roles

Relational leadership (Grogan and Shakeshaft, 2011) resonates with a notion of multidirectional and multidimensional leadership in its emphasis on horizontal rather than hierarchical relationships. Similarly, critical leadership scholarship (CLS) values educational leadership as democratic practice in the potential transformation of hierarchy (Grace, 2000). The nature of what has been termed 'distributed leadership' is much contested (see Fuller et al., 2013 for further discussion), however, in the sense that leadership might emerge depending on circumstances and the range of expertises required leadership need not be equated to formal roles (see Woods et al., 2004). Diverse knowledge(s) held by a range of people might be valued. In the sense that potentially marginalized groups might be represented with parity of esteem there is a focus on leadership for social justice as associational justice (Cribb and Gewirtz, 2003; Fraser, 2007; Grogan and Shakeshaft, 2011). Qualities traditionally ascribed as 'feminine' such as 'awareness of individual differences' and 'informal' (Gray, 1993) approaches resonate with such a leadership discourse. Adjectives traditionally ascribed as 'masculine' such as 'formal', 'conformist' and 'highly regulated' (Gray, 1993) might describe leadership that militates against this approach.

Leadership to empower rather than to control others

Grogan and Shakeshaft's (2011) identification of leadership concern for social justice resonates with the exercise of power to empower rather than to control others. Feminist discourse 'opened up to both men and women the possibility of challenging the "taken-for-granted" world and has exposed hitherto unrecognized interests in domination' (Grundy, 1993, p. 165). Emancipatory leadership practice would involve practitioners and those affected by practice. A dialogic approach (Shields and Edwards, 2005) might ensure potentially marginalized groups were represented in decision-making. The extension of leadership development opportunities would create a professional learning community that resonates with leadership for learning (MacBeath, 2007; Grogan and Shakeshaft, 2011). Collaborative action and critical self-evaluation would mean 'emancipatory educational administrators will become students of their own work and that of their institution, recognizing the hegemonic social construction of that work' (Grundy, 1993, p. 172). How leaders worked with others was the issue:

> [a] feminist style of management rather than women as managers . . . the stereotype of a manager is the bully; someone who doesn't care about feelings, or about how the work is done, who pulls rank – as long as the goods are delivered and he gets his own way . . . the characteristics of a feminist manager . . . would be completely opposite. (Adler et al., 1993, pp. 87–8)

A feminist manager would still make executive decisions and recognize power relations but would value the whole support network. Recognition of individual contributions by team members was an integral part of feminist management. The self-evaluation and self-reflection required to achieve a collaborative approach also resonates with spiritual leadership (Grogan and Shakeshaft, 2011). Spiritual leadership is defined in part as consciousness raising, self-understanding and developing a strong sense of self-identity. In terms of attributes traditionally ascribed as 'feminine' a 'creative' (Gray, 1993) approach is needed to establish a range of forums in which all might engage. Through action research Duffy (1999) created ways to 'engage in forms of critical, self-reflective and collaborative work' (Grundy, 1993, p. 174) to generate the conditions for people to control their own knowledge and practice. She aimed to reverse the 'massive learned helplessness' (Gemmill and Oakley, 1992, p. 114). For some her approach was empowering; for others unnerving. By contrast, a quality that has been ascribed as 'masculine' promotes an 'evaluative' (Gray, 1993) approach. The important consideration is whether evaluation is collective self-evaluation for internal accountability purposes or externally imposed (MacBeath, 2007).

A relational view of morality in which moral practice is rational within given contexts and social and political relations and not according to abstract moral laws or principles

CLS links educational leadership to philosophy, morality and spirituality where educational leadership as a vocation to serve has been located in religious educational cultures (Grace, 2000). Educational leadership requires 'an awareness of philosophical principles and of moral complexity as well as technical competence' (Grace, 2000, p. 242). English school headship has been constructed as 'the articulation of spiritual and moral conceptions of the "good life" and of the formation of "good people"' (Grace, 2000, p. 241). However, what constitutes 'goodness' must be questioned. Headteachers' values are explored further in Chapter 3. However, there is a clear link here with spiritual leadership (Grogan and Shakeshaft, 2011). Leadership approaches traditionally ascribed as 'feminine' such as 'subjective', 'intuitive' and 'tolerant' (Gray, 1993) might suggest they complement a relational view of morality. In the consideration of context and circumstances another 'feminine' attribute 'awareness of individual differences' (Gray, 1993) is clearly key. By contrast, the adjectives traditionally ascribed as 'masculine', 'highly regulated', 'conformist', 'normative' and 'objective' (Gray, 1993) might describe uncritical conformity to rules-bound practices based on normative values and judgements. It is the antithesis of feminist leadership.

Leadership concerned with communitarian and collective activities and values

Pupil engagement with learning and the continued professional development of staff are potentially communitarian and collective activities. Learning has intrinsic value. School-based curriculum development is a way of making 'schooling more relevant to the needs of particular populations' (Grundy, 1993, p. 174). Wrigley et al. (2012) refer to connectedness rather than relevance because 'it indicates both a respect for students' knowledges and interests and the need to scaffold learners into other knowledge forms, genres and media from which disadvantaged students should never be excluded' (p. 99). Emancipatory praxis is knowledge constituted 'by an emancipatory interest . . . which recognizes that freedom is inextricably linked with truth and justice' (Grundy, 1993, p. 166). By contrast, task-driven technical leadership embraces externally dictated performance guidelines and standardized procedures. People-driven practical action enables shared reflection on and analysis of the outcomes of action (Grundy, 1993). Crucial to shared reflection and evaluation is the questioning of meanings that may be hegemonically determined. CLS links educational leadership to ethical practice in aspiring to the common good (Grace, 2000). Western social democratic or liberal humanist values are likely to dominate as: 'inclusivity, equal opportunities and equity or justice, high expectations, engagement with stakeholders, cooperation, teamwork, commitment and understanding' (Gold et al., 2003, p. 99). Adjectives traditionally ascribed as 'feminine' complement a communitarian and collective leadership approach such as 'caring', 'tolerant' and 'non-competitive' (Gray, 1993). Those ascribed as 'masculine' that might work in opposition are 'non-tolerant' and 'disciplined' (Gray, 1993) in the sense of externally imposed discipline. There is further discussion of values in Chapter 3.

Lack of feminist management

Despite set-backs to the progress of a feminist project for transforming schools in a male-dominated, managerial climate, Grace (1995) argued 'feminism, in education, is not simply a trendy and short-lived phenomenon of the 1960s but a continuing oppositional culture for making schools more humane places' (p. 62). CLS and feminist approaches are directly beneficial to pupils. Gold (1997) noted the need for self-reflection by those who acquired power 'if those people who came from less powerful positions than those privileged by our society reflected on the effects of their lack of access to power they would work differently with power when they had it from those who have never had to engage in such arguments' (cited Reay and Ball, 2000, p. 149). Experiencing powerlessness might not be enough. Those who challenged organizational authority were unlikely to be promoted; conformists were more likely to succeed. The promotion process is

> a difficult balancing act in which conformity, collusion, acceptance of the status quo and self-promotion jostled with conflicting ethical stances, criticisms of the organization and the ways in which it operates, and desires to be part of a collectivity. (Reay and Ball, 2000, p. 150)

The assumption that women's values might be undermined by gaining power is problematic if we do not know what they were before. Women might be successful because they are managerial. Reay and Ball (2000) acknowledge women's qualities vary according to position and power. They raise the issue of women's dominance of other women but women might also oppress subordinate men. Women who espouse feminism might be autocratic and unsupportive in practice (Reay and Ball, 2000).

Headteachers' approaches to leadership

Feminist scholarship has been valued by critical leadership scholars (Grace, 2000). However, Hall (1999) articulated frustration that chapters about gender were an 'add on' (p. 156). There is a need for, 'a more integrated analysis of gender and management . . . that recognizes, as essentialist hegemonic critiques do not, the diversity of masculinities and femininities that characterize managers' behaviour' (Hall, 1999, p. 160). Arguing for the inclusion of men and 'a diversity of masculinities' in future research she saw 'any attempt at redefining educational management that fails to recognize their influence on both the definers as well as the phenomenon under scrutiny are doomed to fail' (Hall, 1999, p. 161). Research is needed into

> the connections between men as managers and managers as men. We need to know more about the relationships between home and work, family and career, early socialisation for both men and women. (Hall, 1999, p. 163)

Women have been slow to research men. Examination is needed of the connections between life histories and their impact on how school leadership is exercised by both women and men. Chapters 3–6 specifically explore headteachers' values and life experiences and their influence on headship.

In the section that follows I illustrate how four women and men engage (or not) in feminist leadership discourse. Silvia and Gregory's accounts demonstrate engagement with aspects of feminist leadership discourse; Katherine and Duncan's accounts demonstrate lack of engagement. Blackmore's (1989) feminist reconstruction of leadership frames the discussion.

Women engaging in feminist leadership discourse

Out of nine women only one (not Silvia) described having an interest in feminist politics (see Chapter 4). However, it was clear in five women headteachers' accounts that a feminist leadership discourse dominated. There were elements of a feminist discourse in the accounts of two other women. Of the remaining two, one described herself as an autocrat; another appeared to engage in a masculinist leadership discourse.

Silvia

As headteacher of a large comprehensive school, Silvia was concerned about colleagues' difficulties following major structural change imposed by the local authority. Staff continued to face challenges in their daily work with pupils living in an area of multiple deprivations.

Multidimensional and multidirectional power with leadership practised in different contexts by different people not merely equated to formal roles

Silvia had created spaces for one-to-one review meetings with members of the leadership team outside the line management system. There were opportunities for open reflective dialogue about her leadership practice. However, colleagues found it difficult to feed back honestly to her. They were still 'deeply hierarchical'. In team meetings colleagues were more relaxed, 'they will make jokes and be rude to me but on a one-to-one they still find challenging me quite difficult'. She took the opportunity in these meetings to do some 'teaching around leadership'.

Teachers of the 'highest technical calibre' had an increasing acceptance and understanding of what was needed to improve teaching and learning. Silvia acknowledged the intense emotional labour and fluctuating energy levels among staff. The staff learning programme 'celebrate[d] expertise' with staff generating ideas and leading sessions. Support staff members were greatly valued, 'I have never worked with a support staff of such calibre and commitment.'

Silvia described the school council as a space where pupils might challenge the work of the school. One Year 8 girl was determined not to 'tolerate second rate' teaching.

Leadership to empower rather than to control others

Silvia's work with the leadership team was differentiated depending on levels of self-confidence. She gave fuller explanations to some or put in more feedback loops; made greater demands of others; worked with colleagues around task completion or conversations. Her interest in human behaviour made her responsive to others, 'It helps to grow people better because you are growing them from within, the sort of person that they are – not from a model of what they should be like.'

Significant organizational change before Silvia took up post led to 'traumatic experiences'. Teachers were in a state of recovery. Their personal and professional self-esteem had been damaged. There was a need for a lot of 'healing that needs to go on in the organization around people'. Staff members were systematically valued privately and publically. The line management structure ensured staff requests for support or health were sympathetically responded to.

A relational view of morality in which moral practice is rational within given contexts and social and political relations and not according to abstract moral laws or principles

Silvia believed in being 'real, as well as optimistic' about the school's apparent poor performance and the responsibility for it. She unpacked difficulties, 'around the individuals that are involved, not around a mass'. The school was developing into 'a very human based organization'.

Difficult decisions were based on Silvia's core values, 'ultimately you have to say not am I doing it right? but am I doing the right thing?' She considered the rights of individuals, acted with compassion, tried to explain what was happening and why. Her inner core set of values 'about the rights of the individual, and [pupils'] entitlement to be safe, and the responsibilities of being adults in the organization' were what drove her.

Leadership concerned with communitarian and collective activities and values

Pupils' chances of achieving academically would be improved if they developed as 'self-motivating learners'. A radical Key Stage 3 curriculum had been introduced to maintain 'interest and capacity to access [and support] learning'. Silvia referred to an 'approved answer' about catering for pupil needs. That consisted of target setting; student understanding and ownership of assessment; teacher awareness of individual targets and learning styles; and what was 'traditional' and 'technically, theoretically congruent' with the National Curriculum. Silvia questioned the assumption of a, 'technology of teaching that is appropriate for every teacher'. Nor did a prescribed content enable every child to succeed. The curriculum was rarely created around pupils and learning. An integrated curriculum with a flexible timetable was designed around looking at school as 'learner driven, and not constructed for teacher convenience'. The five higher-grade GCSEs were a 'progression passport', but Silvia refused to 'devote the entire Key Stage 4 curriculum to doing [ICT] GNVQ'. She would not 'deliver children as fodder to a system'. She would do everything she could to provide them with their 'passport to improvement which is the five A* to C's' but refused to de-humanize them or de-skill them. Her concern was for the 'good' of pupils and society as a collective.

Silvia demonstrated self-awareness acknowledging she did things of which she was ashamed. She was prone to irritation but tried, 'to be reflective around that'.

The size of the school precluded Silvia from working personally with the majority of staff so like most headteachers her talk about working with staff focused largely on the leadership team (see Chapters 4 and 5 for further discussion of leadership teams). Silvia demonstrated the difficulties in breaking down existing hierarchical structures (Grace, 2000). Nevertheless, the leadership team was gaining confidence in speaking their minds. Her encouragement of their voices and direct critiques of her leadership demonstrated she was building leadership for social justice (Cribb and Gewirtz, 2003; Grogan and Shakeshaft, 2011; Grundy, 1993). Unaccustomed to speaking back to power some were clearly uncomfortable (Duffy, 1999). Efforts to empower staff included affording them leadership development opportunities and teaching about leadership. This resonates with leadership for learning (Grogan and Shakeshaft, 2011; MacBeath, 2007). Teachers and support staff were highly valued. They were encouraged to share a wide range of knowledges with one another by leading staff development sessions in a non-formal leadership capacity (Grundy, 1993). Faced with difficult decisions regarding people's futures as staff or pupils, Silvia reflected on her personal values to ensure rights and responsibilities were weighed up in any given context (Blackmore, 1989; Grace, 2000). Catering for pupils' differences meant a creative approach to curriculum design. The processes and quality of learning and teaching were central to headship (Grundy, 1993; Grogan and Shakeshaft, 2011). The curriculum was developed to engage young people in learning they valued while simultaneously ensuring pupils accessed high status learning (Grundy, 1993; Wrigley et al., 2012). Silvia referred to qualifications as a 'passport', but disputed educational policy regarding classroom pedagogy and school effectiveness (Grundy, 1993; Wrigley et al., 2012).

Men engaging in feminist leadership discourse

In the case study below I show one man's engagement with feminist leadership discourse. Six of nine men engaged with feminist leadership discourse to varying degrees. They resembled 'Old Collectivists' (Mac an Ghaill, 1994) who had become headteachers. The remaining three almost wholly engaged in masculinist leadership discourse.

Gregory

Gregory was concerned about the damaging impact of the educational system on teachers, pupils and his own children. Some teachers applied for posts as teaching assistants at the special school he led.

Multidimensional and multidirectional power with leadership practised in different contexts by different people not merely equated to formal roles

Gregory's preference was a team-based approach, 'there is a sense of it not being about me'. His role was 'like a gardening role to find the weeds and fix it and you make sure you do the strategic thing but you also look at the detail'. People's motivation came from more than 'just being a consumer'. He identified people's motivation came from their minds and emotions. Those were very 'powerful' when they were engaged. He described his style as 'mixing people who can solve problems with those problems'. Other people had expertise he lacked. He was concerned about staff welfare. A senior leader stepped down to be a drama teacher for a period of recovery from stress. Jobs were created to suit colleagues' strengths. The informal hierarchy appeared different to traditional hierarchies, 'the ranking of people here isn't around their jobs, so if you're a very, very good person, and very committed to the kids then you have huge authority in the place, both with the kids and the staff'.

Achievement was measured in broad terms. Pupils' efforts were rewarded to recognize a range of behaviours and attainments. Nominations for awards were validated by peer review. A whole school communal meeting enabled pupils to engage with the process. They were given a voice in the award of privileges. Two or three major complaints were made on each occasion. The complaints and defences were heard separately. Once awards had been validated letters were sent home to celebrate achievement. Prizes were film shows, meetings with the chair of governors and a platinum pass that gave pupils executive status in school.

Leadership to empower rather than to control others

Gregory was mindful of the impact of emotional labour on staff, 'I'll be quite tolerant of people who aren't perfect'. He did not see 'people [as] machines to be driven for us'. He was critical of management theory imported from industry to education. Systems and workforce reform began with people not functions. The approach was 'opposite' to government policy. Gregory looked for what people could contribute in unconventional job roles, 'my office manager runs discipline. How about that as an odd combination? But she has the commitment and personal integrity and the drive to make those things possible. Now if she left you wouldn't advertise that as a job'. Flexible working practices suited the personal, emotional and health needs of staff. Some moved between teaching and teaching assistant roles as they chose. Gregory talked about treating and paying people well. His job was to find them space and resources to do what they needed to do.

Fundamental to Gregory's thinking was the powerlessness children experienced in their lives. People were motivated by power to influence the direction of their lives but, 'Children have none'. Otherwise he thought they had the same drives and perceptions as adults. They had the same intensity of feeling. Gregory did not distinguish between pupils and adults; what happened to them was equally important. He thought, 'many people would see these things as not so important. That what happens to a child isn't so important'.

A relational view of morality in which moral practice is rational within given contexts and social and political relations and not according to abstract moral laws or principles

One boy, who exhibited violent behaviour, was found space after school to 'wrap[s] the quiet around him like a blanket', to be safe and still. This was preferable to being driven around in a bus waiting for his parents to arrive home. Finding out what was needed and providing it had 'transformed his life and the parents' life and their relationship'. The intervention was not profound 'it just needs noticing what people like; and just giving that extra bit of respect'. Gregory coped with one girl's abusive language by giving her a cup of tea and listening to what she needed. Her behaviour was unacceptable but Gregory focused on meeting her needs rather than disciplining her behaviour. The school provided a system of sanctions for inappropriate home behaviours to support parents.

Leadership concerned with communitarian and collective activities and values

Gregory saw learning as process rather than product. The school's earlier emphasis on academic attainment led parents to question the curriculum's usefulness for some children. The curriculum was redesigned to include basic skills such as telling the time and checking change. Pupils were taught as very small, vertically streamed groups. They worked on tightly focused learning needs every morning. Gregory described a child-centred learning programme offering a range of 'suits . . . tailor[ed] . . . to the individual' rather than a 'bespoke tailoring service'. He emphasized the importance of relationships between staff and pupils and the willingness to try 'extreme' measures to meet needs, such as teaching some pupils outside the school day. Pupils gained higher-grade GCSEs in some subjects such as art.

Pupils' pastoral needs were paramount. Hot chocolate and toast were provided on arrival. Pupils were given cups of tea at times of distress. Toilet facilities were checked for cleanliness throughout the day. Such 'acts of kindness' helped pupils feel good about themselves and feel able to be good.

Gregory enabled colleagues to develop unconventional job roles depending on their range of expertises and interests. Pupils exercised power in validating awards to their peers for attainment and behaviour. They could challenge staff decisions. These processes resonate with leadership for social justice in affording associational justice (Cribb and Gewirtz, 2003; Fraser, 2007; Grogan and Shakeshaft, 2011). Leadership was practised in a variety of contexts and not necessarily equated with formal roles. Indeed the hierarchy of respect was based on colleagues' caring contributions not job roles (Blackmore, 1989; Grace, 2000). In giving both staff and pupils the opportunity to lead Gregory demonstrated leadership for learning (Grogan and Shakeshaft, 2011; MacBeath, 2007). Gregory saw his role as a facilitator and nurturer who enabled others to make things happen in ways they devised. He found the resources. Gregory's leadership was based on an assumption of professionalism, dedication and high levels of motivation. He acknowledged the intensity of emotional labour in the daily work with pupils with a range of SEN. Gregory created flexible working practices with regard to working hours and changing job roles. He did not judge colleagues as 'failing' teachers but valued their contribution to the organization. In that sense he exercised relational morality to consider individual circumstances and context (Blackmore, 1989). He used intuition in his assessment of people as 'good' and made subjective decisions. In his treatment of pupils he was tolerant of unacceptable behaviour in diffusing it and listening to pupils' needs. Gregory's focus was clearly on curriculum design, learning and teaching, educational outcomes and pastoral support. The curriculum had been redesigned in response to parents' concerns about their children's levels of basic skills (Grundy, 1993). Gregory's leadership was based on Buddhist values in seeking opportunities to enact small kindnesses for the common good as a matter of principle (Grace, 2000; Grogan and Shakeshaft, 2011) (see Chapters 3 and 7).

Women not engaging in feminist leadership discourse

Not all women valued feminist or women's ways of working (Fuller, 2010; Grogan and Shakeshaft, 2011; Reay and Ball, 2000). In the next section I demonstrate aspects of Katherine and Duncan's leadership that are antipathetic to feminist leadership discourses. Katherine was not the only woman to engage with masculinist leadership discourses but they dominated her leadership discourse more than others.

Katherine

Katherine was headteacher of a high-performing academic, selective, girls' school. Her concern was to manage a prescriptive curriculum. Her focus was on pupils' educational outcomes as qualifications rather than the process of learning. Regarding staff, some practices were designed to give an impression of consultation and accessibility.

Multidimensional and multidirectional power with leadership practised in different contexts by different people not merely equated to formal roles

Katherine's consultation of senior staff consisted of, 'let[ting] them talk' but ultimately she 'still ma[de] the decisions'. She recounted a 'jovial' conversation, with a senior colleague who described her practice as, 'You're very good at making decisions. You let us sit there, you let us talk and then you suddenly say "Right, I've had enough of this. This is what we're going to do".' Katherine saw it as an accurate summation, 'I wasn't conscious that that was what I did, but I suppose it is what I do, on reflection. I don't suffer fools. I'll let them talk, because it's important that people think that, feel that they've had their say and people feel that I've listened.' She did the same with heads of department. Responsibility for tasks was devolved for pragmatic reasons.

There were no examples of teachers, support staff or pupils exercising leadership.

Leadership to empower rather than to control others

Katherine's 'open door' was meant to be inviting. However, it had a hidden purpose, 'you learn a tremendous amount by listening to what goes on down that corridor'. Workforce reform was an opportunity to increase classroom teaching, 'I don't think that teachers have thought this through yet. I don't think that they realize that a reduction in their admin actually means more teaching . . . at some point I will probably ask them to do more in the classroom.'

Katherine ranked staff importance to value support staff highly, 'In a way they're more important than the teachers.' Barriers between teaching and non-teaching staff persisted, 'we just tried to break down all of those barriers. They will still exist. I will never do away with them totally but at least the guide from here is "these are pupil partners".

A relational view of morality in which moral practice is rational within given contexts and social and political relations and not according to abstract moral laws or principles

Katherine gave automatic public support 'to the hilt' for staff. She thought she might be criticized for that. Nevertheless she thought 'it's important that they see that I trust them. I will defend if I possibly can'. There were no other examples of making decisions within a moral framework.

Her pastoral concerns centred on pupils' lack of self-esteem. The selective system resulted in low self-esteem for able pupils who measured themselves academically against others. The school needed to nurture them and 'convince them that they're good. This is the trouble, one of the problems of the selective school, the ones at the bottom end think that they're poor or will tell you that they're thick. What they mean is in the context of their peers'. Poor self-esteem demonstrated itself as quietness, poor behaviour and serious mental illness demonstrated through anorexia and self-harming. Teenage pregnancy was mentioned in relation to examinations, 'the baby's produced in the middle of the GCSEs helps everybody doesn't it? . . . There's nothing you can do about that, at all.'

Leadership concerned with communitarian and collective activities and values

All pupils went on to further education. Almost all (99%) continued to higher education. There was no sense of learning as a process. Katherine talked about attainment stretching from five grade As at A level to 'scrap[ing]' five higher-grade GCSEs. While there were not many in the latter group there was a need to 'lever [them] over that metaphorical line'. Individual teachers provided individual support. A broad curriculum was retained, 'We don't go for the best five [GSCEs] and hope that they'll get them. What they do is everything'. Pupils were targeted and prevented from joining in other activities until coursework was completed.

Katherine felt bound by the National Curriculum, 'by the time we've delivered what is required of us nationally, we have exceedingly little flexibility'. Decisions regarding the curriculum were 'pragmatic' relating to classroom accommodation; length of lesson and school day; and the GCSE option system. The focus was on organizing a prescribed curriculum.

Katherine worked 'through' heads of year to ensure someone knew the pupils personally. Her job was to work with adults. At the same time, she was 'around. I'm active. I'm visible. I know the naughty one[s], I obviously know the very naughty ones and I know the very good ones. But there is a mass in the middle that I don't know. That is sad but I don't actually think it's my job'.

Katherine constructed her leadership as less autocratic than that of her predecessor (Fuller, 2010). Nevertheless, power was located in Katherine and she accepted that. There was no sense of multidimensional, multidirectional use of power or relational leadership (Blackmore, 1989; Grogan and Shakeshaft, 2011). Structures were hierarchical with Katherine working 'through' others to lead and manage pupils (Blackmore, 1989; Grace, 2000). There was no sense of shared team leadership. This was not leadership for learning in the sense of expanding and developing leadership capacity among senior, middle, teaching, non-teaching staff or pupils (Grogan and Shakeshaft, 2011; MacBeath, 2007). There was no sense of sharing knowledge to empower colleagues in their practice (Grundy, 1993). Nor was it leadership for social justice in the sense of recognizing differences and ensuring representation (Cribb and Gewirtz, 2003; Fraser, 2007; Grogan and Shakeshaft, 2011). Katherine appeared to consult, wanted people to think they had input, but made decisions herself. An 'open door' might usually indicate an approachable leader but here it was a surveillance mechanism. It demonstrated her control. There was also a sense of being cleverer than teachers because they misunderstood her management of workforce reform (see Chapter 5). Katherine planned to use teachers' administration time to increase teaching contact hours rather than to enable planning, preparation and assessment. Katherine ranked staff in status. Members of support staff were higher than teachers. Her reasoning was based on operational management. Without support staff the school could not function; without teachers the building could still open. However, there was some ambivalence in Katherine's discourse about working with staff. She constructed her automatic trust and support of them against external criticism as a weakness. This could suggest her deliberate engagement with a dominant and domineering leadership discourse that came about because of her role (Reay and Ball, 2000; Fuller, 2010). Alternatively, her automatic defence of staff was a highly regulated response rather than one predicated on individual context or circumstances. Defence of colleagues equated with defence of the school and of her leadership position. She did not appear to engage with the moral complexities of her work with staff (Blackmore, 1989; Grace, 2000). Nor did she engage with moral complexities in implementing a prescribed curriculum. The curriculum was managed rather than designed to meet pupils' needs (Grundy, 1993; Wrigley et al., 2012). Katherine focused on educational outcomes as qualifications. The high pressure of a selective school combined with family expectations led to pupils' low self-esteem and in some cases physical and mental harm. Katherine gave no indication of introducing curriculum or pastoral programmes to reduce this. Despite recognizing the selective system was responsible for damage to pupils, Katherine chose to remain in and to perpetuate it. There were no discussions about alternative or flexible approaches (Grundy, 1993). Additional support was supplied by individual teachers on an ad hoc basis. An anecdote provided an accurate summation of Katherine's decision-making practice; but she appeared not to question whether things might be done differently. She demonstrated little self-awareness that might be equated with spiritual leadership (Grace, 2000; Grogan and Shakeshaft, 2011).

Recognizing men not doing feminist leadership

In the final case study I give an example of Duncan's engagement with leadership discourses that could not be described as feminist. He was not the only man to engage with masculinist leadership discourses. However, there are aspects of his account that demonstrate the complexities of his leadership discourse.

Duncan

With regard to pupils Duncan was concerned with raising self-esteem and attainment. Using prior attainment data and targets in every lesson would achieve that. Regarding staff, some practices gave an impression of ruthlessness.

Multidimensional and multidirectional power with leadership practised in different contexts by different people not merely equated to formal roles

Duncan looked for order and logic in structures, systems and decision-making. Team teaching was a valuable example of 'working together collegially'. However, it was 'random' and needed structure. Duncan expressed frustration with the staff perception of a hierarchy with him at the top of the pyramid. He valued team work in differentiating between his membership of a subject team and his leadership of the school. He wanted to be trusted to do his job and objected to the 'challenging in the profession'. Staff professional development was linked with performance management but not as much as 'anyone thought it ought to' be linked.

Duncan did not mention working with the senior leadership team. Nor did he talk about leadership opportunities for staff and pupils

Leadership to empower rather than to control others

Duncan described himself as intolerant of failure, 'sometimes you do actually have to be quite hard on teachers because of the view that children deserve the best'. His reprimand of teachers who completed annual reports late caused 'uproar'. At the same time tackling of the issue was perceived by some as positive. He had been 'successful in moving [staff] on. I think it is easier to move them on than to change them, and last year . . . I had quite a turn over . . . nearly twenty people left and I would say fifteen of them I was quite pleased they left'. They had not shared his vision for the school.

A relational view of morality in which moral practice is rational within given contexts and social and political relations and not according to abstract moral laws or principles

Duncan acknowledged his 'ruthless[ness]' in handling long-term absence. Concern to provide teaching stability for pupils overrode concern for teachers at difficult moments. Some staff were 'genuinely ill' with problems of their own and needing support; but to cover teachers' absence impacted negatively on pupils' education. Duncan's desire for logical clarity and consistency in decision-making led him to question why he responded differently to a terminally ill teacher; he concluded he did not have to dismiss someone who was going to die.

Leadership concerned with communitarian and collective activities and values

Duncan prioritized the quality of teaching and learning over catering for pupils' pastoral needs. Referring to Maslow's hierarchy of needs he acknowledged 'children need to be . . . comfortable before they can start learning'. However, he dismissed this thought to focus on academic attainment, 'I think if you push the academic side and exam results, the rest follows to a large extent.' He was committed to teachers using prior attainment and grade prediction data daily in all lessons. This system would raise pupils' self-esteem, expectations and examination results. Duncan valued the quality of relationships between teachers and pupils, 'probably all children . . . learn best when they feel they are working alongside an adult, and working with them, rather than being confronted with them or bullied by them into learning'. He valued the 'liberal' use of rewards to raise self-esteem. Duncan referred to differentiation; a variety of teaching and learning styles; and using Information Technology as motivators.

Staff development began with the school development plan in which 'every individual member of staff has a certain positioning'. However, Duncan also valued it as a collegial activity.

Although Duncan talked about his frustration that staff perceived a strongly hierarchical structure was in place he appeared not to recognize that was in his leadership discourse. He wanted to be a team member in a subject department but talked about every member of staff have a 'positioning' (Blackmore, 1989; Grace, 2000). He was frustrated by the messiness of a team teaching approach to staff development. Although he valued it as a collegiate activity he wanted it to be systematically carried out. It needed to be managed and organized. There was no reference to working with the leadership team or leadership opportunities for teachers, non-teaching staff or pupils (Grogan and Shakeshaft, 2011; MacBeath, 2007). Duncan's discourse about managing and leading staff was focused on handling poor performance, long-term absence and those who rejected his vision for the school. It was an imposed vision and he was content for staff to leave if they disagreed with it. His talk about the terminally ill member of staff lacked compassion. There were no indications that any staff or pupils' voices were heard. Recognition of difference was not linked to leadership for social justice in the sense of distributive, cultural or associational justice (Cribb and Gewirtz, 2003; Fraser, 2007; Grogan and Shakeshaft, 2011). However, Duncan did talk about learning and teaching as a process that included a variety of pedagogical approaches to meet pupil needs and learning preferences (Grogan and Shakeshaft, 2011; Grundy, 1993). He referred to their readiness to learn. Duncan's discourse focused on using prior attainment and predicted grades in a very systematic way to set targets for pupils' learning in every lesson. This approach was prescriptive; there was no indication of its development in consultation with staff. It suggests a highly regulated, systematic and disciplined approach. Nevertheless, Duncan noted the importance of relationships between staff and pupils to suggest the value of relational leadership (Grogan and Shakeshaft, 2011). That did not extend to his own working relationships with staff. The interests of pupils were prioritized to the extent that Duncan was intolerant of staff limitations. He was more tolerant of the member of staff who was terminally ill precisely because s/he was going to die. This was a managerial response. His concern was to act fairly in the sense of using logic and reason to treat everyone the same.

Misrecognition of feminist leadership discourses

Earlier in this chapter I referred to the possible misrecognition that occurs in focusing solely on where women have achieved headship in the United Kingdom. Symbolic violence occurs for the women and men whose aspirations are not nurtured. There is also a danger of misrecognizing higher proportions of women in some authorities (and senior leadership teams) as indicative of leadership concerned with learning and social justice that is relational, spiritual and balanced (Grogan and Shakeshaft, 2011). Positioning women as school leaders does not automatically result in their engagement with feminist leadership discourses (Reay and Ball, 2000). Nor does it result in their using traditionally 'feminine' qualities and attributes (Fuller, 2010). Similarly, men are capable of drawing on (pro)feminist discourses in their headship (Hall, 1999; Lingard and Douglas, 1999; Mac an Ghaill, 1994). They also draw on traditionally 'feminine' attributes (Coleman, 2002). Gender behaviour is not linked to biological sex; gendered leadership is not linked to biological sex. These four headteachers demonstrated their engagement with quite different leadership discourses. Those differences cannot be attributed to the type of school any more than they can be attributed to biological sex (Collard, 2001). Katherine was the only one of three women leading high performing selective schools in this study who had such seemingly little regard for pupil and staff welfare. In the other two schools one headteacher actively reduced competition and academic pressure; the other provided personal and pastoral support for pupils experiencing academic failure (see Chapter 4). Duncan was the only headteacher of a comprehensive school to show little care for staff members. A more nuanced exploration of headteachers' values and the life experiences that impacted on headship is the focus of the following chapters.

None of the headteachers explicitly described their approaches as feminist; I have interpreted them as such using the framework outlined above. Their accounts are self-reported. Pupils and colleagues might not construct their leadership practices in the same way. There might also be a degree of self-misrecognition by headteachers. Emancipatory intent is not the same as emancipatory outcome (Fuller, 2012). However, there appears to be genuine concern to establish parity of esteem in Silvia and Gregory's accounts.

There is also a danger of misrecognizing the degree of autonomy headteachers appeared to have in their resistance of dominant policy discourses. They were working within macro-level structures concerned with marketized, managerial and performative approaches to school leadership. Katherine's adherence to curriculum implementation and Duncan's systematic use of prior attainment data might be accurate portraits of contemporary headship. Silvia and Gregory's approaches to curriculum design and development that focused on pupil needs might be rare. Nevertheless, they are valuable examples of values-led leadership that focuses on learning for all and seeks social justice. It appears they exercised some agency in their headship in trying to do something different. Perhaps these headteachers reflect the mixed messages of New Labour educational policy with its market-led, performative approach couched in the rhetoric of child-centredness.

Summary and key points for aspiring leaders

The literature relating to gender and educational leadership draws on gender theories that evolved over the last three decades. Feminist discourses of equality and difference led to research, largely by women, into women's career progression and the barriers they might experience. In the United Kingdom there remain many fewer women in secondary school headship than men. Women's success in achieving headship varies across the United Kingdom. There is a need for further qualitative research into the reasons for such wide geographical variations.

Post-structural gender theory explains how women and men perform gender that is not linked to their biological sex. Both women and men draw on traditionally ascribed 'feminine' and 'masculine' qualities and attributes to various degrees. Women and men headteachers drew on aspects of feminist leadership discourse. These accounts reveal an alternative discourse that seeks to empower, that acknowledges moral complexity and values diverse school populations (see Chapters 3–6). Some headteachers were engaged in leadership for learning and social justice; and in relational and spiritual leadership (see Chapter 4 for discussion of balanced leadership). There is also evidence that some women and men drew on masculinist leadership discourse that dominates educational policy. Chapter 3 looks specifically at headteachers' values-led leadership and the negotiation of values conflicts in school.

3

Values-led Leadership

Introduction

Educational policy in late nineteenth- and early twentieth-century England has been characterized as one of 'progressivism, control and correction' (Grosvenor and Myers, 2006, p. 225). One aim might be to provide a 'mechanism for social justice' (Grosvenor and Myers, 2006, p. 244) but there was also a 'moral technology at work' (p. 246). In the latter half of the twentieth century, successive educational policy-makers in England required headteachers, teachers and schools to promote values creating an 'unresolved dilemma for teachers' (Cairns, 2004, p. 6). At the time of this research, the General Teaching Council (GTC, 2004) identified respectful and inclusive relationships with members of the whole school population as key to teacher professionalism. Teachers should actively 'challenge stereotypes and oppose prejudice to safeguard equality of opportunity, respecting individuals regardless of gender, marital status, religion, colour, race, ethnicity, class, sexual orientation, disability and age' (GTC, 2004, p. 2). Desirable characteristics for teachers and pupils included 'a spirit of intellectual enquiry, tolerance, honesty, fairness, patience, a genuine concern for other people and an appreciation of different backgrounds' (GTC, 2004, p. 2). By contrast, current teacher standards require them 'not [to] undermin[e] fundamental British values, including democracy, the rule of law, individual liberty and mutual respect, and tolerance of those with different faiths and beliefs' (DfE, 2011, p. 9). Fundamental British values (FBV) are defined by anti-terrorist policy in the Prevent Strategy (DfE, 2011). A human rights discourse defines behaviour running counter to FBV as 'intolerance of other cultures and gender inequality' (HM Government, 2011, 10.32, p. 68). The new standards are 'designed to make it easier for heads to sack teachers who are members of the British National Party or those with extremist Islamic beliefs' (Paton, 2011). Such values might be similar to those many espouse but further exploration of what they mean to whom is needed. Their identification as 'British' makes them appear exclusive rather than inclusive. Both New Labour and the Coalition government (from 2010) have fallen into the trap of developing 'a catalogue of correct values which school administrators ought to adopt without question' (Begley and Zaretsky, 2004, p. 641).

In Chapters 1 and 2 I have shown how a feminist reconstruction of leadership incorporates concern with communitarian and collective activities and values (Blackmore, 1989). Critical leadership scholarship links educational leadership with ethical practice in aspiring to the common good (Grace, 2000). Headteachers' values, ideas and beliefs contribute to the construction of gendered headteacher identities, or headteacherly habitus within the terms of discourse and power (Butler, 1990). Thus values inform and direct headteachers' engagement in discursive practices. The values underlying such leadership are thought to be social democratic or liberal humanist marked by 'inclusivity, equal opportunities and equity or justice, high expectations, engagement with stakeholders, cooperation, teamwork, commitment and understanding' (Gold et al., 2003, p. 136). As such they are concerned with valuing the individual within the wider social framework. While cooperation and teamwork suggest a shared leadership approach, how far 'shared values such as critical engagement, shared policy-making and forms of accounting that value a broad range of impacts and not just academic achievement' (Fuller et al., 2013) extends is uncertain.

In this chapter I report findings about 18 headteachers' espoused personal values, their sources and impact on leadership. There are four main sections. First, there is an outline of educational leadership theory conceptualized within a feminist and critical discourse (Grace, 2000). The second section outlines headteachers' personal values and their recognition of values differences among the school population. Thirdly, there is discussion of headteachers' potential authentic leadership comprised of self-knowledge, their sensitivity towards values orientations of others and ethical approaches to the resolution of values conflicts (Begley, 2006). I refer to *ethics of care, critique* and *justice* as well as Begley's (2006) definition of *using ethics* to consider headteachers' ethical approaches. There is evidence of misrecognition in some headteachers' uncritical engagement or lack of engagement with the values differences of staff, pupils and families. The chapter ends with a summary of key points as advice for teachers and aspiring headteachers.

Background – Educational leadership theory

A significant shift in thinking about educational leadership is attributed to Hodgkinson's (1983, 1991) conceptualization of leadership as a moral art. Greenfield (1993) argued administrative science was founded on knowledge informed by 'hidden values' (p. 147). Thus interpretative and qualitative research might give 'greater attention to power relations, conflicts and values and moral dilemmas in educational leadership' (Grace, 2000, p. 237). Greenfield (1993) saw the study of intention as 'key to understanding organizations' (p. 127) necessitating exploration of what motivates the actions of people within an organization. A notion of educational leadership as 'moral endeavour' (Heck and Hallinger, 2005, p. 234) has evolved. Alongside its articulation of professional values, New Labour outlined in the headteacher standards a need for a shared school vision that should 'express core educational values and moral purpose and be inclusive of stakeholders' values and beliefs' (DfES, 2004b, p. 6).

Critical leadership studies

Critical leadership studies have drawn on the idea of educational leadership with moral purpose. The body of literature has been described as 'a set of critical responses to developments in a number of countries' (Grace, 2000, p. 236) seen as increasingly managerial. Grace (2000) identifies four main themes: educational leadership as ethical practice: aspiring to the common good; school leadership and democratic practice: transforming hierarchy; beyond patriarchal leadership: the contribution of feminist scholarship; and educational leadership: philosophy, morality and spirituality. A feminist construction of leadership (Adler et al., 1993; Blackmore, 1989, 1999; Ozga, 1993) is valued within a discourse of ethical, democratic and moral leadership. Ethical approaches drawing on the *ethics* of *critique, care* and *justice* are explored further below (Begley, 2003, 2006; Begley and Stefkovich, 2004; Begley and Zaretsky, 2004). A notion of emancipatory leadership has challenged assumptions of what constitutes the common good (Grundy, 1993). Democratic leadership has been justified in the double-stranded connection:

> *From schools to society*: schools need to nurture tomorrow's democratic citizens;

> *From society to schools*: democratic society should, by its nature, enable schools to be democratic cultures inclusive of all who work in or have a stake in them.
> (Woods, 2005, p. 32)

Passionate leadership is motivated 'with a moral driving force in ensuring children becoming all they can become' (Davies, 2008, p. 3). The passion has a moral foundation. It is concerned with all children engaging in learning. Leadership as a moral endeavour and for social justice sees a shift towards a concern for the ends of leadership (Heck and Hallinger, 2005). The goal of scholarship might be to use 'our research, status, and power to transform our profession to take leadership for social justice in schools and even society' (Marshall, 2004, p. 5). This theme of leadership for social justice is found in women's leadership literature (Grogan and Shakeshaft, 2011; Lyman et al., 2012). However, further consideration of what social justice means to whom is needed if 'authentic leadership' (Begley, 2006, p. 584) is to be achieved. It is not enough to assume that social justice means the same to everyone.

Values-led leadership

To discuss values-led leadership we must first consider what we mean by values. Haydon (2007) uses Begley's (2003) definition to consider their influence on action:

> Values are conceptions, explicit or implicit, distinctive of an individual or characteristic of a group, of the desirable which influence the selection from available modes, means and ends of action. (From Begley, 2003, p. 3; cited in Haydon, 2007, p. 8)

Hodgkinson's (1991) categories extended from the 'subrational' (values are based in preferences); the 'rational' (values are based in consensus or consequences); to the 'transrational', fundamental principles that might include 'high-level principles that are somehow based above all our other values' that 'might include justice, equality or dignity' (Haydon, 2007, p. 11).

Accounts of individual headteachers' approaches to leadership have explicitly or implicitly revealed the values lying behind their work (Adler et al., 1993; Hustler et al., 1995; Ozga, 1993; Ribbins and Marland, 1994; Tomlinson et al., 1999). Contradictions between headteachers' practice and the principles they espouse have been highlighted (Hustler et al., 1995). The complexity of gendered leadership by some women in such accounts has already been discussed in Chapter 2 (see Adler et al., 1993; Duffy, 1999; Hustler et al., 1995; Ozga, 1993; Regan, 1990; Ribbins and Marland, 1994). Moving beyond the rhetoric of moral leadership there is a need for headteachers to develop

> a degree of self-knowledge that comes to many of us too late in life and an uncommon sensitivity to the values and beliefs of other individuals and cultures.

The payoff of moral school leadership occurs when understanding the value orientations of others, and the political culture of schools, provides leaders with information on how they might best influence the practices of others towards the achievement of broadly justifiable social objectives, not just efficiency. (Begley and Stefkovich, 2004, p. 136)

Such self-knowledge resonates with spiritual leadership (Grogan and Shakeshaft, 2011). It relies on the self-evaluation by leaders (and those working with them) that Grundy (1993) described as emancipatory praxis. Begley (2006) proposes a framework to consider headteachers' ethical approaches to solving problems. His questions relate to interpreting the problem as an *ethic of critique*; working towards a humane response as an *ethic of care*; and taking ethical action as an *ethic of justice*. There is a need for cultural sensitivity in the recognition of ethics as isomorphs (Begley and Zaretsky, 2004). In other words, transrational values that appear to be common to a number of cultures

are rather vulnerable to multiple interpretations in application from one social context to another. When unexamined values are applied in arbitrary ways justified in the name of democratic process, they can be anything but democratic. The essential, and often absent, component that would make adherence to a value genuinely democratic is dialogue. (Begley and Zaretsky, 2004, p. 642)

The uncritical arbitrariness links with Bourdieu's notion of misrecognition whereby social actors forget to question apparently natural and obvious power relations. Examples of *using ethics* rather than being ethical might be when, 'a cultural ethic is imposed on others; an ethic is used to justify otherwise reprehensible action; an ethical posture veils a less defensible value; and an ethic is used to trump a basic human right' (Begley, 2006, p. 581). Critical thinking and moral literacy are essential in avoiding such traps (Begley, 2006).

Headteachers' personal values and worldviews necessarily impact on their resolution of conflict on a daily basis. Shields and Edwards (2005) note headteachers 'cannot deal with parents, discipline students, or allocate resources without being aware of the difficulty of knowing what course of action is "right" or "good" in a given situation' (p. 37). Relational leadership 'is about facilitating the work of others who share the power and authority to collaboratively craft direction' (Grogan and Shakeshaft, 2011, p. 10). That must be achieved through dialogue. However, Shields and Edwards (2005) caution against taking a simplistic approach. Dialogue is about relationships, understanding, building community and breaking down boundaries. Unless head/teachers acknowledge their own 'situatedness' and prejudices, positive as well as negative, they cannot create and sustain ongoing dialogue. They argue, 'to become open to meanings of another we must foreground our prejudices in their multiple forms and our situatedness, expecting the back-and-forth play of meanings with the other to discover "prejudices" of which we were unaware' (Shields and Edwards, 2005, p. 75). Similarly, Butler (2004) argues the struggle for the 'realization of certain values, democratic and nonviolent, international and antiracist' (p. 36) is what leads us to enter 'a collective work in which one's own status as a subject must, for democratic reasons, become disoriented, exposed to what it does not know' (p. 36). Thus feminist theory makes us constantly question our own status relative to that of others in the world. Understanding the impact of differences on a child's learning or staff member's work is vital to the countless decisions headteachers make and the leadership approach they take if it is to have emancipatory intent (Fuller, 2012). Such knowledge cannot be developed without a deep understanding of the importance of our own and others' situatedness or habitus. Bourdieu's (2005) notion of habitus as 'systems of durable, transposable dispositions' (p. 72) enables us to think about headteachers' dispositions in terms of personal values developed over time from their engagement with collective discourses dominating the social fields of family, education and faith communities and the professional fields of teaching and educational leadership. Headteachers develop a (head)teacherly habitus, in terms of their thoughts and feelings about leading in education, as well as a gender, social class and ethnic habitus (Blackmore, 2010a). They make some choices about how they *do* gendered leadership.

Source of values

Grace (2000) reminds us of the English school leadership culture that prioritized, 'spiritual, moral and pedagogical leadership in education' (p. 241). While he refers to Sergiovanni's (1992) notion of servant leadership as a vocation rooted in Judaeo-Christian-Islamic religions, he acknowledges it is also located in the secular-humanist cultures (Grace, 2000). It is useful here to consider what might constitute the 'religious faith, political or humanist standpoints that underpin [headteachers'] lives and exercise of headship' (Fuller, 2012).

Any comparison of the values promoted by the major religions is likely to reveal commonalities as well as intra-faith denominational differences. All the major religions incorporate values concerned with the sanctity of life and social responsibility. de Botton (2012, 2013) draws on religious values to draw up ten virtues for atheists. Transrational values such as equality, justice and dignity are fundamental to a human rights values discourse (UNDHR, 1948). Booth

(2005) distinguishes between socialist theories and socialist values identifying the latter as permanent. Naming as socialist his inclusive educational values, or 'to talk overtly about politics in discussing education is to break a taboo' (p. 152). Nevertheless, the 'centrality of values in developing practice, and a determination to keep in view the values on which my actions are based and those that underlie the actions of others' (Booth, 2005, p. 151) prevails. Aligning values with broader religious, human rights or political discourses enables us to articulate a shared moral discourse. Apple (1992) talks about standing 'under the ideological umbrella' of dominant discourse in making sense of the world. The alternative is to interrupt the dominant discourse and to shape it (Apple, 2009).

The headteachers

Headteachers identified the personal values that influenced their headship. Fourteen discussed values in connection with their work with pupils and education; 15 discussed them in relation to adults and the management and leadership of staff. In the section that follows I explore headteachers' personal values and their recognition of values differences with staff, and pupils and families. I go on to discuss the findings by drawing on *ethics of care*, *critique* and *justice* as well as the notion of *using ethics* in headship (Begley, 2006).

Headteachers' personal values and their source

Nine headteachers located the source of values in religious faith (though one had become an atheist); three in political conviction; two in human rights. A former Anglican had adopted a human rights discourse. Six did not align their values with a broader discourse. I have grouped the headteachers to describe them as headteachers with *faith values*, *political values*, *rights values* and *other values*. Clearly there are overlaps between these descriptions. *Rights values* might be seen as political; one headteacher identified his values as faith *and* political. Nevertheless it is useful to think about headteachers' responses in this way. I do not mean to suggest that headteachers of faith are a homogenous group. They comprised seven active believers as six Christians, a Buddhist and a Muslim. The six Christians (one woman and five men) represented a range of denominations as Quaker, Seventh Day Adventist, Evangelical Christian, non-Evangelical Christian, Catholic and a non-practising Catholic. Muhsin, Robin and Sam had each taken leadership roles in their respective faith communities. These seven headteachers had *faith values*. The *political values* group comprised two headteachers: a woman engaged in feminist politics at university; and a man whose politics were once Left wing. One man who was both a practising 'cradle Catholic' and socialist was identified as having *faith/political values*. Two women with *rights values* adopted a human rights discourse. The remaining six headteachers had *other values*.

Faith values

Stephanie – *A Quaker liberal educational philosophy*
Ben – *Making life better for all, every person matters and relationships*
Duncan – *Christian values of integrity, honesty, trust and equality*
Gregory – *Buddhist belief in having a duty to do the best you can for the good*
Muhsin – *Charity and being beneficial, harmony, peace, togetherness, community strength and reform*
Robin – *Christian respect for the individual*
Sam – *Love of the Scriptures, respect for religion and happiness*

Political values

Diana – *Exercising humanity*
Robert – *Liberalism, tolerance, empathy with children, anti-racism and anti-bullying*

Faith/political values

Tony – *Christian reconciliation and forgiveness, and socialist values*

Rights values

Rosaline – *Transparency, trust and loyalty, respecting human rights*
Silvia – *Individual rights and compassion*

Other values

Emily – *Respect, integrity, doing your best for others*
Isabella – *Goodness and working together*
Katherine – *Honesty, trust, leading by example and high standards*
Lucy – *Mutual respect and achievement*
Rose – *Equality and achievement*
Philip – *Fairness, equal opportunities, wanting the best for everyone and allowing children to make mistakes* (adapted from Fuller, 2012, pp. 680–1).

The interview process provided headteachers with space for self-reflection. However, it was clear most had a high degree of self-knowledge. They talked at length about their values, the source of those values and their impact on headship. Some reported their values underpinned their lives and consequently what they do as headteachers. Others regretted not living up to their own values noting a gap between values they espoused and their work. Headteachers recognized personal values were derived from family background and a range of life experiences. They were articulated as religious faith, political or humanist standpoints that underpinned their lives not just their exercise of headship (Fuller, 2012). People-oriented values aimed to (Brighouse, 2008, p. 29) 'liv[e] one's life by the highest common factor from religious and humanist traditions' came from generational, faith-based, egalitarian or combined imperatives (Flintham, 2008). In particular, the moral imperative of caring about pupils in relation to social justice motivated most headteachers to try to make a difference. They were motivated by an *ethic of care*; some by *ethics of critique* and *justice* (Begley, 2006). A notion of servant leadership that draws on religious discourse was not restricted to faith schools (Grace, 2000; Sergiovanni, 1992) though Ben did not wear Christianity 'on [his] sleeve'. Two headteachers of faith schools were included in the sample. Diana, Robert and Tony referred to Left-wing politics (Booth, 2005). Like de Botton (2012) Silvia traced her values back to an Anglican upbringing. Values were rooted in her family background moral context; they were imbibed at the dinner table, 'without in any sense being conscious of it, what I ate for my lunch and my tea and my dinner and what if people say about me that I have this powerful values drive that is where it comes from'.

Recognizing value conflicts with staff

Headteachers recognized differences among staff in relation to attitudes and values. While one woman headteacher chose to lead schools that already shared her values, two set about changing the culture in terms of underlying values. Headteachers identified values conflicts with staff regarding behaviour management and pedagogical practice (Begley and Stefkovich, 2004). Values conflicts led some to tackle what they considered poor performance. However, there were also values differences regarding tensions between teaching and non-teaching staff (see Chapter 5). In the section that follows I explore some of the values conflicts between headteachers and staff.

Behaviour management

Stephanie (*faith values – quaker liberal educational philosophy*) chose to work in a school reflecting her core values. Values impacted on her whole approach. Her aims for the school were 'fundamentally about my values'. They impacted on conflict resolution that was central in terms of personal and professional development.

> [I]t is therefore taken very seriously because it is something that is slow growing, and which you can never put a final end to it because it is something that you are looking for all of the time. (Stephanie)

Stephanie advocated a relational morality approach to social justice. Pupils understood differentiated treatment in a way some staff did not.

> [P]articularly younger, inexperienced staff find it quite difficult to not react confrontationally in certain situations regardless of the circumstances and regardless of the whole background information that one has got about it. . . . and the fact that [a pupil did not hand in homework] for perfectly acceptable reasons, in my view, doesn't matter to them and I think it is those sorts of things that I feel that they need a black and white structure more . . . (Stephanie)

Social justice was based on knowledge of context and circumstances; it was never about treating everybody the same. It was likened to the English justice system that required evidence and mitigating circumstances to be considered.

> [A]n awful lot of issues are best dealt with as flexibly and as personally as possible. There is clearly a body of opinion that feels that in terms of children misbehaving that you need a very straight forward code . . . I feel that it is very often unhelpful because I feel that children are very different, so I work my hardest to try to get us to look at everybody as an individual. So I am not of the view that everybody has got to be treated equally in terms that everyone has got to be treated the same. (Stephanie)

Two further *faith values* headteachers noted values conflicts regarding behaviour management. Robin's (*Christian respect for the individual*) staff thought he should be stricter.

> [S]ome staff perhaps, aren't aware of all the facts that might be around a child, might be thinking, "You ought to kick that child, that child out. . . ." . . . And you're thinking, "Well actually I can't possibly do that because of the situation that this lad's in and what's behind it all." But you can't tell them because it's confidential stuff. (Robin)

Duncan (*Christian values of integrity, honesty, trust and equality*) knew some staff did not share his values or vision about the treatment of pupils, 'I want them to be on board with the way I'd like children to be treated in terms of relationships and sanctions and style and use of rewards.' He hoped persistence would convince people but staff turnover was an opportunity to replace those opposed to his vision. Two other *faith values* headteachers gave similar accounts regarding the differential treatment of pupils but their values were not in conflict with staff. Diana (*political values – exercising humanity*), decided not to exclude a pupil (see below). The decision led to values conflict with a colleague.

Inclusive education

Rose (*other values – equality and achievement*) ensured staff understood the value of their work with pupils from difficult home backgrounds. It was her responsibility to

> constantly try[ing] to ensure that staff here, through those sorts of stories [about children's home circumstances that lead to poor and unacceptable behaviour] and other things that go on, really do see what an important job it is that we do in education, and that is also to do with making sure teachers here have high self esteem about what they are doing and about the values. (Rose)

When she was newly appointed, she was surprised to find, 'their values seemed to be at odds with their profession and working in a comprehensive school'. She respected values were deep rooted but wanted staff to 'come on board with my values' regarding comprehensive schooling. Her values included social inclusion; high expectations of achievement regardless of socio-economic background; equality; and anti-elitism. Some would not take on her values. Over time they left the school and/or teaching altogether. A more homogenous group still contained diversity. A sense of shared school values was established. She worked with teachers,

> whose values are a little bit outside my own as long as they commit to the values of the school, and they don't display values to do with say elitism or p'raps to do with our socially more challenging children [in] inappropriate ways and basically they have a positive 'can do' approach to our youngsters who step over our doors. That is my bottom line and I get very concerned if staff don't really do, have that. (Rose)

She disaggregated a discussion of values from a notion of effective teaching practice. There was no such thing as 'a perfect teacher'; different teaching approaches suited different pupils. Teachers engaged in a consensus-building exercise to develop a shared sense of what constituted good teaching and learning practice. It was not constrained by an inspection framework.

Lucy (*other values – mutual respect and achievement*), like Rose, found some staff attitudes antithetical to inclusive education in a comprehensive school. She sought

> relationships that were about mutual respect not only between the staff but between the staff and the children. That, in terms of all this spitting in children's faces [accidentally while telling them off] and being really surprised when children turn round and say to 'F' off, and backed them up a corner and spitting in their face and where do they go? Especially children who are not articulate. (Lucy)

Silvia (*rights values – individual rights and compassion*) estimated a high proportion of staff were committed to the values of creating an inclusive learning community.

> That is the quality and calibre that we have and the commitment in the support of staff to the visions and values of the school, in the vast majority of them. That is true of the supporting staff too. . . . I think there are a much higher proportion of teachers here who are on message and a much smaller proportion of teachers who are, in terms of our values and visions that are beyond saving. They are not beyond saving professionally it is just that this isn't the right place for them to be. (Silvia)

Schools with different approaches suited different teachers. Duncan, Rose and Silvia noted staff left when they realized the school ethos was changing to incorporate inclusive pedagogical practices.

Working conditions

Muhsin's *faith values* (*charity, being beneficial, harmony, peace, togetherness, community strength* and *continued reform*) meant he worked long hours to benefit the school and wider community. There was resentment of teachers who shared his faith but not his commitment. They were unprepared to work longer hours than contracted. He complained about teachers' human rights and trades union discourse.

> Sometimes I feel you know that these systems of rights and sometimes rightism or 'This is my right' or 'These are my rights, these are my rights.' This rightism has covered the people's life more than they think about duties. (Muhsin)

Muhsin described teachers as uncharitable. Some had accused him of harassment and sought union support. Muhsin was available beyond the school day; he expected the same of teachers. He equated teachers' concern about terms and conditions with lack of care for pupils.

Recognizing values conflicts with pupils and families

Fourteen headteachers discussed their values in relation to working with pupils. Valuing equality of opportunity impacted directly on the decision to work in comprehensive schools. Education was a way for pupils to improve their life chances and achieve social mobility (see Chapter 5). Philip (*other values – fairness, equal opportunities, wanting the best for everyone* and *allowing children to make mistakes*) considered that the transmission of values benefited pupils. It offered them alternatives.

> I think you have to say here is a model of life, and I am standing up in front of you and giving you. Consider it, view it, you can reject if you wish later, but it works for me and it is within the law and it is for the good of as many people as we can make it. (Philip)

Personal philosophy and faith informed advice to pupils. Muhsin placed great value on career choices valuable to the wider community, 'I teach and I encourage them to be charitable and to be beneficial'. For Robert (*political values – liberalism, tolerance, empathy with children, anti-racism* and *anti-bullying*), morality and educational purpose were more important than abuse of uniform and smoking. However, some misdemeanours called for a tough stance and headteachers discussed fixed term and permanent exclusion from school. In each case headteachers had worked with other schools to give pupils another chance. Values conflicts occurred between headteachers and pupils/families with respect to educational aspiration (see Chapter 5). Values differences linked to faith and ethnicity are discussed further in Chapter 6. In this section I explore other values conflicts headteachers recognized in their work with pupils and families (Begley and Stefkovich, 2004).

Meeting individual needs

Gregory (*faith values – Buddhist belief in having a duty to do the best you can for the good*) felt privileged to have a role in which he could do 'good' for others. In Chapter 2, I demonstrated his engagement with aspects of a feminist leadership discourse. I referred to his establishment of parity of esteem with pupils and parents.

It is worth exploring further his account of resolving values conflict between a 'combative' boy, his family, the school and local authority. Difficulties in a number of schools had been 'hugely distressing' for the boy and his family. Legal actions between the family and local authority had followed. First Gregory noticed the violent behaviour occurred on the mini-bus journey home. He suggested the boy should be dropped off first but the parents were not home by then. That resulted in the boy travelling round for an hour. The local authority refused to fund a single taxi for him because it was not an educational need. Clearly Gregory thought that did not make sense as the family had cost the authority 'a fortune in legal bills and other sorts of bills'. Gregory paid for the taxi out of the school budget so the boy could stay after school for an hour instead. Gregory described the impact:

> [I]n the meantime we also found out, we noticed that he likes hot sweet tea. It's a thing that he loves. So he has a cup of tea and he plays with the computer by himself. And he loves the quiet and he wraps the quiet around him like a blanket. It's an extraordinary thing to see. That's transformed his life and the parents' life and their relationship. It's not anything very profound. It just needs noticing what people like and just giving that extra bit of respect. (Gregory)

Working with the boy and his family to meet his and their needs was a dialogic process that Gregory saw as 'not anything very profound'. It required adults to listen and notice. Where the local authority lacked flexibility, Gregory exercised his duty to do the best he could for the good by funding the boy's taxi fare. In Chapter 2, I referred to the school's support of parents in disciplining children.

Gregory:	We work with parents very closely. It's unusual but we do Saturday morning detention for children who aren't cooperating, aren't working. It works very well. We send taxis for them. We have a major award system but we have sanctions. But we also work with parents and if the parents have any difficulty we run sanctions for the parents as well. So we work very closely in that.
Interviewer:	So if a child does something at home?
Gregory:	So particularly if they're very disruptive. Some of our children . . .
Interviewer:	That's a very close partnership.
Gregory:	It is. It's amazing how it cements a partnership. How the child realizes they really do have [to] change because there's not a division.
Interviewer:	There's something just outside the family that is going to support the adults in the family.

Gregory: One of the child's weapons is embarrassment, or whatever, shame. Children can bully families. That's another thing that's not uncommon, especially Special Needs children, who tend often to be spoiled, because they're [*sic*] Special Needs.

Such close partnership working was likely to narrow values differences between headteacher and families.

Diana (*political values – exercising humanity*) engaged in feminist politics as an undergraduate. She talked about the exercise of humanity in her relationships with pupils and parents. Securing their learning and achievement was the driving motivation but she was concerned for pupils, who lacked the social skills to mix well.

> [I]t is constantly those personal values thinking, 'I like them. I like working with them.' I love doing the dinner queue. Do you know I like the fact that the little ones will come up and say 'Miss have you seen this?' And the big ones are just there for a bit of banter you know. I just think they're just such great, it's such a great opportunity to work with young people in that way. (Diana)

Values conflicts between headteacher and parents were associated with pupil misbehaviour. The parents of some excluded pupils accepted the decision; they shared the same values regarding nonviolence.

> [T]heir parents were just, weren't acquiescent, but were just completely understanding of where I was and why I had to make this decision. And do you know in the end we've managed I think to, just to place all the boys in different schools without going through a permanent exclusion. But that their view, their attitude, just they're positive, they're with us. They're horrified by their children's behaviour and accepted that I had to make this decision. (Diana)

By contrast, the mother of a boy bullying younger pupils refused to engage in dialogue about his behaviour.

> [W]e've got a very challenging mum at the moment; very challenging. Whose son is very difficult and bullies people. She's refused to work with us. She's got a solicitor onto us. She won't work with us about her son. She just constantly picks holes in anything we do and writes long letters of all the things we've failed to do. He was involved in another serious incident two weeks ago where he bullied two more, younger children. (Diana)

Reflecting on her decision not to exclude him, she concluded she was right even though a senior colleague accused her of 'running scared from the parents'. The school had not exhausted all possibilities to resolve the conflict. The mother's disengagement delayed the boy's access to additional support. It meant concerns remained for the 'two Year 7 boys that are terrified that he's going to come up and grab them by the neck to get another 20p out of them'. She reflected deeply,

> I really had to question myself, 'Would I have done it differently if the parents had been somebody with whom we'd had a different relationship?' And I really do think I wouldn't have done it. We might have got further with the child by now and that might have affected my decision. But it's that sense that actually different parents do impact on how you view and treat the child but hopefully not to an extent where we make different judgements. (Diana)

Rosaline's (*rights values – transparency, trust and loyalty* and *respecting human rights*) motivation came from acknowledging a privileged background meant 'you owed a debt'. Her father was committed to public service and shared his philosophy with her during her youth. Concern for human rights came from study of sociology, psychology and human ethology. The most basic human rights regarding health and nutrition informed Rosaline's introduction of health education to improve pupils' diets at a special school. Extreme responses to sensory stimulation led to a rigid approach to eating for pupils with autism. Consequently some struggled. One child ate only chips or crisps; another chocolate biscuits. The impact was demonstrated in bowel problems with one child needing to wear nappies. Parents perpetuated the problem telling staff,

> All he'll eat is chips. That's all you need to give him. Or he'll eat his crisps. (Rosaline)

They accepted children's unhealthy diets. Pupils needed to learn how to be healthy. In her resolution of the conflict Rosaline empathized with parents.

> We have parents who will rattle around and they're discontent with their lot. They have been blessed with what is probably a, very definitely is a, youngster who certainly didn't meet their expectations when they were carrying. So you've got all of those difficulties but you've also got youngsters who are incredibly difficult to live with; really difficult. (Rosaline)

She acknowledged parents' emotions. Trying to stimulate staff participation in the healthy eating project, she asked for their views.

> In fact my very words were 'Are you happy for your child to have McDonalds every day?'
>
> 'Yes'. (Rosaline)

Some of their children had similar diets. Her task was to 'mov[e] hearts and minds' among staff and families towards a shared set of values around the health education of pupils with SEN. She achieved that through staff development activities. Another conflict occurred with the local authority. Again she empathized with parents seeking access to the school and its resources.

> Sometimes I get quite compromised because I could give advice to parents because I have a sympathy at a human level and I know that that would be frowned on by my bosses so it's quite difficult. The most I could do is say, 'if you look up this, this and this you might find that there is a way through.' And go that way. But the difficulty is it's only those people with enough bottle to go or/and are able to really. You need the emotional bottle but you also need the intellectual and the resources to be able to go to a tribunal because it's not nice. (Rosaline)

Barriers were highest for those without access to cultural, social and economic capital. Rosaline was forced to reconcile her *rights values* that led her to support families with her employment responsibilities working in the local authority. Open dialogue with parents, as Rosaline might like it, was not always possible. Limited resources resulted in regulation of their distribution.

The values Philip (*other values – fairness, equal opportunities, wanting the best for everyone* and *allowing children to make mistakes*) acquired from a very secure family background underpinned the work of the school.

> [I]t is all you have got I think, at the end of the day. This is what I believe. And you have to nail your colours to the mast, and say 'this is it; this is what I believe in'. And [the] vision of the school that you want and the way you want it to perform. And the people within it are very much based on the values that you have. That I think is the responsibility that figures large with heads, they are the one person in the school that are looked to, to set the ethos and pattern of the school. I think schools often reflect the values that heads have. (Philip)

His values would last him for life; he had tested and confirmed them. Pupils made mistakes in school because community values were in conflict with school values.

> They don't necessarily come to school with the same values that you have. If somebody steals their pen, it is okay to steal somebody else's, whereas in my world stealing is wrong full stop. (Philip)

Nevertheless, 'school is a place for children and children make mistakes and therefore we live with their mistakes and we try and put them right and we guide them'. He offered his values as an alternative choice for pupils in their futures. Learning, continued learning, creating opportunities, self-improvement, ambition, self-esteem and achievement were valued in school. The socio-economic aim of establishing a career and supporting a family was promoted. Philip saw that as an ideal that was not 'so straight jacketed that it doesn't allow for variations'. What constituted a family was one such variation.

> I am not saying that a family must be a replica of my family, families are sometimes uncle, son and dog, whereas the stereotypical family of a mother and father and two children, one boy, one girl, is way off the mark. . . . I do believe in groups of people that I call families living together and being supportive. (Philip)

He believed in values of 'rightness' and 'wrongness'. If a child misbehaved he worked with families and staff to resolve the conflict through dialogue.

> [T]hat isn't the end of the world for me. 'Let's stop and consider our actions and try and put things right and move on'. (Philip)

Like Stephanie and other headteachers, his approach led to conflict between him and staff.

> That is often hard for other staff to bear, they often expect me to react harshly, and more severely with children than I probably do, so I am the advocate of the child as well. Where they would want to get rid of them it is me who goes the extra mile, 'let's think of another way of dealing with this. Let's just sleep on it. Let's not over react'. We're talking about a child here, that hasn't got the same wherewithal as the adult to stand back and be objective. (Philip)

Recognition, non-recognition and misrecognition of values differences

All 18 headteachers identified the personal values on which they based their leadership. There was a clear sense of moral purpose in their motivation to work in the education of children and young people. In each of the above examples there is evidence of headteachers' recognition of values differences between themselves and staff and pupils/families. In some cases there was acceptance of differences; in others there were attempts to change pupils' behaviour and attitudes to learning, or to change staff attitudes to teaching and working with pupils. There is further discussion of headteachers' recognition of families' dispositions towards education in Chapter 5. In Chapter 6 there is discussion of headteachers' recognition of differences relating to ethnicity. However, the absence of a discourse of values conflicts is of further interest here.

Non-recognition

Values differences between headteachers and staff were not recognized in the discourse of five men headteachers (three *faith values*; one *political value*; one *faith/political value*). In each case there was much talk about their value of staff and recognition of difference with respect to job roles, skills and knowledge. In each case their discourse celebrated diversity regarding teaching ability and the level of colleagues' commitment to pupils' education in its broadest sense. There was a sense of assumed professionalism and the support and nurturing of staff. In three cases there was talk of using flexible working practices to support staff. The absence of a values differences discourse cannot be constructed as headteachers' lack of awareness of staff differences. They resembled the 'Old Collectives' who engaged with feminist discourse who had become headteachers (Mac an Ghaill, 1994). It is more likely this reflects headteachers' length of time in post. A shared school ethos could have been developed through the appointment of like-minded staff. Gregory described his approach to appointing staff in looking for 'goodness'.

> [Y]ou wouldn't employ a good person who was a very poor mathematician . . . But the first quality I would look at is goodness. (Gregory)

In Chapter 2, I described the informal hierarchy connected to contribution rather than job role. Gregory also criticized the NPQH for its lack of a values base.

> I said, 'All that you're assessing, except whether a person is good, it's missing.' . . . someone with all those qualities, but you wouldn't necessarily want him [*sic*] in charge of a school. Therefore you can't assess that. I think people assess it immediately and absolutely and children certainly assess it in grown-ups and in each other. (Gregory)

Values differences between headteachers and pupils/families were not recognized by three headteachers (one woman and two men) with *faith values* and one *other values* woman headteacher. One worked in a selective school with high academic performance. Parents were likely to select the school precisely because they shared its values. One worked in a faith school. Parents were likely to share the *faith values* of the headteacher. The other two worked in comprehensive schools. They each recognized differences among the pupil population. One was concerned for the impact of poverty in pupils' lives (see Chapter 5); the other celebrated the talents of an ethnically diverse population (see Chapter 6). Non-recognition of values differences does not equate with non-recognition of difference. However, non-recognition could lead to misrecognition in selective and faith schools where assumptions are made about shared values. Muhsin's Muslim staff did not share his Islamic values in terms of preparedness to work longer hours. Muslims are not a homogenous group. Nor are highly academic girls; their desires, interests and needs clearly differed in one school where there were emotional and mental health difficulties.

An ethical approach

In this section I consider how far headteachers' values-led leadership discourse was located in a feminist and critical framework (Blackmore, 1989; Grace, 2000). Identification of values suggests they were aware of their 'situatedness' (Shields and Edwards, 2005). There was evidence of a relational approach that valued dialogue (Grogan and Shakeshaft, 2011). In some cases parity of esteem was established that suggested leadership for social justice (Cribb and Gewirtz, 2003; Fraser, 2007; Grogan and Shakeshaft, 2011). I draw on the ethical leadership literature to consider ethical approaches (Begley, 2006).

Working with staff

The accounts of headteachers cited above in the section *Recognizing values conflicts with staff* demonstrate how they approached those values conflicts (Begley and Stefkovich, 2004). They interpreted problems within an *ethic of critique* (Begley, 2006). With regard to pupil behaviour management and inclusive approaches to children's learning they minimized and marginalized dissenting voices to the extent that staff might leave their jobs. Staff turnover created opportunities to appoint staff who shared headteachers' values. It was easier to replace people than change their values. The arenas of conflict were professional and organizational. The values in conflict were headteachers' engagement with relational morality and staff members' desire for clarity, transparency and regulation in the award of sanctions (Stephanie, Robin, Duncan, Diana, Philip);

and non-elitist/elitist approaches to education (Rose, Lucy, Silvia). In Chapter 2, there was some discussion of headteachers' value of staff (and parents') voices regarding curriculum and staff development. In her disaggregation of values and effectiveness, Rose valued staff voices that might otherwise be marginalized in a prevailing culture of managerial performativity (Begley and Stefkovich, 2004). She consulted staff in the development of a shared understanding of what constituted 'good' teaching and learning outside the external accountability framework (MacBeath, 2007). Her value of staff voice might be interpreted as rational in its concern for consensus. Gregory's approach to appointing staff was based in transrational *faith values* in doing the best he could for the good. However, there is also a rational outcome in the positive consequences of his (and the staff's) approach to pupils' education. Implicit in these examples is the *ethic of care* for children's welfare, personal development and futures (Begley, 2006).

There are also examples of headteachers *using ethics* to justify their approaches to staff management (Begley, 2006). Headteachers' values were largely imposed on the staff. They were non-negotiable regarding pupil behaviour management, an inclusive approach to pupils' learning in comprehensive schools, and the appointment of staff. In some cases their consideration of pupils within *ethics of critique, care* and *justice* superseded the consideration of staff and their values differences (Begley, 2006). The exceptions were headteachers who accepted values difference as long as they did not infringe the overall work and values of the school; and the few headteachers who actively engaged staff in shared vision building (see Chapter 5). However, in these examples headteachers did not appear to *use ethics* to deliberately disguise otherwise reprehensible action; to veil a less defensible value; or to trump a basic human right (Begley, 2006). Nevertheless, Duncan's treatment of long-term absenteeism described in Chapter 2 does appear to be an example of *using ethics* to prioritize the interests of pupils over those of vulnerable members of staff.

In Chapters 4–6 there is further discussion of headteachers' recognition of differences among staff that demonstrates their engagement in dialogue across differences (Fraser, 2000; Shields and Edwards, 2005). Approaches to tackling poor staff performance have been located within an *ethic of justice* in terms of fairness towards staff who make greater contributions (see Chapter 4). Some headteachers worked within an *ethic of care* for staff in accommodating flexible working practices for the execution of family responsibilities (see Chapter 4). However, in some cases there was a clear sense that the consequences of their flexibility would be beneficial to the organization and secure personal loyalty (see Chapter 4). Some consulted staff in vision building and change management (see Chapter 5). Rational motives of concern for consequences were evident for some headteachers.

Working with pupils and families

The accounts of headteachers cited above in the section *Recognizing values conflicts with pupils and families* demonstrated how they approached particular values conflicts. In each case they worked ethically (Begley, 2006). Each headteacher drew on an *ethic of critique* in their consideration of who the stakeholders were (Begley, 2003, 2006; Begley and Stefkovich, 2004; Begley and Zaretsky, 2004). The voices that might be unrecognized or unarticulated were the boy with SEN travelling on a mini-bus (Gregory); the boy who bullied other children not receiving support *and* the victims of his bullying (Diana); children with unhealthy diets (Rosaline); and the child who stole (Philip). In each case the headteacher recognized the child/ren. Parental voices are potentially unrecognized and unarticulated. However, it is clear several headteachers tried to work on a dialogue across differences, even when it was particularly challenging (Fraser, 2000). Conflicts occurred across a range of personal, cultural, community, professional and organizational arenas (Begley, 2006). The values in conflict are not always easily named. Gregory's case is about respect for personal dignity and disregard of it by the local authority. Diana's example is concerned with non-violence and violence. In Rosaline's case the conflict might be opposing understandings of a human rights discourse. Rosaline sees the child's right to a healthy and nutritious diet being infringed; the child and parents (and the school staff) might see their right to make unhealthy food choices being infringed. Philip's is about obeying and disobeying the rule of law. The turbulence caused by values conflicts in these examples impacts largely on the pupils and their schooling. However, behaviours associated with values outside those of the headteacher/school also impact on other pupils such as the victims of bullying (Diana) and the daily professional lives of staff including the headteachers. In their humane responses each headteacher responded with an *ethic of care* based largely on transrational values.

There is a possible exception here. Clearly Diana's headship is built on an *ethic of care*. However, her justification for not excluding the boy who bullied other pupils is also based on rational values of concern for consequences. The boy's mother sought legal advice and Diana must be sure the school has done everything it could; there will be scrutiny of decisions and actions by a third party. It may be this rational concern for consequences overruled a transrational value (non-violence) decision that would prioritize care for the victims of bullying. The deputy headteacher's accusation that Diana was 'running scared' implies her decision was based on rational values as concern for the consequences of excluding him. Diana's dilemma was to recognize the bully's needs as well as those of his victims. It resonates with Gregory's concern to listen to the child with SEN who was regularly violent on the mini-bus journey but it was framed differently. Diana's discourse was located within those of the educational and legal systems; whereas Gregory's disrupted the educational system discourse at local authority level.

In these instances ethical action was undertaken with respect to individual rights that also maximized benefits for other stakeholders in line with an *ethic of justice*. Both Rosaline and Gregory took action that countered local authority instruction in the interest of individual pupils and families. They made 'subjective' and 'intuitive' decisions about the redistribution of resources that might result in limiting access to resources by others who had equal or greater need. Each responded personally to the needs of people with whom they interacted drawing on traditionally ascribed 'feminine' qualities (Gray, 1993). As budget-holder Gregory is accountable for financial management. By contrast, Rosaline disregarded the needs of other unknown families by redistributing cultural capital (knowledge about how to argue a case) to maximize some parents' chances of securing a place for their child at her school. In these examples of headteachers' values conflicts with pupils and families there appears to be little evidence of headteachers *using ethics* to justify actions (Begley, 2006). Rosaline will educate staff about the need for healthy eating habits among the pupils, and thereby educate the pupils (and possibly their families) about healthy habits. She will not try to impose healthy eating against anyone's will.

Misrecognition of ethical leadership

Uncritical engagement with values-led leadership discourse disguises the potential for unethical practice with respect to some headteachers' interactions with members of the school population. In Chapter 2, I showed how far Katherine and Duncan might be from engaging in a feminist leadership discourse. Katherine might have misrepresented her leadership as built on *other values – honesty, trust, leading by example* and *high standards*. Her conceptions of honesty and trust included misleading staff about the consequences of workforce reform. What she described as openness, transparency and consultation practices do not equate with practices associated with feminist and ethical leadership discourses. This is an example of the isomorphic nature of values (Begley and Zaretsky, 2004). Openness to Katherine meant telling staff to ask questions. It did not mean sharing knowledge with staff systematically so they gained greater understanding of their work (Duffy, 1999; Grundy, 1993). Consultation resulted in Katherine making the decisions regardless. She was 'let[ting]' people talk; she was seen to listen. Her conceptualization of not being 'dictatorial' was to show she was 'working alongside people' while retaining the power. There is a gap in understanding between Katherine's description of leadership practice and that described by her colleague (see Chapter 2) that suggests lack of self-knowledge (Begley, 2006; Grogan and Shakeshaft, 2011).

Duncan's use of ethics to justify decisions that prioritized the needs of pupils barely disguised lack of care for vulnerable members of staff (Begley, 2006). The Christian *faith values – integrity, honesty, trust* and *equality* did not appear to apply to some staff. In Chapter 2, I showed Duncan's frustration that staff constructed school leadership as hierarchical. They may have noted his 'ruthless' handling of long-term absence and his welcome of increased staff turnover. Both sets of circumstances were likely to have reinforced their construction of power as located in the position of headship and in his person.

Summary and key points for teachers and headteachers

The literature relating to ethical and values-led educational leadership associated with feminist and critical leadership scholarship (Blackmore, 1989; Grace, 2000) has provided a frame through which to consider headteachers' recognition of their personal values and values differences between them and the school population. Headteachers drew on *faith values, political values, rights values* and *other values* in their leadership discourse. Some had arrived at their values later than others. For example, Silvia exercised agency in rejecting her family's Anglicanism; Diana embraced feminist politics as a young woman; and Gregory embraced Buddhism as a young man. Philip had 'tested and confirmed' the values he gained from a secure family background to recognize families that did not have to resemble his own.

Some demonstrated efforts to engage in dialogue across differences to practice relational leadership (Fraser, 2000; Grogan and Shakeshaft, 2011; Shields and Edwards, 2005). In so doing there is a glimpse of 'authentic leadership' in their self-knowledge and recognition of the values orientation of others (Begley, 2006).

In focus was their care for pupils' best interests. Some headteachers were open to dialogue that conflicted with their own notions of what constituted pupils' best interests (Shields and Edwards, 2005). Headteachers' understanding of pupils' best interests sometimes conflicted with the best interests of staff. Headteachers used *ethics of critique, care* and *justice* to justify their decisions with regard to staff management (Begley, 2006).

In the same way that both women and men drew on aspects of feminist leadership discourse in their leadership practice in Chapter 2, so women and men engaged in ethical and values-led leadership discourse. Some of these accounts reveal the moral complexities of values-led leadership. They also reveal potential misrecognition of values-led and ethical leadership by some with regard to staff management.

What Diversity Means to Headteachers: Gender

Introduction

In its exploration of what diversity means to headteachers, this chapter is concerned with headteachers' discourse about gender. It explores connections and gaps between headteachers' life experiences and their discourse about gender-related differences among staff and pupils. In Chapter 2, I focused in part on the inequalities in women's achievement of headship in secondary schools. Their sociocultural roles have impacted on multilevel barriers to advancement (Coleman, 2002; Cubillo and Brown, 2003; Shakeshaft, 1987). Headteachers' experiences of unequal gender relations in the fields of family, education and the workplace might have influenced their recognition of differences among the staff population. They might impact on decisions about access to leadership and continued professional development (CPD) opportunities. They might also influence leadership for learning (Grogan and Shakeshaft, 2011; MacBeath, 2007) and leadership for social justice (Grogan and Shakeshaft, 2011).

Headteachers are accountable for the overall effectiveness of schools measured by the achievement of pupils, quality of teaching, behaviour and safety of pupils and quality of leadership and management (Ofsted, 2013). Whether motivated by external pressure or personal values in an inclusive approach to educational achievement, headteachers are likely to be concerned with the attainment of groups or individual pupils who achieve differently from others. Headteachers' recognition of differences in the pupil population will impact on decisions about pedagogical practice, curriculum design, timetable organization and grouping arrangements. They might be engaged in leadership for learning (Grogan and Shakeshaft, 2011). MacBeath (2007) focuses on an inclusive learning culture. Learning relies on 'effective interplay of emotional, social and cognitive processes' (MacBeath, 2007, p. 253); and is sensitive to context and varied ways of learning. It is a process. Leadership capacity arises from 'powerful learning experiences' and opportunities to exercise leadership 'enhance learning' (MacBeath, 2007, p. 253). There is an important distinction between the accountability of external pressure applied through inspection and a professional imperative concerned with a shared approach to self-evaluation and its congruence with core values, sustainability and succession (MacBeath, 2007). Meanwhile a narrative about gendered pupil attainment persists.

From the mid-1990s the dominant discourse about gender and achievement in English schools has separated children into two homogeneous groups as girls and boys. Like the discourse about women's under-representation in secondary headship, it is an essentialist discourse based on binary opposites of biological sex. The media represents girls outperforming boys at GCSE (Richardson, 2011), A level (Paton, 2010) and university entry (Ratcliffe, 2012). An apparent gender equality discourse has led to a narrative of 'problems of educating boys' (Skelton and Francis, 2009, p. 103). In 2009 the New Labour government published three leaflets designed to dispel myths and share the realities about gender and education with teachers and school leaders (DCSF, 2009a). They offered research evidence of what works in raising achievement (DCSF, 2009b); and ways schools might narrow the gap in attainment between girls and boys in English (DCSF, 2009c). The aim was to 'open up dialogue about gender issues in education' (DCSF, 2009a, p. ii). Myths about boys' achievement, a gendered curriculum and assessment regime, differences in learning styles, preferences for teachers of one sex or the other, competition, single-sex classes and biological differences between the sexes were exposed. Whole school recommendations were made regarding pupil behaviour, valuing diversity through a commitment to equal opportunities, fostering an achievement culture, encouraging pupil involvement and ensuring shared values and aims permeated school life (DCSF, 2009b). Further recommendations were made to narrow the attainment gap in English that related to pedagogy, individual and sociocultural approaches (DCSF, 2009c). Here I explore whether headteachers' discourse about gender was connected to concerns about pupils' learning.

This chapter is divided into four main sections. The first provides a reminder of some aspects of feminist and critical leadership discourse. It explains how Bourdieu's thinking tools of field, habitus, forms of capital, misrecognition and symbolic violence have been used to consider headteachers' discourse about gender. The second section explores the impact of gender-related experiences and roles on leadership and the recognition of differences among staff and pupil populations. Thirdly there is a discussion of the misrecognition of unequal gender relations that results in symbolic violence (Bourdieu and Passeron, 2000). Finally there is a summary of key points as advice and guidance for teachers and aspiring headteachers.

Background

Feminist leadership theory

In Chapter 2, I referred to literature about *who* does leadership and *how* leadership is done. Barriers to women's advancement have been reinforced by women's sociocultural roles (Coleman, 2002; Cubillo and Brown, 2003). On a practical level headteachers need a balanced approach to managing family responsibilities and professional roles (Grogan and Shakeshaft, 2011). Much literature was based on distinctions between women and men as they are biologically sexed. Gender performance is not linked to the physical body but that does not mean we should not be concerned about the experiences of women. While the category of women has been exclusionary there remains a need for a 'double path in politics' concerned with entitlement regarding sexuality and gender that 'subject[s] our very categories to critical scrutiny' (Butler, 2004, pp. 37–8). Questions about *which* women achieve headship and which do not with regard to social class and ethnicity remain. Likewise there remains a need to consider which girls and which boys do or do not achieve in school.

The kind of relational leadership that works alongside people to empower rather than to control (Blackmore, 1989; Grogan and Shakeshaft, 2011) requires open dialogue. Such dialogue recognizes the 'importance of remaining open to one another, meeting the Other with "absolute regard", and taking neither a relativistic nor a dogmatic approach to life, but a celebratory and integrated attitude' (Shields and Edwards, 2005, p. 159). It establishes participatory parity in working towards leadership for social justice (Fraser, 2007; Grogan and Shakeshaft, 2011; Marshall, 2004). Such values-based critical leadership work is built on *ethics of critique, care* and *justice* (Begley, 2006; Grace, 2000). It requires self-knowledge (Begley, 2006; Grogan and Shakeshaft, 2011). In Chapter 2, I showed how women and men might engage (or not) with feminist leadership discourse (Hall, 1999). Shields and Edwards (2005) argue that 'situatedness' or habitus informs an individual's dialogic interactions with others.

Bourdieu's thinking tools

I have used Bourdieu's thinking tools of field, habitus, forms of capital, misrecognition and symbolic violence (see Chapter 1) to explore connections and gaps between headteachers' experiences of unequal gender relations and their discourse about gender-related differences. There might be glimpses of past interactions between social fields (family and education) and habitus (an individual's way of being and doing). Insights are possible into continuing interactions between the social fields and professional fields (teaching and educational leadership) and habitus (Reay, 1995). The complex interplay between past and present might be seen as headteachers de/reconstruct narratives of personal and professional life histories (Reay, 1995). The convergence of individual and collective trajectories might be demonstrated in headteachers' self-reported accounts as girls, boys or pupils; and as women, men, teachers or headteachers. Specific experiences and roles that influence the formation of a (head)teacherly habitus will be explored (Blackmore, 2010a). Forms of capital (economic, cultural, social) available to them, or not, depend on status in a given field (see Chapter 5). There might be direct experience of symbolic violence associated with unequal gender relations. The extent of headteachers' recognition of unequal gender relations and how far that fed into their discourse about gender differences is explored.

The re-theorization of 'gender habitus' considers the possible coexistence of change and continuity in gender relations and identities by acknowledging 'the contradictory effects and dissonance of crossing different fields' that results in 'a more uneven and less seamless relation between habitus and field' (McLeod, 2005, p. 12). It counteracts the notion that field simply reproduces habitus. The adoption of traditionally ascribed 'masculine' characteristics, or 'masculinist' leadership discourse by some women might be explained by their crossing and re-crossing of social and professional fields (Fuller, 2010; Reay and Ball, 2000). So too, might men's adoption of traditionally ascribed 'feminine' characteristics and 'feminist' leadership discourse (Coleman, 2002; Gray, 1993; Hall, 1999).

The headteachers

In this section I report findings regarding 18 headteachers' recognition of gender-related differences in their experiences in the family, education and the workplace; and among staff and pupils. There are two distinct groups of headteachers. Eight headteachers who recounted an experience of unequal gender relations are identified as *gender aware*. Those who did not, comprise a group of ten *gender unaware* headteachers. There are four main focuses. The first is on headteachers' recognition of sociocultural roles and their impact on leadership, followed by their recognition of the impact of sociocultural roles on staff. The second is on headteachers' awareness of unequal relations in the fields of family and education followed by their recognition of unequal gender relations impacting on staff members. Thirdly, I focus on headteachers' recognition of unequal gender relations in the professional field followed by their recognition of unequal gender relations impacting on staff in the workplace. Finally, I focus on headteachers' recognition of gender differences among the pupil population.

Headteachers' self-recognition – Sociocultural roles in the family

Seven of the eight *gender aware* headteachers (Diana, Emily, Isabella, Lucy, Rose, Philip and Robert) referred to the impact of their sociocultural roles on headship. Katherine did not. Nine of the ten *gender unaware* headteachers also did so. They talked about balancing their sociocultural roles with headship; the additional pupil perspectives they gained; using their families as touchstones for school standards; empathizing with parents; the impact of family relationships on professional relationships; and engagement with a broader discourse about education.

Gender aware headteachers (Diana, Emily, Isabella and Rose) and *gender unaware* headteacher Robin described balancing their sociocultural roles as children, wives/husbands and parents with their professional responsibilities. As a single woman, Emily described the tension between caring for an elderly father and working long hours, 'you're pulled in all directions'. Headship affected Isabella's home life. Rose and Diana had supportive husbands. Diana's husband shared parenting responsibilities.

> My husband is completely committed to me and my job as well as to his own job and career. We have a very even spilt on childcare. (Diana)

They invested in home-based 'good-quality childcare'. Robin freed up time for his children in the evening.

> [B]eing a husband and father is more important than one's job but sometimes the job tries to muscle in fully . . . I [got] to work very early . . . that meant that when I got home I would be able to give some time to the children and when they went to bed I'd get on with some work again. (Robin)

Their children's behaviour and experiences directly informed headteachers' interactions with pupils. Having children gave Diana a sense of perspective about pupil behaviour. Diana made a direct link between her son and pupils.

> [W]hen I'm dealing with a stroppy 14-year-old my life experience is there as well. My son doesn't like going to bed at night; my son does this; my son is challenging, but I love him and I would hope that when he was in school his teachers could see past it sometimes. (Diana)

Gender aware Lucy directly compared her children's access to cultural capital with that of pupils in school (see Chapter 5). *Gender unaware* Silvia now agreed with a speech by a union official that identified the interaction between parenthood and teaching as positive. It angered her as a young teacher in its exclusion of non-parents, 'but actually my own experience of parenting has been exactly what she felt hers had been, . . . which I might not have got if I hadn't been a parent'. *Gender unaware* Gregory's children had school experiences making him focus on details in classroom pedagogy and pastoral needs, 'Things that they complain about I try and fix; for instance, I know their horror of school toilets so we have our school toilets cleaned five times a day.'

Families provided touchstones for school standards. Fatherhood was the 'acid test' that increased the sense of urgency making *gender aware* Philip,

> question everything, you are never satisfied with what you are doing, there is always the what if we did something different? And there is always ways of improving, you should never be satisfied with what you've got. That was more truer (*sic*) after I had children than before. (Philip; from Fuller, 2012, p. 682)

Similarly, *gender unaware* Duncan and Sam questioned whether standards at their schools were good enough for their own children.

Gender aware Rose empathized with parents, 'I am very aware of my role as a mother and do talk to our parents about that . . . I know exactly how they feel because I've been there myself' (Fuller, 2012, p. 682). Similarly *gender unaware* Rosaline empathized with parents seeking resources for their children with SEN (see Chapter 3).

Family relationships impacted on relationships with pupils, parents and staff in a positive and fluid way depending on context and circumstance. Diana valued family life that enabled her to handle workplace conflict.

> I needed to be with my husband and my kids and I needed to say, 'This is what matters. What those [people] have just said or done out there doesn't matter. This is what matters.' It gives me such a strong sense of self that I then bring back. (Diana)

Similarly, *gender unaware* Stephanie described the changing interaction of personal and professional roles.

> [B]eing wife, being a mother and being a daughter, all of which carry with them different responsibilities and different demands have moulded the way that I work in my career. I suppose those roles have also, as they have changed, have also changed the way I thought about young people and I have thought about other people in the profession. (Stephanie)

Gender unaware Tony's roles as parent and grandparent influenced leadership as much as professional relationships. Like Sam, *gender unaware* Muhsin articulated a paternalistic approach.

Gender aware Robert's extended family of teachers gave him access to wider educational leadership discourses that spanned phases of education, private and state systems across generations. There was room for much disagreement about educational policy and leadership development.

Recognizing sociocultural roles in the family among staff

Five *gender aware* and seven *gender unaware* headteachers recognized the importance of colleagues' sociocultural roles in the family. Of those, four *gender aware* and five *gender unaware* headteachers enabled flexible working practices to cater for parenting and other family needs. Two appealed to colleagues' sense of parenthood in their work with pupils.

Gender aware Diana's agreement to part-time working for new mothers was automatic, 'It just wouldn't even cross my mind to say no to them.' The predominantly male staff might see flexibility as a 'soft option' but paternity leave and reduced hours were available to fathers. Diana altered staff hours to accommodate continuing childcare even though it caused timetabling difficulties. Staff could work at home, 'If they've got kids and want to be at home for the hours between 4 and 6 and then want to work again then fine'. Parents could take time off to attend their children's school performances or graduation ceremonies. One off absence from meetings was negotiated. Unpaid leave enabled unusual absence and was motivated by a sense that families mattered. However, decisions were not wholly altruistic. Diana noted the personal loyalty that flexibility engendered.

> But now she's mine. She's going to say the head was really good about [unpaid leave]. She'll come back in January invigorated and really committed rather than thinking . . . I just think people don't always think about what you get out of people. (Diana)

Part-time hours were offered to alleviate poor attendance, 'It's made a phenomenal difference to [one teacher's] attendance . . . her health and how she sees herself. . . . it was worth it to get the three days out of her that became quality'. *Gender aware* Lucy was similarly understanding about the demands of motherhood. She facilitated occasional absences referring to times she missed her children's school performances, but would not accommodate regular lateness or absence.

> [Y]ou reckon you can come to work and you have got three children under five then I am afraid I do see it as your responsibility to fulfil and take your time at work and not expect the rest of the staff to all soak up every time there is a problem; because I don't see that as managing your responsibilities. (Lucy)

Her concern was fairness to other staff. *Gender aware* Emily empathized with a member of staff. She would, 'bend over backwards to be helpful'. Like Diana she noted the loyalty flexibility engendered, 'it pays for itself because people recognize that you'll do what you can to help them'. Isabella trusted a colleague to pay back time taken when her daughter got married.

Gender unaware Stephanie understood the demands of motherhood. She supported a colleague with four children under school age with a record of regular unpunctuality, 'I view that rather differently to if one of my single members of staff who once every three weeks phoned up and said they were going to be half an hour late'. Family life prevented some women from taking up professional development opportunities that single women might take.

> [T]hey are likely to perform better at school if we can free them up from as much as we possibly can. In another five years' time it will be different for them and I think that everybody understands that. (Stephanie)

Only one man discussed the childcare needs of staff. Despite personal experience of balancing fatherhood with headship, *gender unaware* Robin regretted agreeing to part-time hours for new mothers.

> [T]he next time I have a request like that I'll probably say 'No'; because the boys lost out, undoubtedly lost out. It was so difficult to find two, a pair of part-timers sufficiently good to be able to cover the full groups. (Robin)

He was prepared to lose an excellent teacher. However, he temporarily accommodated another teacher's lateness to school due to her child's ongoing serious illness. Other *gender unaware* headteachers veered from local authority guidelines in granting requests for absence on an individual basis. Duncan did not need to know the reason,

> We don't work strictly to the LEA guidelines; we will be quite sympathetic there. I think we are probably quite generous; I like to try and regard teachers as professionals who can make their own judgements about their attendance. (Duncan)

This contrasts with his unsympathetic approach to staff illness (Chapter 2). Ben believed, 'people know that their family comes first and if they need support they'll get it'. Support was provided long term for staff caring for sick relatives at Gregory's school,

> We go more than the extra mile for that. Especially if people are dying near staff members, they can go for months and we will support that . . . that's because we deal in people. (Gregory)

Senior colleagues were also knowledgeable about personal circumstances mediating with headteachers when necessary.

Two headteachers appealed to colleagues' sense of parenthood in their working practice. *Gender unaware* Rosaline asked staff whether they would allow their own children to eat unhealthily (see Chapter 3). *Gender unaware* Sam wanted staff to treat pupils as they would treat their own children.

Connections between headteachers' awareness of their sociocultural roles and those of staff

Headteachers' sociocultural roles fed into and interacted with professional roles in many ways. There was a discourse about balancing roles but it was not the only discourse (Coleman, 2002; Grogan and Shakeshaft, 2011). Family roles and relationships impacted on dialogic interactions with pupils, parents and staff demonstrating empathy (Fuller, 2012). Headteachers used their children to consider pupils' perspectives. Here is an indication of how some men used their sociocultural roles in their professional practice (Hall, 1999). Families energized headteachers and shaped headteacherly habitus. Two women noted the interaction between family and school relationships. They described shifting gender performances intersecting with other aspects of their identities. Their discourse resonated with post-structural gender theory (Butler, 1990). They demonstrated the impact of crossing back and forth between social and professional fields (McLeod, 2005).

There were links between some self-recognized sociocultural roles and those of staff. Flexible working practices were described by four *gender aware* headteachers and five *gender unaware* headteachers. However, there were limits for *gender aware* Lucy and *gender unaware* Robin even though they acknowledged the difficulty of balancing roles. By contrast, *gender unaware* Stephanie was particularly tolerant of unpunctuality. Equally, other *gender unaware* headteachers afforded a degree of flexibility that might enable colleagues to establish balance (Coleman, 2002; Grogan and Shakeshaft, 2011).

Headteachers' self-recognition – Unequal gender relations in family and education

Four *gender aware* women described the symbolic violence that accompanied unequal gender relations in the fields of family and education. Rose's father blocked her ambitions for higher education. She was determined to demonstrate he was wrong,

> I was bloody-minded and I was going to prove me right. As he saw it all the expense he was spending on my education at the higher end would be wasted when I got married. And it wasn't. (Rose)

Diana's study of a male-dominated subject led her directly into feminist politics.

> [U]niversity for me made me very aware of gender things. . . . I got very involved in feminist politics for example just because you seek out other women with whom you can spend some time. (Diana)

A job interview revealed the prevailing sex discrimination in industry.

> [T]hey immediately set about asking me how I would cope in an environment that would be very male orientated. Do you know? It just threw me. I hadn't had that kind of really outright, you know, 'would you be able to do it? You're different'. (Diana)

Lucy's educational aspiration was attributed to her mother. Lucy's grandfather had encouraged Lucy's mother when she won a grammar school scholarship.

> [Lucy's grandmother's] attitude (because she had three brothers) was 'well you don't go, what a waste of time, there's no point in a girl going'. But [Lucy's grandfather] had insisted she go, . . . These sorts of things, . . . made my mum . . . absolutely adamant that any daughter she had was going to have equal opportunities. (Lucy)

Lucy benefitted from her mother's experience of sex discrimination. Lucy's grandmother questioned the value of a girl being educated in the 1930s. Lucy's grandfather insisted on equality. Lucy's admission to grammar school was constructed in gender terms, 'Nearly all of the girlfriends that I went to junior school with were either pregnant or married or whatever by the time I left school.' Similarly, Isabella remembered the girls' futures in her class, 'I remember standing there and thinking, I don't want what my friend who had got pregnant wanted etc at 16, 17 – I thought I have got to get out of here.' Lucy and Isabella witnessed the limits placed on their contemporaries' life choices by the dominant sociocultural role of early motherhood.

Recognizing unequal gender relations in the education of staff

Of the four *gender aware* headteachers who recognized unequal gender relations in the fields of family and education only two recognized unequal gender relations in those fields among staff. Diana recognized women support staff left school without qualifications to raise families. They had not fulfilled their educational and career potential,

> that whole cycle of support staff in schools if you look at they're predominantly female. They tended to leave school with very few qualifications. They had their children very young. They're all now coming back to work with grown-up children . . . what you see as you start to scratch under the surface is many of them are very talented, very skilled. (Diana)

She and Isabella enabled teaching assistants to complete foundation degrees by giving financial support and time off to complete academic work. Diana noted the importance of providing opportunities for clerical staff to improve their skills.

> I do think they've got to develop their skills too. That's about them becoming the individuals they really want to be rather than the individuals they've fallen into being. (Diana)

Connections between headteachers' awareness of unequal gender relations in the fields of family and education and their recognition of it among staff

Direct experiences of sex discrimination did not automatically lead to recognition that colleagues might have experienced it too. Women headteachers were more likely than men to say they have experienced sex discrimination (Coleman, 2002). However, Diana and Isabella did use their experiences to recognize the women in non-teaching roles who had not accessed education in the way they had. They actively supported their access to tertiary education. Both acknowledged women's talent demonstrating some awareness of women's exploitation as cheap labour following workforce reform (Gunter and Rayner, 2007). These femininities might be constructed as working class (see Chapter 5). Diana and Isabella worked with women to empower them, in a desire for social justice (Blackmore, 1989; Grogan and Shakeshaft, 2011). Distributive justice was achieved by their provision of resources as funding and time (Cribb and Gewirtz, 2003).

Headteachers' self-recognition – Unequal gender relations in the workplace

Six *gender aware* headteachers recognized the impact of unequal gender relations in the workplace. Positive and negative professional role models as women and men headteachers either inspired them or demonstrated how not to do headship. Rose was influenced by the inclusive leadership of a former headteacher colleague:

> a very inclusive leader, an outstanding teacher . . . I just always knew how good a leader he was and I knew that was the sort of leader I wanted to be . . . the focus was always on the kids and the learning and very much on the children and yet he managed to make everyone in the team feel very wanted, involved so you got the best of both worlds and we were a very strong team as a result and achieved a great deal. (Rose)

Emily described one woman's negative role model from which she learned to be loyal and supportive of staff. Katherine described a woman predecessor's autocratic style that led to aggression from staff. They learned from negative role models but the impact of direct experience should not be underestimated.

Three *gender aware* women and two *gender aware* men recounted negative experiences of working with men enacting hegemonic masculinities. Diana described her humiliation having been refused permission to miss an after-school meeting on return from maternity leave.

> [N]ot only did I feel completely humiliated because I went to ask but it just blackens the relationship I think. It would have made no odds if I was in that staff meeting or not to anyone, other than that he wanted to make a point. (Diana)

Whereas, working with a male colleague taught Katherine resourcefulness and adaptability.

> I was the traditional young female head of department with a male second in department who was very awkward. I learnt man management skills and . . . how to approach different people in different ways. (Katherine)

Emily gained confidence from her confrontation with a powerful male figure.

> I learnt to stick up for myself . . . having to stick up against somebody who was essentially a very big powerful man – both physically and mentally and there's little old me and – and I did it. So I think knowing I could hold my own in that kind of setting was good. (Emily)

Robert described the stress induced by working with a headteacher, who was

> a complete monster of a head. He was a bully. I was second deputy. . . . He induced three nervous breakdowns amongst the staff. It was the only time in my life that I have ever felt stressed to the point of it actually beginning to worry me. He just handled people ruthlessly. He was a coward at heart. He would use other people to bully. (Robert)

Philip criticized a headteacher unable to make eye contact with women.

> I worked for a head who never spoke to women, men were very comfortable in his company; he was a man's man. He could talk rugby and knew lots of things. He never spoke to women. When he spoke to women they felt uncomfortable. When he spoke to them he looked over them, never looked them in the eye. (Philip)

These experiences of difficult gender relations were not just between powerful men and subordinate women. Katherine's subordinate blocked her. Robert's difficulties were between a powerful man and subordinate men, as well as women presumably.

Isabella actively subverted the dominant gendered leadership discourse. Having worked for women's leadership development, she recounted her profound understanding of gender inequalities. The assertiveness courses she led nationally were

> very influential, to help me, as well as help colleagues – to say 'you can do this job'. Because at [the] time, of course, it wasn't fashionable to have a feminine head, you had to be hard. You didn't have a female deputy being a curriculum deputy either – it was a man's job. It was very much challenging a lot of the established traditional values of what teaching was. (Isabella)

Recognizing unequal gender relations among staff in the workplace

Headteachers did not construct differences among staff by biological sex. They constructed differences by job role as members of senior or middle management, in teaching and non-teaching roles (see Chapter 5). They referred to skills and knowledge (see Chapter 5); attitudes and values (see Chapter 3). Four *gender aware* and two *gender unaware* headteachers recognized gender differences among particular colleagues in specific roles as senior leaders, middle leaders, teaching and non-teaching staff.

Senior leaders

Three *gender aware* and two *gender unaware* headteachers recognized gender differences among senior colleagues. *Gender aware* Lucy and Diana tackled poor leadership team performance soon after their appointment. They subverted the dominant 'masculine' leadership discourse by taking the single most powerful position. Both aimed to develop leadership capacity to promote inclusive classroom pedagogies. Lucy described hostility from, 'a group of strong, happened to be male, managers'. She sympathized with the insecurities change brought; but not the patronizing attitudes, refusal to cooperate and obstruction to technological advances.

> I could understand the insecurities but I couldn't accept the refusal, downloading the examination, downloading the disc, 'is she talking about computers? We don't do computers here, dear'. (Lucy)

A painful review process led to the removal of two senior colleagues. Lucy found the process, 'very, very threatening and quite intimidating'. It left her feeling deskilled questioning her ability. Her struggle was to establish an inclusive learning and achievement culture when the school's culture had been, 'a boys' own club and 20 years worth of tradition about . . . "well children don't attend here. You can't expect . . . it's always been . . .". Lucy regretted direct confrontation with one colleague.

> [H]e pushed and pushed and pushed until really I had to take him out, in ways I wouldn't have done. Although he wasn't working for me, I knew, over the years from when parents came in, in time past he'd done a brilliant job. He was just tired. He'd done 30 odd years. I'm not surprised. Instead of being prepared to sit on the sidelines he was obstructive. (Lucy)

Lucy's construction of these senior men was as hostile, obstructive and patronizing. During this period of change women might also be hostile, Lucy described 'quickly pick[ing] up the person lurking behind you with the lipstick of dynamite'. Women might be equally hostile.

Diana handled a similar situation differently. She wanted to replicate the dynamic management team she left. Two deputy headteachers were given, 'a really hard time'. Neither lacked capability so Diana 'couldn't go after them like that'. There was an acknowledged period of waiting until each retired. A re-structured leadership team enabled one deputy headteacher to perform an operational and administrative role. The governing body supported Diana's appointment of new members to the leadership team. With hindsight she thought,

> I took a line that I think that ultimately was wrong. I took a line of 'What you're doing guys isn't good enough' and actually [they] probably could have . . . made it. (Diana)

She regretted a 'battling environment' concluding her best stance was to identify positive qualities and build on them. Her construction of these senior men was as ineffective, uncreative and lacking in their relationships with pupils.

Gender aware Isabella recognized the potential for unequal gender relations in the workplace. Having supported a colleague's promotion to assistant headteacher, she regretted losing her quickly to further promotion elsewhere. The colleague, 'got a Vice Principal somewhere and she deserved that; that's what it's about'. She constructed this senior colleague as ambitious and capable.

Gender unaware Ben and Silvia recognized gender differences relating to senior leaders. Ben described a woman assistant headteacher as a 'great leader' in teaching and learning development, and 'one of our IT guys' had led staff development about using technology in the classroom. He valued the leadership capacity of women and men and non-teaching support staff. A man deputy headteacher was described as a 'great mother' or 'medicine woman'; he took responsibility for staff welfare. The colleague's cultural background was northern English, his subject background physical education. Neither are spaces where masculinity is constructed in terms of women's roles. He constructed this senior man as caring, supportive and knowledgeable. Silvia described the leadership contribution of the school business manager doing dinner duty in terms of non-hegemonic masculinity.

> [H]e is a tiny Irish man and when first started there he was totally nervous, he says it has transformed his feeling about the place, the kids know him, he just

has to look at somebody and their hat comes off and the coat comes off. He can't believe what has happened to him. (Silvia)

Silvia empowered this man whose physical stature and initial lack of confidence might have undermined his authority in school. She constructed him as physically small and initially lacking in confidence; his increased confidence came from interacting with pupils.

Middle leaders

Three *gender aware* headteachers referred to middle leaders with regard to recruitment; role change and empowerment. Diana had appointed numerous women to a predominantly male-dominated staff. One man was appointed as head of department because of the positive and different gender role model he provided. He had

a very gentle way of working with the boys. Actually I got kind of desperate in some ways to have male role models that aren't hard, firm, down the line. (Diana)

An equally capable woman candidate might have been a safer choice. She was

very organized, very crisp, very clear. We'd know where she was, we'd know where the kids were. (Diana)

Diana made the choice to 'get myself out of a mindset'. She resisted appointing someone who might be like her and others. She constructed the man as gentle and flexible; the woman as managerial.

Isabella listened carefully to a colleague complaining about her future in the profession. She did not want to be 'a middle-aged woman in a tracksuit on the field'. Together they worked out an alternative career path, 'She's retrained; she had put a lot of effort in and we have put a lot of effort, time and energy into her'. Isabella's engagement in open dialogue enabled the colleague to share her fear and frustration. Together they created an alternative career path. Isabella constructed the woman as hard-working and capable.

Philip constructed a leadership discourse of empowering others, 'real power comes in empowering other people that is where the strengths lie'. He encouraged a woman head of department to take risks, make decisions and take responsibility. If things went wrong he would provide support.

[Y]ou encourage people to take responsibility and do things that they want to do. Very much you're just a facilitator as headteacher. You're the one that tries to give them the wherewithal. (Philip)

He constructed the woman as capable with potential for additional leadership responsibility.

Teaching staff

Isabella acknowledged her dialogic interactions were imperfect. She offended one woman by referring to a dress as, 'nice and sleazy' but noticed the response and rectified it. Her powerful position gave additional weight to her words and additional discomfort. Similarly, Rose's visits for informal chats prompted one teacher's concern, 'I sometimes think, what have I done wrong?' These two women noted the impact of their powerful position on colleagues' interpretation of words and actions. They were aware of their unintended impact on other women.

Non-teaching staff

Philip enabled a senior classroom assistant to become a form teacher. He constructed the additional role as a professional development opportunity the woman sought. However, he also went on to discuss the blurred edges between teachers and non-teaching staff (see Chapter 5).

Connections between headteachers' awareness of unequal gender relations in the workplace and recognition of gender differences among staff

Two *gender aware* women systematically dismantled male-dominated, 'masculine' and masculinist gender regimes within the senior leadership team and wider staff population (Connell, 2006). They changed tack when initial approaches met further opposition (Hall, 1996). Hostility and obstruction (not just by men) led Lucy to use direct confrontation having tried to change attitudes through professional development. By contrast, Diana was met with ineffectiveness and lack of energy. She ultimately opted to change the gender regime by recruiting new senior and middle leaders. More women were appointed but she altered her approach on recognizing alternative male role models were needed. Both women recognized gender was not fixed to the body as it was biologically sexed. Each referred to women and men doing gender opposite to expected and traditionally ascribed qualities (Francis, 2010; Fuller, 2010). Their gender discourse drew on post-structural gender theory. However, they also described experiences of sex discrimination that drew on feminist theories of equality and difference. *Gender aware* Isabella's previous work in women's leadership development ensured she recognized women's needs. Their careers were developed by way of open dialogue and relational leadership (Grogan and Shakeshaft, 2011; Shields and Edwards, 2005). Her leadership discourse was of empowerment (Blackmore, 1989). The women to whom she referred were in non-teaching and teaching, middle and senior leadership roles. Isabella engaged in a discourse about gender differences that acknowledged multiple femininities as they intersected with social class (Connell, 2005). She also drew on feminist theories of equality and difference in her historical account of gendered leadership. However, Isabella never once mentioned a male member of staff. *Gender aware* Philip constructed two women as capable of taking on additional responsibility. In one case the woman was paid for that responsibility; in the other she was not. There is a danger that Philip had not recognized the potential for exploitation of women as cheap labour following workforce reform (Gunter and Rayner, 2007).

The two *gender unaware* headteachers who recognized gender differences among staff constructed non-hegemonic masculinities. In each case they were linked with men in powerful positions. Ben used women's roles to describe a caring and supportive senior colleague; and Silvia referred to an initial lack of confidence in one senior non-teaching colleague. Both demonstrated understanding of gender as unfixed to biological sex (Butler, 1990). Neither drew on feminist theories of equality and difference.

Headteachers' recognition of gender differences among pupils

Here it is useful to distinguish between school types as headteachers inevitably used generic terms such as children, pupils and students that referred to one sex or another in single-sex schools and did not distinguish between the sexes in mixed schools. Four *gender aware* headteachers worked in mixed schools; four in single-sex schools. Seven *gender unaware* headteachers worked in mixed schools; three in single sex.

Gender aware headteachers in mixed schools (Isabella, Lucy, Rose and Philip) recognized gender differences among pupils with regard to social class and ethnicity although some only referred to one sex or the other. Isabella talked only about Black girls (see Chapter 6). Rose talked about boys with respect to family circumstances, behaviour, curriculum needs and ethnicity. She talked at length about provision for working-class boys in a post-industrial society. Music technology, leisure and sport were seen to reduce the

> very heavy 'laddish' culture in this school, boys are boys believe you me, but
> there isn't that sort of 'laddish' negative, 'laddish' culture and we think that the
> music has played a big role in that. We have got about five bands on the go,

they're always on the go with new bands going, they spend a lot of time down there. (Rose)

Philip referred to a generic sense of (possibly White) adolescent masculinity.

[H]e doesn't like you to stand up and say how well he did but he would like you just to wink at him and say, 'Well done, I saw that.' Then you haven't embarrassed him, but he still got the positive stroke. (Philip)

Lucy was the only *gender aware* headteacher of a mixed school to talk about both girls and boys. She contrasted the work of a girl that was, 'immaculate, [she] writes me a novel every week; it is all underlined', with that of a boy whose relationships were unstable and, 'just about got himself [to school] let alone his planner and his homework, or equipment or anything else'. Her discourse appears to draw stereotypes of a conscientious, hard-working girl and a disorganized boy. However, Lucy's discourse was more nuanced than that. She also referred to a girl's challenging behaviour to construct multiple femininities.

Gender aware headteachers in single-sex schools (Emily, Katherine, Diana and Robert) recognized the intersections of social class and ethnicity with gender. They referred to academic attainment. Some pupils' families at Emily's school were well educated with very high academic expectations that impacted painfully on girls achieving less well.

And that can be terribly hard to have sometimes. They're people who have triumphed over adversity but sometimes they're people who've had the silver spoon and they've been lucky in everything through life and it can be a real, come uppance for them and very, very hard. (Emily)

Academic failure was not getting into Oxbridge. Similarly, as already discussed in Chapter 2, Katherine described the dangers of academic pressure.

[I]n a girls' school that's high achieving with it come the neuroses, the anorexia, the self harm, because, not because of the type of school it is, but because of the type of girl that they are. They've got tremendous pressure on them. We don't put it on, they put it on, and the family put it on. (Katherine)

She did not connect teenage pregnancy with the low self-esteem she described among Year 7 girls who found their cultural capital did not match that of their classmates. Emily contrasted impoverished and affluent girlhoods (see Chapter 5). She also recognized national heritage, racialized and faith girlhoods (see Chapter 6). Katherine never mentioned ethnic differences. Emily and Katherine referred to relationships with the opposite sex. Joint activities with a local boys' school were organized for Emily's pupils. The bus journey enabled informal social interaction with boys. Emily believed girls should not see boys just, 'as sex objects'. They should be friends and workmates. Katherine's acknowledgement of unplanned pregnancy demonstrated boys played a part in pupils' lives. However, there was an assumption of heterosexuality by both headteachers.

Diana constructed impoverished and middle-class boyhoods that equated with lack or acquisition of cultural capital. She referred to ethnic identities. Robert constructed socially mobile and diverse ethnic and faith boyhoods (see Chapter 6). Diana and Robert also constructed multiple masculinities in descriptions of boys' lack of social skills, eccentricities or a spectrum of gender performance. Diana's pupils were

> those boys who stand in the playground alone who walk around by themselves. They don't need any other grouping. They're not 'bright' or 'not-bright', they're not 'White' or 'Black', they're just kids who for whatever reason haven't made it in terms of knowing how you approach somebody and hang out with. (Diana)

Robert thought boys seen as 'eccentrics . . . find their niche somewhere in the school'. He empathized more naturally with budding actors than those aiming for military careers, but gave boys equal time and support. Choice of career would impact on boys' future access to economic, cultural and social capital; it also impacted on their performance and Robert's construction of masculinities. He recognized a need for

> a cross-section, so there are people who are very literate and academic. There are people who are good scientists and engineers. You've got people who are 'people people' and in caring professions. You do need some military people and some intending policemen, otherwise society will collapse and each one deserves encouragement in the framework, which you're creating for them. (Robert)

Robert referred to girls' high levels of academic achievement at the 'sister' school where they outperformed his boys. Diana never mentioned girls.

Gender unaware headteachers in mixed schools (Rosaline, Silvia, Ben, Duncan, Gregory, Muhsin, Tony) recognized a variety of gender differences. Working with pupils according to individual need in a special school, Rosaline noted biological difference was meaningless in providing equal opportunities. She used biological sex to monitor progress, 'but I don't find it as constructive in terms of the conventional means of dealing with boys and girls and equal opportunities and all the rest of it because it's actually opportunities for all whatever you are'.

However, two headteachers referred to a 'gender gap' in academic attainment. Duncan focused on the varied attainment of girls and boys; their apparently different learning styles; experimentation in single sex classes; and differentiated teaching materials.

> [T]here is a certain type of literature that appeals to boys and a certain type of literature that appeals to [girls] and they would target the groups accordingly. I think as well, there is a way boys learn better and a way that girls learn better in terms of teaching and learning strategies. (Duncan)

By contrast, Tony was sceptical about a gender gap in attainment and various strategies designed to counteract it.

> [B]oys have always done worse than girls. Even when I was at school the girls did better until you were at sixteen. At university you tended to even out a bit. We exhibit the gender difference [in the school]. (Tony)

Gender was constructed in relation to social class. Ben constructed impoverished girlhood; Duncan constructed underachieving, football-playing boys. Despite an earlier essentialist discourse of gender difference regarding learning styles, Duncan acknowledged the complexity of gender performance.

> [T]he developing view that kind of sexuality (*sic*) isn't polarized, you could get boys whose learning styles and all sorts of attitudes if you like, are drifting towards the female side and the other way around. So it is slightly more of a spectrum than we ever thought it was some twenty years ago, but as a generality I think you could say they have different learning styles. (Duncan)

Duncan and Tony referred to the intersection of gender and ethnicity. Duncan referred to Black boys; Tony to Pakistani girls (see Chapter 6). In an Islamic school, girls and boys were segregated. Muhsin recognized the intersection of gender with national heritage and faith.

In Ben's school there was gender equity in the reward system. A girl and boy from each year group were selected on the basis of consistent effort and contribution to the school to become 'student of the year'. It was the only example of a headteacher specifically outlining an explicitly equitable approach. Girls and boys were also represented on the school council at Silvia's school. Her descriptions appeared to draw on stereotypes of mature and articulate girls and immature, self-centred boys. One girl was indifferent to school but, 'She is going to be a great trade unionist, she's going to be a great "them and us" sort of person'. Another used the council to question the quality of teaching and learning. By contrast the boy, 'just can't help interrupting all the time but it is because he constantly, he is desperate to understand what is going on and make a contribution, but he is still a really little boy, so everything has to be interpreted in terms of his own personal experience' (Silvia).

Gregory referred to both a boy and a girl when highlighting the importance of respecting pupils and ascertaining their needs. Each was prone to disruptive and abusive behaviour; each given the opportunity to articulate their needs over a cup of tea. The boy's story was reported in Chapter 3. Another involved a girl.

> [S]he used to come and she used to be calling me [names]. For her it was [accepted]. She got up and had a cup of tea and came back and she'd be fine. Now that's not to say that I would accept that language from everybody. But from her at that time. (Gregory)

Gender unaware headteachers in single-sex schools (Stephanie, Sam, Robin) recognized gender differences regarding social class and ethnicity. Stephanie actively discouraged academic competition. She was anxious

> not to create an aggressively competitive atmosphere in the school so that the emphasis would always be on the celebration of success, without the sense that you have trodden on everyone else's head to get there. (Stephanie)

A consequence might be to lower anxiety levels. Her approach contrasts with Katherine's apparent powerlessness regarding pupils' emotional welfare (Chapter 2). Stephanie also recognized 'multi-faith' girlhoods. She never mentioned boys. Sam's vision for girls was to compete on an equal basis with boys.

> It's a very simple vision – that every individual girl leaves here with all the necessary tools to survive in life, to compete on an equal basis with all the blokes and even do better than they. (Sam)

He recognized lack of educational aspiration among girls and their families. He also recognized faith and Black girlhoods relating to specific Caribbean island origins. Robin recognized working-class boyhood where parents worked long hours. He also recognized Sikh boyhood. Girls joined the sixth form as a minority population. Robin did not think

> they lose by being in such a minority. They get looked after by the boys. The boys are very protective of the girls, probably too protective in the sense that it means that they'll run and help when they shouldn't run and help. (Robin)

Boys' overprotectiveness of girls might also indicate sexual attraction between them.

Connections between headteachers' awareness of unequal gender relations and gender differences among pupils

Among *gender aware* headteachers in mixed schools only one talked about both girls and boys. Lucy gave the most balanced account of gender difference in recognizing multiple femininities and working-class masculinity. However, she did not recognize the intersection between gender and ethnicity. Three out of four *gender aware* headteachers in single-sex schools referred to both sexes. Inevitably their recognition of gender difference was more fine-tuned. All four recognized the intersections between gender, social class and ethnicity (Connell, 2005). Two recognized the intersection of gender with heterosexuality. Two distinguished further to identify eccentric or socially unskilled masculinities. Neither was bound by conventional social categories.

There were more diverse gender difference discourses among *gender unaware* headteachers in mixed schools. One drew on an essentialist discourse of gender difference about girls and boys' learning preferences as well as post-structural theories of intersectionality (Connell, 2005; Crenshaw, 1991) and a notion of gender that is not linked to biological sex (Butler, 1990). Only one headteacher engaged in a gender equity discourse that draws on feminist theory of equality. Like Lucy, both Silvia and Gregory gave accounts of both girlhood and boyhood though Silvia acknowledged her discourse drew on gender stereotypes. Gregory, like Lucy, gave an account of disruptive and abusive girls.

All three *gender unaware* headteachers in single-sex schools recognized intersections between gender, social class and ethnicity (Connell, 2005). One headteacher actively reduced academic competition. An unintended consequence might be to reduce anxiety. A traditionally 'feminine' notion of 'modest' and 'non-competitive' achievement was nurtured. It was located in faith values connected with pacifism (see Chapter 3). By contrast, Sam wanted girls to compete on equal terms with boys. Robin may have underestimated the impact of girls learning helplessness from overprotective boys.

Non-recognition and misrecognition

Sociocultural roles

Despite recognition by four women and one man that their sociocultural roles resulted in balancing leadership with family responsibilities, there was little recognition of that among staff (Coleman, 2002; Grogan and

Shakeshaft, 2011). Five headteachers referred only to colleagues' professional roles. That included two *gender aware* women and one *gender aware* man. Experiencing or witnessing unequal gender relations was not enough to ensure headteachers were concerned with unequal gender relations in the workplace. Diana was the only headteacher who did not question the right to flexible working practices for new parents. Her discourse about unequal gender relations demonstrated how gender habitus was layered over time to include experiences in education; the recruitment process in industry; and the humiliation caused by an inflexible headteacher colleague (Reay, 1995). Her heightened awareness was enhanced by engagement in feminist politics. Like Emily, she noted the personal loyalty flexibility engendered; her approach might not be wholly altruistic. Apparently liberal attitudes might be more manipulative than first appears (Cliffe, 2011).

Unequal gender relations in the family and education

Only two *gender aware* women recognized the possibility of unequal gender relations in the education of staff. Diana and Isabella rectified it in their practice of leadership for learning (Grogan and Shakeshaft, 2011; MacBeath, 2007). They engaged in distributive justice by providing resources for women whose education and career potential had been curtailed (Cribb and Gewirtz, 2003; Grogan and Shakeshaft, 2011).

Unequal gender relations for staff in the workplace

The gender regimes of the senior leadership teams Lucy and Diana inherited were constructed as 'masculine'. As headteachers, they did not always empower others. They resorted to exercising power to control in order to create an inclusive learning culture where there had been none (Blackmore, 1989; Grogan and Shakeshaft, 2011; Hall, 1996; MacBeath, 2007). They used aggressive language in their accounts with phrases such as 'take him out' and 'go after them'. The women choreographed their headships to suit the context and circumstances (Hall, 1996). They adopted 'masculine' approaches because the role required it (Fuller, 2010; Reay and Ball, 2000). Use of these tactics and language reinforces the women's power base to give them a 'masculine' headteacherly habitus. Isabella and Rose each caused offence but noticed it. Their self-awareness led them to correct the situation (Begley, 2006; Grogan and Shakeshaft, 2011). Each of these four women were *gender aware* headteachers.

Gender differences among pupils

Headteachers engaged in various gender discourses that drew on feminist theories of equality and difference; multiple femininities and masculinities (Connell, 2005; Mac an Ghaill, 1994); and post-structural gender theory that disconnects gender performance from biological sex (Butler, 1990). An equality discourse led to monitoring pupils' progress by biological sex; an equitable rewards system and representation on the school council; and desire for girls to compete equally with boys. There was some concern for parity of esteem and associational justice in two headteachers' accounts (Cribb and Gewirtz, 2003; Fraser, 2007; Grogan and Shakeshaft, 2011). A discourse of intersectionality (Connell, 2005; Crenshaw, 1991) resulted in the recognition of multiple femininities intersected by social class, ethnicity and (hetero)sexuality; and multiple masculinities intersected by social class, ethnicity, (hetero)sexuality, sociability and career choice.

Misrecognition of unequal gender relations

So far I have discussed recognition and non-recognition of gender differences relating to particular gender theories. Misrecognition occurs when social actors forget to question the arbitrariness of status and power relations in the field. Gender and sex differences barely featured in most discourses of differences among staff. Unequal gender relations featured even less. In their adoption of an equality discourse headteachers might have forgotten to engage critically with the unequal gender regimes in their schools. They cannot be unaware of the gap between women in the teaching workforce and women as headteachers. In any case, there is misrecognition in headteachers' refusal to honour flexible working practices following maternity leave. There is evidence of headteachers *using ethics* to present an argument about fairness to staff as a whole (Begley, 2006); and of using managerial arguments to refuse flexible working. So too, there is misrecognition in the assumption new mothers do not want to advance their careers while children are young; that single women have no family responsibilities. It may be that fathers and single men relish the opportunity for flexible working practices. A family friendly approach as advocated by Grogan and Shakeshaft (2011) might benefit all. In Chapter 5, I discuss the misrecognition of the intersection of social class with gender regarding non-teaching staff. The impact of the intersection of ethnicity with gender is also misrecognized in headteachers' virtual non-recognition of ethnic differences among staff (see Chapter 6).

There is also misrecognition of the emotions of gender transition (Connell, 2006). Women's exercise of power to control to achieve their objectives marked a shift from their preferred approach (Hall, 1996). The four headteachers who recounted the awareness of power were *gender aware*; less gender aware headteachers are unlikely to question the powerful impact of their actions and words on others (Whitehead, 2001).

There was misrecognition of unequal gender relations among pupils. Although multiple femininities and masculinities were recognized and the intersections between gender, social class and ethnicity noted there was not much evidence of headteachers' understanding of unequal gender relations among pupils; or provision for gender difference (Fuller, 2012). Headteachers largely labelled pupils. Some empathized. Only two referred to equitable practice. The strongest discourse was about working-class boys; followed equally by working-class girls, BGM girls and BGM boys. In each case fewer than half the headteachers recognized these pupils. Uncritical or lack of engagement with an unequal gender relations discourse demonstrated headteachers' misrecognition of the roles schools play in perpetuating stereotypes and unequal gender relations. There was no discussion of teaching pupils to deconstruct gender stereotypes for example. Nor of monitoring over/under-representation of girls and boys in particular subjects.

Summary

Gendered headteacherly habitus

Headteachers hold powerful positions. How they perform gendered leadership impacts on large populations of pupils and staff. Just as members of staff drew on a range of gender narratives to construct gendered headship (Fuller, 2010) so some headteachers drew on a range of experiences that demonstrated engagement with gender discourses in the fields of family, education and the workplace. Their variable status in those fields afforded or limited access to economic, cultural and social capital. Personal accounts of sex discrimination and/or bullying in the family, education and the workplace led to intense feelings of humiliation and stress for some. Such experiences of vulnerability and passion, grief or rage led headteachers to reflect deeply (Butler, 2004). In the main, the perceived misuse/abuse of power was located in hegemonic masculinity – as middle-class (probably White) men holding powerful positions as father, interviewer, headteacher(s)

(Connell, 2005). However, powerful women, as former colleagues, also adopted qualities that might be traditionally ascribed as 'masculine' (Reay and Ball, 2000). The headteachers in this study overcame difficulties associated with unequal gender relations to progress to headship. Their experiences informed their gendered headteacherly habitus.

Interactions with non-hegemonic masculinities and multiple femininities also influenced gendered headteacherly habitus. Headteachers acknowledged the influence of working-class masculinities and femininities, and middle-class femininities in their backgrounds (see Chapter 5). Two headteachers identified the influence of global majority and ethnic minority femininities and masculinities (see Chapter 6). The men headteachers in the study did not all conform to hegemonic masculinities as White and of middle-class origin (Connell, 2005). Two women who failed to comment on gendered power relations described their fathers' powerful influence. These women acknowledged privileged backgrounds. However, that did not mean there were no struggles. One described the impact of learning difficulties that obstructed her education.

There was no simple correlation between the recognition of unequal gender relations in headteachers' backgrounds and recognition of unequal relations among staff and pupils. There were headteachers who connected their experiences of reduced status in the fields of family, education and/or the workplace with those of staff and/or pupils. There were those who did not. Similarly, there were headteachers with no experiences of unequal gender relations who recognized them in staff and/or pupils. With regard to establishing participatory parity whether headteachers recognized both sexes as staff and pupils is important (Fraser, 2007). Two men never mentioned either sex; one man never mentioned women; two women and two men never mentioned men. There was a distinct lack of explicit recognition of unequal gender relations. There was little reference to gender as performance.

In their non-recognition of gender inequalities, there was a danger that eleven headteachers (three women and eight men) misrecognized gender relations in the fields of family, education and the workplace. Headteachers' experiences of unequal gender relations did not necessarily translate into awareness in the workplace. The dominant discourse of gender inequality in teaching and educational leadership overpowered that of family and education experiences. It seems the 'headteacherly' habitus is influenced more by the professional field than by gender habitus in some cases. Or else the adoption of an equality discourse blinded headteachers to gender issues. Headteachers failed to recognize the impact of powerful performances of hegemonic masculinities on women and men. By contrast, the professional field's influence on 'headteacherly' habitus of some gender unaware headteachers might be positive in making them more gender aware.

In their discourse about differences among pupils, six headteachers (five women and one man) never mentioned one sex or the other. In single-sex schools, three women only talked about their school population. In mixed schools one woman only talked about girls; one woman and one man only talked about boys. Pupils missing from this discourse about differences became invisible. It might not be surprising for headteachers to talk only about the sex of their school population, but four headteachers of single-sex schools *did* talk about the opposite sex with regard to relationship building; academic competition; and equality of access to employment. The differing status of women and men in the professional field, and of girls and boys in the social field of education affords them different levels of access to economic, cultural and social capital. Chapter 5 goes on to examine headteachers' discourse about differences with regard to social class.

5

What Diversity Means to Headteachers: Social Class

Introduction

This chapter is concerned with headteachers' discourse about diversity with respect to social class. In Chapter 2, I outlined inequalities in women's achievement of secondary school headship. I noted a more nuanced examination of *which* women achieve headship was necessary. Women whose families have 'always' been middle class might be more likely to achieve headship. Socialization and stereotyping barriers apply to class inequalities as well as gender. Class inequalities in the fields of family and education might influence headteachers' recognition of differences among staff and pupils. Class distinctions, as internalized dispositions, might influence headteachers' engagement with leadership for learning (Grogan and Shakeshaft, 2011; MacBeath, 2007) and leadership for social justice (Grogan and Shakeshaft, 2011).

Headteachers are concerned with the attainment of pupils. The 'floor target' requiring 40 per cent of all pupils to gain five higher grade GCSEs was imposed in 2011 with the ambition it should rise to 50 per cent by 2015 (BBC, 2011). That target applies regardless of pupils' prior attainment, SEN and socio-economic background. A narrative about pupil underachievement persists. While the dominant discourse has been about gender and educational achievement, evidence shows social class and ethnicity should be factored into analyses of pupil attainment. Educational disadvantages perpetuated by lack of economic, cultural and social capital need recognition. In an effort to break the link between disadvantage and low attainment, New Labour shared research findings about early years development and home deprivation, the potential for one-to-one tuition, quality of teaching, patterns of behaviour, community aspirations, broadening the range of qualifications and recognizing links between children eligible for FSM and SEN (DCSF, 2009d). Disadvantaged children attained less well in schools not seen as disadvantaged. Here I explore whether headteachers' experience of social class inequalities was connected to their concerns about pupils' access to learning. Headteachers' recognition of class differences might impact on decisions about pedagogy, curriculum design and school organization.

This chapter is divided into three main sections. The first outlines what is meant by social class in terms of economic, cultural and social forms of capital (Bourdieu, 1986). Bourdieu's thinking tools of field, habitus, forms of capital, misrecognition and symbolic violence are used to consider headteachers' discourse about class. I provide an overview of the socio-economic factors used in some analyses of pupil attainment. The second section explores headteachers' experiences of social class inequalities in the fields of family and education, framed by Bourdieu's (1986) forms of capital. Headteachers distinguished between staff members by job role, skills and knowledge. Recognizing staff as senior and middle leaders, teaching and non-teaching staff is a classed distinction. I focus on headteachers' recognition of these groups. Headteachers distinguished between pupils' socio-economic statuses as well as perceived 'ability'. In the third section there is discussion of headteachers' misrecognition of unequal social class relations (Bourdieu and Passeron, 2000). Finally the chapter ends with a summary of key points as advice and guidance for teachers and aspiring headteachers.

Background

Forms of capital

By social class I refer to an internalized disposition informed by an individual's access to various forms of capital in the social fields of family and education, and in the professional fields of teaching and educational leadership. As outlined in Chapter 1, three forms of capital are identified as economic, cultural and social capital (Bourdieu, 1986). Economic capital has monetary value. Cultural capital has monetary value but is also institutionalized as educational qualifications. It exists in an embodied state as 'long-lasting dispositions of the mind and body' (Bourdieu, 1986, p. 47); and in an objectified state as goods such as books, access to computers and the internet. Social capital as social connections might be converted into economic capital. It impacts on the development of long-lasting dispositions; and enables access to power and influence. Cultural capital provides a possible explanation for the,

> unequal scholastic achievement of children originating from the different social classes by relating academic success i.e., the specific profits which children from the different classes and class fractions can obtain in the academic market, to the distribution of cultural capital between the classes and class fractions. (Bourdieu, 1986, p. 47)

It is of interest in an education system that prioritizes educational qualifications as the measure of success. In England, headteacher effectiveness is measured by the acquisition by pupils of institutionalized cultural capital in the form of qualifications that lead to further and higher education, employment and training.

In Chapter 4, I used Bourdieu's thinking tools of field, habitus, forms of capital, misrecognition and symbolic violence to consider headteachers' discourse about gender. Here I consider how headteachers' varied status in the fields of family and education impacted on their access to forms of capital and subsequent development of a (head)teacherly habitus (Blackmore, 2010a).

Social class identity

Reay (1997) conceptualizes class as 'encompassing complex social and psychological dispositions that interact with gender and race to inform and influence everyday practice' (p. 226). Bourdieu's notion of habitus describes a set of dispositions that are 'powerfully internalized and continually played out in interaction with others across social fields' (Reay, 1997, p. 226). Maguire's (2005) exploration of women teachers' class identities demonstrated their 'plasticity' and the complexities of class boundary crossing among women teachers of working-class origin. Social class is seen as a 'complex amalgam of economic and material conditions as well as embodied lived experiences and subjectivities' (Maguire, 2005, p. 4). The women's 'classed "footprints behind" still mark[ed] the "footsteps forward"' (Maguire, 2005, p. 7) particularly where women worked with working-class children. Teachers could,

> call up identities patched together from their class trajectories, their role and occupation, their gendered subjectivities and a range of other attributes: notably 'race'/ethnicity, age, (dis)ability and sexualities as well as mothering, other

dimensions of caring and critical material conditions. In some contexts they can 'play' with their identities. (Maguire, 2005, p. 8)

With 'hybrid' class identities, women could 'move between class-cultural contexts' (Maguire, 2005, p. 8). Their breaks were with class rather than gender norms. Their experience contrasts with that of middle-class women who achieved headship from the last quarter of the nineteenth century (Watts, 1998). The conflation of teaching with discourses of care and mothering meant women could imagine working with children (Maguire, 2005). Links between teaching, care and mothering might once have applied to primary schooling but secondary schools have long been gendered as 'masculine' (Gray, 1989). The dominance of performativity and managerialist discourses throughout education mean teaching cannot be seen as a feminized profession just because it is dominated by women (Lingard and Douglas, 1999; Skelton, 2002). Modernization means it is no longer a good career choice for women, particularly those with children (Conley and Jenkins, 2011; McNamara et al., 2008, 2010). For working-class men who work in female-dominated occupations such as teaching, their construction of success has been located in a discourse of upward social mobility (Lupton, 2006). Teaching has been constructed historically to exclude or include particular masculinities and femininities (Martino, 2008). The question of which women and men achieve headship is complex.

Social class and education

Children's educational outcomes measured by the attainment of nationally recognized tests and qualifications have been analysed for variation by gender, social class and ethnicity. Skelton et al. (2007) used receipt of FSM as an indicator of social class. However, eligibility for FSM was found to be an imperfect proxy for low income households. It indicated low income only before benefits were received (Hobbs and Vignoles, 2010). Benefits pushed household incomes up sufficiently for up to half of children eligible for FSM to move out of the lowest household incomes. The use of FSM as a proxy for social class might be problematic for the distribution of resources to schools and the reporting of educational attainment. Nevertheless, it remains an indication of state dependency (Gorard, 2012). In addition to FSM, contextual variables such as attendance, motivation and attitudes towards school and parental involvement have been used to explore underachievement (Smith, 2003). Others have used neighbourhood data to give a 'relatively versatile indicator of a child's individual circumstances' (Kingdon and Cassen, 2010, p. 408). Mensah and Kiernan (2010) have measured family environment using information about income, maternal qualifications, employment, housing tenure, neighbourhood, family structure, ethnic origin and home language. Strand (2011) considered four main blocks of variables as family background including home social class, maternal education, entitlement to FSM, home ownership and family composition; parental attitudes and behaviour (likely to create the context for student attitudes and behaviour); student risk and protective factors associated with low or high attainment; school context and neighbourhood deprivation. Such analyses have attempted to specify families' access to economic, cultural and social capital.

The headteachers

In the following sections I report findings regarding 18 headteachers' discourse about social class. Their experiences of unequal class relations might impact on their recognition of social class differences in the school population. Headteachers draw on life experiences in the fields of family, education and/or the workplace to construct aspects of their headteacherly habitus and leadership discourse. First, I look at headteachers' recognition of their social class backgrounds with respect to economic, cultural and social forms of capital. Secondly, I look at their recognition of differences among staff. Thirdly, I look at their recognition of differences among pupils.

Headteachers' self-recognition

Sixteen of eighteen headteachers recalled family background influences on headship. Twelve referred to social class; parental occupations or being raised in relative poverty or affluence. Eight headteachers constructed family backgrounds as working class. They experienced class inequalities. Four constructed family backgrounds as middle class; however, two women struggled to access higher education and witnessed class injustice in education. Those women have been included in the *class aware* headteacher group. Another described a complex set of circumstances that impacted on his education and subsequent headship. He has been included. In total there are eleven headteachers in the *class aware* group (Diana, Emily, Isabella, Lucy, Rosaline, Rose, Ben, Duncan Gregory, Robin and Tony). Five gave no clear indication of class background or experience of class inequalities; they are grouped with those from middle-class backgrounds as seven *class unaware* headteachers (Katherine, Silvia, Stephanie, Muhsin, Philip

Robert and Sam). I have separated the forms of capital for the purpose of analysis. However, they clearly interact with each other, and with gender and ethnicity, to inform internalized dispositions that inform headteacherly habitus and impact on leadership discourse.

Economic capital

As secondary school headteachers they earned considerably more than the median national wage (at the time of writing £26,200 (ONS, 2012a)). Salaries are dependent on size and location of school, but leadership team salaries range from £37,461 at a small school outside London to £112,181 for a headteacher in a large school in inner London (NUT, 2012). Ben acknowledged his relative wealth, 'at this particular moment in time [I] do different things that society thinks I should be paid more than anybody else for doing that'. However, Muhsin's description of long hours of voluntary work, 'if I would have gone to business I would have been [a] millionaire now', is a reminder that headteachers' full unofficial working week extended to an average of 62.4 hours (Halliday-Bell et al., 2008). Education was the means to upward social mobility for some headteachers in the *class aware* group.

Eight headteachers achieved social mobility. Parental occupations included manufacturing jobs, skilled trade or manual working-class jobs such as working in a chip shop, cleaning, coal mining, agricultural labour and lorry driving. Two men described relatively impoverished backgrounds. Rose described a 'traditional-middle-class' background, but witnessed the injustice of selective education at 11. Rosaline's schooling was disrupted by being an armed forces child with undiagnosed dyslexia. Nevertheless, she referred to a 'privileged' upbringing. Gregory was orphaned during his secondary schooling. He referred to being so 'scruffy' a deputy headteacher gave him money to buy a shirt. The scruffiness was a symptom of ongoing depression. Lucy found social mobility painful,

> I say I pretty well survived it. It isn't without its impact, and I think all of those times you go into situations, where you are not equipped socially, you have sort of got your wits about you so you survive but that feeling of intimidation, that feeling of powerlessness, that feeling that comes with not being the right class. (Lucy; from Fuller, 2012, p. 681)

By contrast, in the *class unaware* group Silvia's father was a headteacher and Robert's family worked 'in the City (London)'. Attendance at an independent boarding school suggested his family was relatively wealthy. Five headteachers did not refer to their economic backgrounds.

Cultural capital

Two *class aware* headteachers referred to grammar school education. Rose constructed it as 'elitist'. Early recognition of educational injustice was fundamental to her commitment to comprehensive schooling.

> [E]ven at eleven I could recognise it was an awful thing to do to kids. . . . I realised it was an elitist school and that that wasn't the sort of school I would want to work in or lead. (Rose)

Lucy described the division between grammar and secondary modern schoolgirls, but for her it was a valuable route to higher education. Diana's comprehensive schooling showed her what education could do to change life chances. Seven class aware headteachers were first-generation graduates. Tertiary education was Emily's, 'way out of the dreary grind of drudgery'. Lucy and Isabella escaped early motherhood (see Chapter 4). However, Lucy was 'teased mercilessly' because of her accent. Rose's place at teachers' training college was compensation for not going to university (see Chapter 4). Rosaline's access to university was complicated by dyslexia. She described her frustration at being able to answer orally when written responses were required.

> [B]eing dyslexic you're not gonna achieve 'As'. Even if they're in your head you can't get them down on paper. (Rosaline)

Emily described academic failure and subsequent empathy with pupils. Education enabled an alternative future away from factory or shop work for Ben; or a 'route towards the professions' for Duncan. Tony attended teacher training college.

Of the *class unaware* group, Stephanie attended grammar school and Robert valued a liberal arts education that shaped his cultural values, liberal politics and liberal approach to headship. Sam's teachers inspired him to study modern foreign languages leading to his migration from Trinidad to France. The remaining headteachers in the group made no links between education and headship.

Social capital

The class aware group acquired social capital through higher education. At university Robin met

> people of all sorts, all sorts of statuses. I went to a comprehensive and I went from there to Cambridge and I therefore met people of widely differing status. (Robin)

Tony's contemporaries became headteachers. Such networking was already established in Rose and Rosaline's middle-class families. Rose's mother's family enabled her to access tertiary education. Rosaline's wider family gave her access to high-profile educationists, journalists and politicians that, 'all rubbed off'.

Headteachers augmented social capital in the professional field by networking formally and informally with influential individuals and organizations. Among class aware headteachers, the NPQH, 'allowed [Isabella] to open a lot more doors, and networking'. Friends and former colleagues provided role models. Four described valuable networking among headteachers in geographical, faith or school-type groups and the benefits of collaboration between schools. Ben outlined the complexities of an intricate and fluid network of local schools working collaboratively. Multi-agency networking enabled access to economic capital for the school. Increased collaboration between schools was positive. Lucy noted:

> schools are moving now towards working together rather than this sort of drawbridge and portcullis up, and boiling oil on the battlements. I think it is a much healthier climate. (Lucy)

Additional local, national or international roles provided further social capital. Ben modelled headship on the 'social entrepreneurship' he observed growing up in an area of multiple deprivations. Business investment had provided additional resources such as new buildings and new staff that led to a new ethos. As headteacher, he persuaded businesses to invest in pupils' education. He turned social capital into economic capital for his school. Additional roles were aligned to education, augmented what could be achieved in headship, but were not a prerequisite of the job. They extended social capital. Public service outside education included work for the Duke of Edinburgh youth scheme; The Prince's Trust; charities; churches; and as Justice of the Peace.

Among *class unaware* headteachers, Silvia's headteacher father attended university 'with everybody who was anybody'. Robert's influential social capital was gained at boarding school. Only Katherine from the *class unaware* group described networking locally to enhance curriculum opportunities for pupils. Some of the remaining headteachers networked nationally. Sam participated in an international exchange programme. He contributed to a national consultation process about developing assessment tests (see Chapter 6). Other organizations included headteachers' associations; single-sex or independent school societies; school governing bodies; university councils; subject societies; and the consultation group for the reform of the University and Colleges Admissions

Service (UCAS). Public service outside education included non-executive membership of a National Health Trust; churches; and interfaith debate groups.

Headteachers referred to the acquisition of a range of economic, cultural and social capital that resulted from their changed or existing status in particular social fields. Headteachers from working-class backgrounds recognized they acquired cultural capital through secondary and tertiary education. Higher education also provided access to social capital. Economic capital was acquired in the professional field of teaching, increasing in line with advancement into headship. Social capital increased with headteachers' engagement with a range of public bodies. There were no indications of anything other than encouragement from working-class families suggesting they were transitional working-class families (Maguire, 2005). In other words, parents valued achievement over domesticity for girls. Similarly men's social mobility might be valued by their families (Lupton, 2006). Ironically, two middle-class women were obstructed; one by her father's sexist attitude, the other by her learning difficulties. These two recognized the importance of acquiring cultural capital. They experienced the pain and injustice of obstruction.

For some women and men all three forms of capital were readily available in the family and education. Middle-class women have accessed higher education to become headteachers for over 125 years (Watts, 1998). Of particular interest, is the non-recognition by *class unaware* headteachers of the importance of capital. Only Robert and Sam valued the impact of education on the development of a headteacherly habitus. In the sections that follow I examine headteachers' recognition of class differences among the school population. I begin with staff.

Recognizing social class differences among staff

Headteachers distinguished between staff by leadership, teaching and non-teaching roles; in relation to attitudes and values (see Chapter 3); and by way of skills and knowledge. These distinctions bear further analysis framed by forms of capital (Bourdieu, 1986). Distinctions between job roles as senior or middle leaders and managers, as teachers or non-teaching staff indicate considerable differences in earnings. Senior leadership team members are the highest paid employees in schools (see above for the range of salaries). The starting salary at the time of writing for newly qualified teachers is £21,588 rising to £45,000 on the upper pay scale in inner London for experienced teachers (NUT, 2012). Support staff pay is determined locally. The recommended range is from local government pay spine point 4 – £12,145 to spine point 49 – £41,616 (NJC, 2009). The lowest paid staff in schools are in non-teaching roles as teaching and learning support, care, clerical and catering assistants. Some earn the minimum wage. Such distinctions also relate to cultural capital; some teachers have acquired the knowledge, skills and attributes required for promotion to leadership posts. Teaching is a graduate profession whereas only 15 per cent of teaching assistants have accessed higher education (Webster et al., 2010). There is much overlap between the forms of capital staff might access. However, I have focused the discussion of leadership work through the lens of economic capital. The distinction between teaching and non-teaching staff is discussed through the lens of cultural capital. Finally, headteachers' talk about the value of CPD is discussed in terms of social capital. I examine links and gaps between *class aware* headteachers' accounts and their recognition of staff differences.

Economic capital

Leadership and management teams

Headteachers' discourse about differences has already focused on gendered leadership teams (see Chapter 4). In senior leadership teams (excluding headteachers) there is an almost even split between women and men. Women secondary school deputy and assistant headteachers are reported as 49 per cent of the total (DfE, 2012). All the headteachers referred to members of senior or middle leadership and management. Eleven referred to line and performance management. Five referred to non-teaching leadership and management roles of bursar, business and office managers. Headteachers' discourse about staff differences was highly classed in its focus on status. However, there was some variety of approaches to working with and in teams.

Class aware headteachers, Diana, Lucy, Isabella and Rose sought diversity among the leadership team to enable collaborative and creative work that challenged preconceptions. Isabella ignited the 'spark' in colleagues' thinking but listened to alternative ideas. Rose used Belbin's (1981, 1993) analysis of team roles to share knowledge about successful teamwork. Collective engagement with theory influenced recruitment,

> I have got a team now where I have got a very diverse range of learners on the team, and the team is better for it. I need that so do they. (Rose)

Diana and Lucy worked with external consultants to develop leadership teams. Diana enabled dialogue,

> I do let these silences run sometimes, or I throw out this question and I just wait. I let them all argue with each other for quite a long time before I intervene. I

think that's been really healthy. . . . It's been very hard to do. I still at the end will
pull back to my direction and I know I do that. (Diana)

Ben, Tony and Duncan saw leadership teams as an opportunity to flatten
hierarchical structures. Ben offered up his leadership priorities for scrutiny.

[T]he team look at what I do and decide whether or not it's good value for money
. . . I just don't believe in this single person can lead and do everything. (Ben)

Tony thought clarity of role and responsibility facilitated a shared approach.

We work together. Here's the leadership team. Here's what their responsibilities
are. Here's the subject leaders, their responsibilities; the pastoral leaders, their
responsibilities. . . . We all mix together. (Tony)

When the person and role did not fit Tony changed the role not the person. I have
already described Duncan's difficulty changing staff perceptions of a hierarchical
structure (see Chapter 2). The remaining four headteachers did not mention
leadership team work. I have already discussed *class unaware* Katherine and
Silvia's contrasting leadership team work in Chapter 2. No other *class unaware*
headteachers mentioned leadership team work.

The range of leadership and management job roles gives an appearance of
highly structured, and managed school organizations. However, headteachers'
discourse about working with and in teams revealed efforts by some to work
collaboratively in open dialogic interactions (Shields and Edwards, 2005). Some
worked horizontally with senior colleagues (Grogan and Shakeshaft, 2011). One
opened up leadership work for scrutiny by the team (Grundy, 1993). Reducing
school hierarchical structures was not easy though there was a desire to do it
(Grace, 2000). Some men's work with leadership teams demonstrated their
desire to work in (pro)feminist ways (Hall, 1999). We have already seen that
not all women headteachers engaged in feminist leadership discourse (Reay and
Ball, 2000).

Leadership development opportunities

Leadership development was discussed in relation to individual colleagues (see
Chapter 4). Dialogue with leadership teams was an opportunity for leadership
development. Two *class aware* headteachers described systematic approaches.
Rose extended opportunities to the wider school staff; Ben extended them among
the leadership team. Rose invited two members of staff to apply for a four-term
secondment to manage a school development project. Ten members of staff had

accessed leadership team work that way. They gained leadership development; the leadership team benefited from hearing teachers' voices

> that makes sure that we have got the voice of the teacher in the leadership team when we are making all our decisions, they are not just there to lead a project they are there to reflect that voice. That is very easy for us when we get into our roles as leaders (we are not in the classroom full time) to forget the pressures and the realities. (Rose)

Ben developed a system of job shadowing. All members of the leadership team documented ten key priorities. The document enabled colleagues to shadow or take over in the event of staff absence. It was an extension of the method used to scrutinize his priorities. *Class unaware* Silvia and Philip described leadership development. In Chapter 2, I discussed Silvia's teaching around leadership. In Chapter 4, I described Philip's encouragement of middle managers.

Each valued leadership development that enhanced capacity within the school (MacBeath, 2007). One sought staff voices in a way that resonates with participatory parity through representation and associational justice (Cribb and Gewirtz, 2003; Fraser, 2007). There were elements of democratic leadership practice (Woods, 2005).

Working with teacher leaders

Class aware Rose and Ben saw the capacity for teachers to be leaders. Ben saw leadership in teachers' daily interaction with children. There were opportunities for whole school engagement in building

> a shared vision that people understand and in terms of distributed leadership can have the youngest new member of staff influencing what goes into that vision, or the youngest child in the community as long as they have an opportunity to feed their ideas into it. (Ben)

The school was full of leaders emerging as 'bobbing corks'. They surfaced depending on expertise and need. I have already described Rose's work with teachers to develop a school-wide understanding of 'good' teaching in Chapter 3. Gregory was a facilitator enabling highly motivated professional colleagues to develop ideas and ways of working (see Chapter 2). Similarly, two *class unaware* headteachers, Philip and Sam, saw themselves as facilitators. Philip located real power in empowering others (see Chapter 4).

These five headteachers described leadership for learning where all members of the school community were learners from headteacher to teachers to pupils (Grogan and Shakeshaft, 2011; MacBeath, 2007). All were potential contributors to leadership. Headteachers recognized a shared moral purpose as a strong motivating force for staff (Grace, 2000). Opportunities for increased economic, cultural and social capital came from engaging directly with the headteacher and leadership team. Ben described his leadership as distributed in the sense it emerged depending on need and expertise (Woods et al., 2004).

Cultural capital

One of the biggest distinctions headteachers made was between teaching and non-teaching staff. They distinguished between graduates and largely non-graduates in the workforce; as qualified teaching or unqualified staff. Workforce reform that reduced teachers' administrative tasks was underway (DfES, 2003b). Discourse about non-teaching staff is gendered and classed. As non-teaching staff (including teaching assistants, administrative staff, technicians, other support staff and auxiliary staff) women outnumber men at 78.9 per cent of the workforce (DfE, 2012). Women teaching assistants far outnumber men at 85.4 per cent; women administrative, technician and other support staff including auxiliary staff make up 75.6 per cent (DfE, 2012). Only 15 per cent of teaching assistants are graduates (Webster et al., 2010).

Working with teachers

The dominant discourse was of valuing teachers' professionalism and commitment. However, six class aware headteachers talked about tackling poor teaching performance. Lucy and Diana used teacher capability procedures. Lucy demonstrated her intent to others,

> I do think it is important to tackle poor performance. I think it is important for those people who have given you 100% every day that you don't allow people who are not pulling their weight, or are in fact being quite obstructive . . . you've got to take that on. I think you only really have to do one really heavily. (Lucy)

She enabled a head of department to relinquish management responsibility to become an advanced skills teacher (AST). Diana reflected on the exercise of humanity and respect,

> I've had to deal with a capability on a teacher who wasn't competent but you do that all the time remembering that this is a person. He has a child, he has a life. So although in the end we reached a point where he had to go, I do feel I dealt

with it with some humanity and remembering that it never reaches a kind of aggression or shouting or madness or unpleasantness. (Diana)

Emily referred to 'doing the dirty deed' with respect for individuals. Tony and Gregory adapted roles to suit valued staff. Duncan awarded a pay rise to be equitable even though he thought it unwarranted. He followed a hard line in tackling long-term sickness (see Chapter 2).

Class unaware Philip valued different teaching styles to suit pupils' learning preferences.

> [T]eachers are amazingly creative people and if they can find a way in they will. If they can find a way of teaching that works then they will do it. They are all individuals, you have got the quiet, noisy, the shouters, the whisperers, those that will just stoically continue and never give up, you have got the gifted communicator who can talk to teenagers and so on and so forth. . . . It is valuing that some people are different and saying it's okay to be different, there isn't one blueprint that fits all and the very nature of the game of teaching is finding a key which will unlock that huge fountain of enthusiasm which children have and that is why teachers stay in teaching . . . It is not about pay and it is not about discipline, it just went well and you knew that the children one hour after you started knew more than they did an hour before, and they were better for that. (Philip)

Similarly, Silvia and Sam valued the variety of skills, knowledge and expertise among teachers. Only Muhsin was frustrated by teachers' apparent lack of commitment to working beyond their contractual hours (see Chapter 3).

Headteachers exercised power in determining outcomes for teaching staff through recruitment, promotion and performance management. Power was not always used to empower; it was also used to control and might result in job loss. Feminist leadership discourse acknowledges tough decisions are made (Adler et al., 1993). There was concern to exercise humanity. *Class aware* headteachers drew on a discourse of fairness to tackle poor performance and in one case long-term absence. They made difficult ethical decisions about what was in the best interests of the majority. They exercised an *ethic of justice* (Begley, 2006). No *class unaware* headteachers talked about tackling poor performance.

Working with non-teaching staff

The implementation and impact of workforce reform (DfES, 2003b) featured highly. The expansion of non-teaching staff brought opportunities and challenges. Class aware Isabella saw opportunities for teachers to, 'plan, prepare, argue, talk, think'. She facilitated dialogue during a period of change. Teachers should talk in teams, with line managers and, 'they can talk in their unions, they can talk in the staff room informally, or they can come in here'. Teachers enjoyed non-teaching tasks so Isabella did not underestimate the impact of change, 'here's me taking it away from them and forcing them more into something, that they, that was actually quite a relief for [them], and it is about having these open debates with staff as well'. Ben, Gregory and Robin described change management. Ben's ongoing dialogue with staff about roles and responsibilities meant the school was well prepared. Gregory took the opposite approach to government recommendations.

> The model that they take is that you take all the functions in the school and assign them logically and then you fit people into that or not. You might sack people or they go or whatever. That's the opposite, the exact opposite of what we do. What we do is settle people in and see if we like them, they might [not fit] the first time and then we have to change the roles around them, till they're working flat out in a way. So we tune the place round the people. (Gregory)

A people-centred approach prioritized contributions rather than roles and tasks; though Gregory expected staff to work at full capacity. An example was that of well-motivated assistants who performed multiple unconventional combinations of teaching and non-teaching roles. They were rewarded financially. Robin made savings on teachers' salaries to appoint sufficient non-teaching staff to comply with workforce reform. He wanted to be open, transparent and inclusive but acknowledged he controlled the information flow and subsequent reactions. He shared the difficulties of leadership with the working group protecting himself from criticism.

> [M]y using a working group which is fairly widely representative and my deliberately saying certain things are confidential and I'd rather they didn't go out, and certain things I just say well it doesn't matter about that, is really trying to manage my information flow. Trying to make sure that the really difficult questions feel that, people feel involved with in order to try to ensure that when there's full consultation and the whatever is agreed by the governors goes out to all staff, they have people that they can turn to and say 'well why did you do this? And why did you do that? And this is stupid, it's so and so forth'. I will have my defenders out there. So not only is it good to be open and inclusive, which is what I'm trying to do, and accept that I don't have all the good ideas and others may and therefore involve them, it's also I've done it also for my own self-protection. (Robin)

The increase of non-teaching staff at Duncan's school was constructed as an intervention to support learning. There was often more than one adult in classrooms. A stranger would not know who the teacher was. There were tensions between teaching and non-teaching staff.

> It is easier for me to sit in an ivory tower and say we are all staff together. The practicalities probably are there are some sensitivities . . . they do use the staff room, but I think they feel uncomfortable doing so . . . within the school we try to generate a culture whereby we are all adults and we are all working in the school. There probably is in some respects a bit of a division. (Duncan)

Emily located teachers' superior attitudes towards non-teaching staff in cultural capital.

> [I]t's the difference between the graduate and the non-graduate and again it's been some of the older folks who've had a 'non-teachers are our sort of servants' kind of attitude. It's been really, really hard to break that down from both angles, from people not seeing themselves as subservient but also people being seen as subservient. (Emily)

Lucy was angered by a union representative objecting to open dialogue about school performance.

> [O]ne of the union reps turned to me and said 'I respect your right to say this but not with ancillary staff present'. Well, I am happy to say that wouldn't happen today. You have to make it clear that there is no space in this school if that's how you feel about somebody working here; because in that statement there's all that sort of anger. (Lucy)

Like Diana and Isabella, Rosaline invested in staff development for non-teaching staff (see Chapter 4). She struggled to professionalize care staff motivated by money.

> People that come into care provision sometimes come because they feel they can't do anything else. It's very lowly paid to start with. We pay quite well but you do get a very mixed bunch. You've got to move them onwards and upwards and sometimes, actually all they want is the money. (Rosaline)

Class unaware Katherine saw workforce reform as an opportunity to increase teachers' contact time (see also Chapter 2).

> I think they just see it as a reduction in their jobs. I don't think they appreciate that it actually means that at some point I will probably ask them to do more in the classroom. (Katherine)

Support staff were more important than teachers. Barriers between teaching and non-teaching staff persisted, 'I will never do away with them totally but at least the guide from here is "these are pupil partners"'. Philip valued non-teaching staff:

> [W]e are all doing the same job, we do different parts of it, which is something I say quite often, the fact that I am headteacher and there's an NQT, and there is a huge number of teachers and classroom assistants in between, we are still basically doing the same job which is teaching children, without the children we haven't got a job. (Philip)

There was a deliberate 'blurring of the edges' between the two groups. A senior classroom assistant was a form tutor (see Chapter 4).

> The children don't come up to you and say, what's your qualifications then? Let's see your degree before I let you teach me. They might in some areas but they don't here. Everybody really has to earn their respect around here whether you are a teacher or non-teacher and you don't get respect just because you've got a suit and stand at the front. You have to do more than that. (Philip)

The influx of non-teaching staff necessitated additional or altered management structures, systems and personnel. In several schools, non-teaching staff held management positions. Diana's personal assistant managed non-teaching staff; a bursar supervised aspects of non-teaching work in another school. Business managers in two schools undertook lunch-time duties that raised their esteem among children and teaching staff. Some were members of senior management teams. That did not necessarily equate with parity of pay. Diana's personal assistant was not paid an equivalent senior management salary. The barrier to improving salary and status was her lack of degree.

Headteachers engaged in a discourse of staff professionalism that largely valued and trusted colleagues in their work. However, where there was poor performance there were two distinct approaches. Some adapted job roles to suit colleagues they valued. Some made adjustments to working arrangements having listened carefully to colleagues (see Chapter 4). A dialogic approach resonated with relational leadership (Grogan and Shakeshaft, 2011; Shields and Edwards, 2005). Others undertook capability procedures resulting in loss of employment. Ethical arguments about fairness justified action (Begley, 2006). The negotiation of tensions between teaching and non-teaching staff was also handled differently. Some headteachers engaged in open dialogue to hear teachers' concerns (Shields and Edwards, 2005); though one used such mechanisms for other purposes. Others were dismissive of teachers' anxieties.

They used discourses of equality, mutuality and inclusion to undermine teachers' concerns (Begley, 2006).

Social capital

Seventeen headteachers identified CPD as a mechanism for catering for staff differences. It consisted of induction and mentoring, support for independent academic study, courses in and outside school and collaborative team work. *Class aware* Lucy used CPD to change a prevailing culture. Rose developed shared understanding of what constituted good teaching and learning that was not limited to inspection frameworks. Duncan reflected on the balance between personal and organizational development priorities. Staff gained social capital by working with well-respected headteachers. References constituted currency that enabled promotion. *Class unaware* Robert expected junior colleagues to be ambitious, 'I want them to be heads of department in a good school . . . I've certainly moved on plenty of people into senior positions in other schools; it's very much part of the role.'

Headteachers exercised power deciding whether and to whom they extended CPD opportunities. Staff acquired cultural capital. Where staff worked with other schools, Higher Education Institutions and other agencies they extended professional networks thus acquiring social capital. Teachers and non-teaching staff were recognized as continuing learners (MacBeath, 2007). In the section that follows I examine headteachers' recognition of class differences among pupils.

Recognizing social class differences among pupils

Class aware headteachers worked mainly in comprehensive schools (Diana, Isabella, Lucy, Rose, Ben, Duncan, Gregory, Tony); with Emily and Robin in selective schools. *Class unaware* headteachers worked in selective schools (Katherine, Stephanie, Robert) and comprehensive schools (Silvia, Muhsin, Philip, Sam). Twelve explicitly recognized class differences between pupils. They referred to pupils' socio-economic status as relative poverty or affluence; pupils' literacy levels and 'ability'; and parents' dispositions towards education.

Economic capital

Class aware Diana referred to impoverished households where worklessness prevailed. Education was, 'their route out; we are their route to something else'. Rose was committed to comprehensive education and helping pupils achieve regardless of, 'disadvantages that they might have got in terms of their economic background, their family circumstances'. Gaining qualifications might secure escape from poverty and hardship, 'Working in the inner cities at that very tough end of things, you see for the kids there the *only* [her emphasis] way that they can move out of those circumstances is by education.' There was a gap between perceived affluence in the school's catchment area and the reality of pupils' backgrounds, 'You go into some of their houses and they are appalling.' Lucy was frustrated by similar assumptions.

> I used to feel like going up and down with a chainsaw 'cause I got so fed up with people telling me how lovely the trees were. When I couldn't get anybody seemingly to take seriously what I saw were huge issues here, but because they were behind all these nice trees that was okay. (Lucy)

The discourse of social mobility was strong for these women. Education was an escape and means to acquire future economic capital.

Duncan described the socio-economic background of most pupils as 'poor working class'. Families could not replace school shoes at Tony's school. Gregory provided free refreshments to ensure basic needs were met. Only Ben referred to 60 per cent of the population being eligible for FSM as an indicator of economic disadvantage. Rented housing and parental occupations were other indicators. Ben questioned the impact on children regarding Every Child Matters (DfES, 2003a) outcomes, 'In any defined community if any of your children don't have any of [the Every Child Matters outcomes] they're likely to be in trouble with the police or in need of psychiatric care at some stage in their life.' There was multi-agency support for one child.

> The wrong benefits were coming into the family when it was investigated. A bucket was being used to flush the toilet, the toilet wasn't working properly. (Ben; from Fuller, 2012, pp. 679–80)

Incentives with economic value were rewards for pupil effort. Ben's discourse about access to economic capital extended to the distribution of school resources. Short-term government funding made initiatives economically unsustainable. Local property businesses needed to invest, 'If they work to make a community where life is better for all then the outcome is likely to be that their property process (*sic*) will go up and their occupancy rates will go up.' Working in comprehensive schools and a special school these men understood the impact of poverty; some redistributed resources to support pupils' well-being. In selective schools, Emily and Robin each referred to relative poverty. Emily distinguished between affluent and poor families. She was intolerant of those with privileges, who did not value them.

> [T]he more privilege you have the more I expect you to give back . . . that would be at one extreme. And then I see other kids who are desperately struggling against poverty and one parent families and monetary hardship who give their all who really appreciate what we offer. (Emily)

Robin referred to illegal acquisition of electronic gadgets as an indicator of multiple deprivations. Fifty per cent of the children came from backgrounds with the 'highest levels of multiple deprivation' that was 'unprecedented' in a selective school.

Class unaware Philip identified families as 85 per cent 'working class' in a comprehensive school. He shared the social mobility discourse that aimed to, 'hopefully get them qualifications that will help them earn their own living'. In selective schools, Katherine supported families with second-hand uniforms and subsidized school trips; though travelling expenses prevented poor families from applying for places. Stephanie identified a range of economic income as well as parental occupations. Robert believed the system of assisted places achieved social mobility more effectively than comprehensive education. Pupils from disadvantaged backgrounds, described in terms of neighbourhood and parental occupation, gained places at Oxbridge. Apparently nobody knew which pupils had free places. Their homes were in areas of the city 'not probably high on your list of potential places to live'.

In the recognition of economic disadvantage among pupils headteachers engaged in an *ethic of critique*. Their humane responses suggest an *ethic of care*. Where headteachers took action to benefit the majority while respecting the rights of the individual they engaged an *ethic of justice* (Begley, 2006). There was a strong discourse of social mobility among headteachers, not only among those who had achieved it themselves. Ben focused on the redistribution of resources or distributive justice (Cribb and Gewirtz, 2003; Fraser, 2000; Grogan and Shakeshaft, 2011). Others saw acquisition of cultural capital as the route to greater social equality.

Cultural capital

Parents' cultural capital

Class aware headteachers recognized families' low educational aspirations. Diana was concerned about low expectations.

> I suppose we still really struggle with the 15 and 16 year olds working class, disaffected, could be bright lads. We really struggle to say education is worthwhile. They want to get out. (Diana)

Duncan wanted to raise the self-esteem and confidence of pupils who were 'not encouraged to do well academically'. Robin described pupils' difficulties when parents worked long hours. It was

> very difficult for them to get the attention from the parents. That doesn't mean the parents aren't loving. And it's very difficult for them to find a place to work. (Robin)

Lucy and Ben worked with parents in family-learning projects. Lucy focused on basic skills 'trying to get the parents on board in learning as well, and also the encouragement of getting internet access at home'. At Ben's school a parent was teaching others in family-learning sessions, 'many of the parents who thought they could only do a bar job or cleaning job actually now realise that it was their life circumstances that prevented them from being successful, not that they were in their terms "thick"'. Lucy compared her children's home resources with those of pupils.

> They come home they need to make a video and if we haven't got the equipment we knew somebody who had. Then I look at some of these little [pupils], who have got no table at home let alone anyone who is running around 'Would you like a cup of tea sweetheart? While you do your revision' [with] everything shut in, own bedroom, internet access, television, the works. (Lucy)

Additional support at school was designed to 'level [the] playing field'. Lucy believed

> this is about equipping them to do it and I would say helping them with their course work to the level that I helped my own children at home. I feel no pangs about it because I think they need that support. (Lucy)

By contrast, some parents were highly educated with influential careers and high expectations of academic success. Diana noted:

> middle class kids always [turn] out to be those learners because actually they're learning it at home and motivation's different. So they know how to learn. They know what to do. They know how to approach an essay. They know how to revise without having an awful lot being taught to them. (Diana)

Emily described the family background of a pupil, who failed to gain a place at Oxbridge, 'both parents were PhDs and both parents had been to Oxbridge, older brother had and it was just what happened in that family and it didn't happen to her'.

There were similar concerns among *class unaware* headteachers. In comprehensive schools, Philip and Sam distinguished between levels of parental support. Philip's focus was on lifelong learning.

> [C]radle to the grave, on opportunity, on bettering ourselves, on having ambition, the right sort of pride; the right sort of feelings about yourself and achievement. You try to instil the need for a career and earn one's own living and support one's family and so on. (Philip)

However, Silvia described some less affluent children as 'very much committed and they understand the nature of schools as places to learn'. All the selective school headteachers referred to pupils from less advantaged backgrounds that implied lack of cultural as well as economic capital. Parents sent their children to selective schools; they applied for assisted places schemes. There was generally a match between parental aspirations and Stephanie's curricular aims. Katherine identified 'terrific difference[s] in aspiration and expectation'. The pressure to achieve academically came from families (see Chapters 2 and 4). Robert's commitment to developing high educational aspirations was demonstrated by interviewing every child about examination and university choices.

There was no perception of a simplistic correlation between social class and educational aspiration. Having economic and cultural capital was usually associated with educational aspiration. Clearly some parents lacking institutionalized cultural capital were favourably disposed to support their children's educational outcomes. They might be transitional as opposed to traditional working-class families (Maguire, 2005). Lucy and Ben were engaged with family-learning projects that extended into the community (Grogan and Shakeshaft, 2011; MacBeath, 2007; Shields and Edwards, 2005).

Children's acquisition of cultural capital

Class aware Lucy and Isabella used pupils' prior attainment data to track progress. Diana identified '[not] academic kids, they are good, they can become good learners'. They needed to learn how to learn. Increased English teaching compensated for low levels of literacy. All three focused on classroom pedagogies to cater for pupils not suited to traditional teaching methods. The pressure to gain higher grade GCSEs meant Diana thought, 'we're ripping away all the independent learning'. Lucy thought examination results impacted on pupils' 'life chances'.

An 'alternative curriculum' in Diana's school included vocational courses such as brick-laying, motor vehicle maintenance or catering; or academic school-based vocational courses in ICT, engineering or media studies. The benefits were in motivation and improved behaviour,

> they've got something a little bit more interesting in their lives that means, 'Yeah it's worth it. I've got something out of my course in construction. And maybe I can cope with coming back to school and just doing . . .' They're just doing the core and a couple of other subjects, which they've picked. (Diana)

Isabella targeted such programmes for students with SEN, behavioural difficulties or persistent absence. Emily saw no need for vocational courses at a selective school; nor did she talk about classroom pedagogy.

In Chapter 4, I described Rose's use of the curriculum to appeal to boys in a post-industrial society. However, she was concerned about the attainment of all children, 'We have never judged our success just on the traditional five A-C benchmark.' She resisted pressure to focus solely on 'the top end'. Helping all children gain qualifications remained the core purpose of the school even if it required breaking the law to offer alternative programmes outside the National Curriculum. The difference between courses was explained to pupils and families to facilitate informed choices about the blend of academic and vocational courses.

> [B]y and large mostly they do choose, they do know what suits them and what they are going to succeed at. But we talk to them and their parents and we have very little difficultly once we explain the difference between the vocational course here or that GCSE course there. It is making sure they have made the right choices but giving them first choice. (Rose)

Ben's school provided vocational education long before national educational policy promoted it. Its introduction at Robin's selective school was unsuccessful. The vehicle maintenance course was a 'disaster' because it was taught at a lower ability level than pupils needed.

Lucy recognized children with SEN. The school was popular for families of vulnerable children. More able children with conditions such as Asperger's syndrome were taught in 'top sets' as were children with a range of emotional difficulties, 'some of the brightest children have got all this baggage with them'. A child with Down's syndrome was equally likely to achieve a school award in Ben's school. Indeed Ben talked about achievement in very broad terms never mentioning qualifications. Robin included a special school in his local network of schools. Duncan and Tony talked about working with children with a range of special and behavioural needs. Each referred to additional resources designed to support pupils. Both headteachers of special schools identified differences between children with SEN in having a vast range of abilities, behaviours and achievements. These impacted on curriculum design and content; teaching and learning approaches; and school organization and management. Parents at Gregory's school questioned the focus on GCSEs when basic life skills were not developed (see Chapter 2). There was a need to identify strengths and weaknesses, 'children who may seem to have very, very low ability indeed in some areas, who are absolutely marvellous and fantastic influence on people around them.' In a similar asset-based approach, Rosaline focused on what children 'can do' as opposed to what they cannot.

> [T]hey're all going to be really good at certain things and you build from that rather than labour what they can't do. I suppose I've always felt that education is about building on the positives and using that positive to some extent compensate or adapt, find ways round the shortfalls. (Rosaline)

The children were vertically grouped around language and social needs.

> [Y]ou've got youngsters who are brilliant at IT or brilliant at maths and there's this developmental delay in that. But it is the personal, the emotional bit, the relationships bit. (Rosaline)

She replaced a primary school curriculum with a traditional secondary school curriculum.

Class unaware headteachers working in comprehensive education also engaged in discourse about the curriculum and learning. Silvia, Philip and Sam discussed the importance of an inclusive curriculum. At Silvia's school, pupils had four hours of non-traditional learning per week to support reading and mathematics, work-related learning, motivational workshops, use of Information and Communication Technology (ICT), and work on overcoming difficulties. As a topic-based curriculum it focused on competencies, learning to learn and independent learning. It ignored much of the National Curriculum. In Chapter 2, I discussed Silvia's refusal to narrow the curriculum under the pressure to improve GCSE results. However, the five or more higher-grade GCSEs remained students' 'passports'. In Philip's school, a third of children arrived below the nationally expected literacy level. He described a 'long tail of under achievement'. Two alternative curriculum pathways were designed to keep children engaged with school with a view to securing further education, employment and training opportunities.

> [W]e knew why they weren't attending; they couldn't cope with 11 GCSEs and the rigour of a metronomic timetable. Tick, tick, tick maths now, English now, history now, bored and fed up and all the rest of it. (Philip)

Sam entered newly arrived pupils with no or little English for A levels in languages such as Dutch, Portuguese, Urdu or Punjabi to build their confidence (see Chapter 6). Pupils engaged increasingly with independent learning to take greater personal responsibility. Technology provided access to learning and teaching that suited some pupils more than traditional classroom approaches.

Katherine, Stephanie, Muhsin and Robert focused on academic achievement. Katherine recounted pupils' academic success. There was no curriculum provision for pupils struggling with emotional and behavioural difficulties (see Chapter 4). By contrast, Stephanie reduced competition (see Chapter 4). Robert claimed 90 per cent of A level grades were A and B grades; pupils gained first-class degrees. His school was aligned with the examination system but not an 'exam factory'. Pupils took ten traditional examination subjects aged 16. Robert greatly valued extracurricular activity that children would remember long after they forgot academic subject lessons. Muhsin's office wall contained pictures of boys who achieved well.

Pupils' acquisition of cultural capital as educational qualifications was constructed as the means to further and higher education, employment and training. Almost all headteachers engaged in that discourse. The discourse about learning as process occurred among comprehensive school headteachers regardless of whether they were *class aware* or *class unaware* (Grogan and Shakeshaft, 2011; MacBeath, 2007). The choice of classroom pedagogies was important in enabling an inclusive curriculum for pupils lacking cultural capital. No selective school headteachers engaged in a discourse about pedagogy or learning. Curriculum choice and a broad range of qualifications were constructed as a way to motivate pupils and engage them in school. There were attempts to draw on existing funds of knowledge to enable pupils to acquire high status academic qualifications (Wrigley et al., 2012).

Social capital

The most explicit indication of social capital among families came from Robert's description of an 'old boys' network'. An 'old boy' officiated at prize giving; 'old boys' socialized. One parent's influence secured national newspaper front-page headlines for a story about independent school children accessing higher education.

In the section that follows I discuss the consequences of non-recognition and misrecognition of social class differences in schools.

Non-recognition and misrecognition

Unequal social class relations in the family and education

Only two *class aware* women recognized the possibility of unequal social class relations in the education of staff. I have already discussed Diana and Isabella's attempts to address this in Chapter 4.

Unequal social class relations among staff in the workplace

Recognition of staff by job role suggests a highly classed discourse of difference focused on status. Seven of eleven *class aware* headteachers discussed their work with leadership teams. They saw it as an opportunity for collaborative work (Grogan and Shakeshaft, 2011) and an opportunity to break down hierarchical structures (Grace, 2000). In particular, Rose and Ben worked in ways suggestive of democratic approaches to leadership (Woods, 2005) and shared knowledge about working practices that empowered colleagues through emancipatory praxis (Blackmore, 1989; Grundy, 1993). They both saw leadership capacity among teachers in non-formal leadership roles though Rose also extended formal leadership roles on a temporary basis (Blackmore, 1989; MacBeath, 2007). Only two *class unaware* headteachers talked about leadership teams; both were discussed in Chapter 2 as contrasting examples of leadership approaches. Nine headteachers did not talk about their work in and with leadership teams.

Six *class aware* headteachers discussed tackling poor performance among teachers. They used a mixture of formal processes and change of job roles. Headteachers referred to drawing on their core values to ensure they behaved with respect for a colleague's dignity (Begley, 2006; Grace, 2000). None of the *class unaware* headteachers referred to tackling poor performance. The coincidence of the research with workforce reform meant non-teaching staff were recognized in headteachers' discourse about staff differences. All those who talked about non-teaching staff were positive about their contribution to school life. There were three responses to the perceived tensions between teaching and non-teaching staff. They align in part with the two headteacher groups. Five *class aware* and two *class unaware* headteachers noted the tensions. One *class aware* headteacher enabled teachers to discuss their concerns (Grogan and Shakeshaft, 2011; Shields and Edwards, 2005). Two noted the tensions and promoted a discourse of mutuality regardless of job role; two were particularly intolerant or manipulative in their responses. The two *class unaware* headteachers were particularly intolerant or manipulative. The four headteachers who were intolerant or manipulative *used ethics* to justify their irritation that teachers might object to the deprofessionalization of teaching (Gunter and Rayner, 2007). There was lack of concern among most that non-teaching staff were being used as cheap labour (Gunter and Rayner, 2007). Among all seven headteachers there was an equality discourse suggesting everyone was equal regardless of status or salary. One headteacher thought pay did not matter to teachers. Two other *class aware* headteachers used an ongoing dialogic approach to workforce reform (Grogan and Shakeshaft, 2011; Shields and Edwards, 2005).

Social class differences among pupils

All headteachers recognized class differences among pupils in some way. There was concern for pupils with low socio-economic status perceived as lack of economic, cultural and social capital. Ben's account of multiple deprivations included reference to FSM eligibility, quality of housing, parental occupations and household income to suggest his recognition of a range of factors and their potential impact on pupils' lives not just their education (Strand, 2011). Six *class aware* and two *class unaware* headteachers engaged in a social mobility discourse. Two were headteachers of selective schools. Social mobility was constructed as a social justice discourse (Grogan and Shakeshaft, 2011). Enabling pupils to acquire cultural capital was seen as distributive justice (Cribb and Gewirtz, 2003). For Lucy and Ben, social mobility extended to families. They actively redistributed resources as economic and cultural capital to pupils and families in distributive justice (Cribb and Gewirtz, 2003; Grogan and Shakeshaft, 2011). They and four other *class aware* and three *class unaware* headteachers of comprehensive schools promoted inclusive education that focused on an accessible curriculum and pedagogies that would enable all pupils to learn (Grogan and Shakeshaft, 2011; MacBeath, 2007; Wrigley et al., 2012). The two special school headteachers, both *class aware*, engaged in an asset discourse to enable pupils to build on their strengths. By contrast, four selective school headteachers, *class aware* and *unaware*, focused only on educational outcomes.

Misrecognition of unequal social class relations

So far I have discussed recognition and non-recognition of social class differences relating to feminist and critical leadership discourses. The question remains whether misrecognition occurs in these headteachers' discourses of social class difference.

Some headteachers' adoption of an egalitarian discourse concerning the staff body would appear somewhat disingenuous. Headteachers might intend the establishment of respectful working relations but to claim everyone as equal partners is to misrecognize social class inequalities regarding their relative access to economic, cultural and social capital. In fact, the school staff body is highly structured with salaries commensurate with qualifications, experience and levels of responsibility. Headteachers recognized the relative status of staff by making distinctions largely by job role. Schools are hierarchical organizations. Six headteachers claimed an equality discourse that is hard to justify; though two also acknowledged their well-paid positions. Misrecognition occurs when unqualified staff are deployed in teaching and leadership roles. First, the salary structure does not allow them to be rewarded adequately for the additional responsibility; second the teaching profession is undermined by their undertaking the work (Gunter and Rayner, 2007). From both angles misrecognition of the division of labour leads to symbolic violence. Unrecognized and unpaid leadership development opportunities might be disguised as leadership for learning (MacBeath, 2007) or distributed leadership.

Only one *class aware* headteacher explicitly recognized the impact of broader structures in perpetuating class inequalities among pupils and families. He used his social capital to develop community-based schooling that included families and local businesses, turning his social capital into economic capital through social entrepreneurship. Ben and Lucy looked beyond the school gates to engage families in learning (MacBeath, 2007). Misrecognition occurs when headteachers fail to engage with families not favourably disposed to education. Distinctions were made between the transitional and traditional working and workless classes (Maguire, 2005). Socially mobile headteachers might not recognize themselves as transitional working class; they might assume all families can achieve social mobility when structural barriers are virtually insurmountable for some.

Headteachers recognized differences in pupils' socio-economic status. However, they did not necessarily understand the impact, or provide for different needs. In comprehensive schools, headteachers were concerned with the process of learning, classroom pedagogies, curriculum variation and grouping structures regardless of whether they were *class aware* or *class unaware*. They engaged in leadership for learning (MacBeath, 2007). In some cases the redistribution of resources to support pupils' learning could be seen as leadership for social justice (Grogan and Shakeshaft, 2011). Instances of pupil voices were rare. How far pupils participated in decision-making about curriculum choices is difficult to determine. Misrecognition might occur through the development of alternative curricular. The intention is to motivate, the outcome might be to reproduce social class inequalities by unwittingly restricting pupils' engagement with high status knowledges (Wrigley et al., 2012). Headteachers responded to a combination of externally driven accountability measures and personal values to engage in an inclusive approach. However, the pressure to prepare pupils to pass academic qualifications overrode the need for deep conceptual or 'slow' learning (Wrigley et al., 2012). In selective schools there was no discourse at all about cognitive or metacognitive processes. Headteachers of selective schools were concerned with educational outcomes but there was an underlying assumption the system largely worked for those who gained entry. The discourse of social mobility one headteacher engaged in overstated the impact of assisted places to misrecognize the social reproduction taking place.

Summary

Classed headteacherly habitus

Leadership performance impacts on pupils and staff. Some headteachers drew on their experiences of social class inequalities in the fields of family and education in headship. There was less evidence of inequalities in the workplace *en route* to headship. I have shown how headteachers' relative status in those fields afforded them economic, cultural and social capital. Personal accounts of inequalities due to family background led to feelings of intimidation, frustration and anger. Headteachers had reflected deeply (Butler, 2004). Lucy recognized the intimidation she felt being the wrong class; Ben recognized the value of social entrepreneurship in sourcing investment to improve the quality of education in the area of multiple deprivations where he lived. Experience of social class inequalities was not exclusive to the working class. Two middle-class women experienced obstructions to their education. For them, the feelings of injustice and frustration were powerful too. Inequalities were located in social structures – as education and employment opportunities. However, these headteachers overcame difficulties to acquire sufficient cultural capital to progress to headship. Their experiences of upward social mobility informed their classed headteacherly habitus (Lupton, 2006; Maguire, 2005). *Class aware* headteachers were more aware of their acquisition of capital through education.

Class aware headteachers were also more likely to value the social capital of collaborative working with other local schools. They sought flattened hierarchical structures and described leadership team working more than class unaware headteachers in the main. They were more likely to discuss tackling poor staff performance. This suggests that they might be more aware of the impact of their use of power on others. *Class unaware* headteachers have not been without power; they might be less conscious of using it. It appears that among some headteachers class habitus impacted on headteacherly habitus with respect to staff management. Those who have acquired power appear to have reflected on their use of it (Gold, 1997 cited in Reay and Ball, 2000).

Class aware headteachers Diana and Isabella recognized non-teaching staff as women who left school without qualifications (see Chapter 4). Isabella also recognized her implementation of workforce reform caused tensions for teachers. Ben and Gregory's ongoing dialogues with staff ensured they were ready for workforce reform and would implement it in ways they saw fit. However, another *class aware* headteacher readily acknowledged his use of a working party to control communication and for self-protection during change management. Tensions between teaching and non-teaching staff were constructed as teachers' discourses of inequality. Headteachers from both groups spoke disparagingly of teachers' concerns.

Some headteachers did not fully understand the impact of class inequalities on pupils. The classification of pupils by ability or motivation might reproduce social inequalities. However, there was no simple correlation between a headteacher's social class background and their recognition of class inequalities among pupils. There were headteachers who connected their experiences of reduced status in the fields of family and education with those of pupils. There were those who did not. Similarly, there were headteachers who did not recount experiences of social class inequalities who recognized them in pupils. In particular, Silvia was concerned with deep conceptual learning as opposed to the acquisition of academic qualifications. Her classed headteacherly habitus was informed by her personal values (see Chapter 3). It may be that Philip's classed headteacherly habitus was influenced by his professional work with working-class children. This may constitute evidence of the professional field informing classed headteacherly habitus. With regard to establishing associational justice and participatory parity whether headteachers recognized class inequalities among families is important (Cribb and Gewirtz, 2003; Fraser, 2007). All headteachers recognized variations in socio-economic status. However, it is not clear how far headteachers engaged in dialogue with families from a full range of backgrounds.

The differing status of staff in the occupational field and of pupils in the field of secondary school education affords them different levels of access to economic, cultural and social capital. Chapter 6 goes on to examine headteachers' discourse about differences with regard to ethnicity.

6

What Diversity Means to Headteachers: Ethnicity

Introduction

Chapters 4 and 5 explored connections and gaps between headteachers' experiences of gender and social class inequalities and their discourse about differences in the school population. In this chapter, the focus is on headteachers' experiences of inequalities in ethnic and 'race' relations and their recognition of differences among staff and pupils. In Chapter 2, there was discussion of inequalities relating to women's achievement of headship in secondary schools. Further exploration of *which* women achieve headship reveals they are overwhelmingly White (DfE, 2012). Multilevel barriers apply to ethnic inequalities as well as gender and social class. The gap between the proportion of BGM pupils and leaders remains substantial in London and nationally (Coleman and Campbell-Stephens, 2010; Johnson and Campbell-Stevens, 2010). Ethnic inequalities in the fields of family, education and the workplace might influence the formation of a headteacherly habitus and the adoption of a particular leadership discourse. Headteachers' recognition of differences among staff might influence their access to leadership development opportunities (MacBeath, 2007). Regarding pupils, ethnic distinctions might influence headteachers' engagement with leadership for learning (Grogan and Shakeshaft, 2011; MacBeath, 2007) and leadership for social justice (Grogan and Shakeshaft, 2011).

In 2005, the New Labour government issued a paper about ethnicity and education (DfES, 2005). It contained demographical information, information about children's profiles by ethnic group on arrival at school and attainment data at each key stage thereafter. Information about GCSE subject entry, school attendance, exclusions and special educational needs was included. A specific section about Mixed heritage pupils referred to attainment, exclusions and perceived needs. Teachers' low expectations of Mixed heritage pupils were based on stereotypes of fragmented homes and 'confused' identities. Experiences of racism from teachers and White and Black peers targeted pupils' Mixed heritage. They were invisible at policy level with no guidance in place about terminology or monitoring of achievement. There was a failure to reflect Mixed heritage experiences and identities in the curriculum and school. The gap between the proportion of ethnic minority teachers and pupils was highlighted.

This chapter is divided into three main sections. In the first I define what is meant by particular terms. I go on to consider the literature about BGM and BME leaders and the achievement of BGM/BME pupils. The second section explores headteachers' experiences of ethnic inequalities in the social fields of family and education and professional fields of teaching and educational leadership. Bourdieu's thinking tools of field, habitus, forms of capital, misrecognition and symbolic violence are again used to consider headteachers' discourse about ethnicity. Few headteachers recognized ethnic differences among staff. Not all headteachers distinguished between pupils' ethnicities. In the third section I discuss the non-recognition and misrecognition of unequal ethnic/'race' relations that result in symbolic violence for members of the school population (Bourdieu and Passeron, 2000). Finally there is a summary of key points as advice and guidance for teachers and aspiring headteachers.

Background

Definition of terms

Changes in the use of different terms to describe ethnicity and 'race' have important consequences for teachers and headteachers (Gillborn, 1990). It is important to define what is meant here by ethnicity, ethnic group and 'race' in the discussion of headteachers' recognition of different ethnic and racial identities. 'Ethnicity' is 'the fact or state of belonging to a social group that has a common national or cultural tradition' (*Oxford Dictionaries*). However, earlier etymological usage from the fourteenth to the nineteenth centuries made reference to 'heathendom, heathen superstition' (*OED*). I take my definition of ethnicity from the idea of a particular group's shared 'sense and expression of ethnic difference' (Gillborn, 1990, p. 7) in contrast to that of non-members of an ethnic group. Such differences might be marked by language, history, modes of dress or physical characteristics (Gillborn, 1990). A distinction between ethnic groups and ethnic minorities is also necessary. 'Minority' implies fewer members of an ethnic group but also gives a sense of reduced power and potential for marginalization. The phrase 'global majority' is increasingly used to point out that ethnic minorities in the West are not minorities globally (see Campbell-Stephens, 2009; Johnson and Campbell-Stephens, 2013). BME is used widely (see Bush et al., 2006; Campbell-Stephens, 2009; Johnson and Campbell-Stephens, 2013; McKenley and Gordon, 2002; Shah, 2009) but,

> is contentious for some because it fails to differentiate between groups based on their cultural background and position in the racial hierarchy. We have used this term when citing particular research studies or government reports. (Johnson and Campbell-Stephens, 2013, p. 35)

The Investing in Diversity programme for aspiring BGM leaders used the term global majority to reflect 'the reality that people of color are a majority in the world and increasingly in the urban contexts of western countries' (Johnson and Campbell-Stephens, 2013, p. 36). However, BGM does not include White ethnic groups who might 'see themselves as culturally distinct from other groupings in society' (Giddens, 1989, p. 243). Gillborn (1990) identified the largest and longest established ethnic minority in the United Kingdom as people of Irish descent with Italians, Jews, Ukrainians and Travellers also as important groups. The terms ethnic group and ethnic minority are 'frequently equated with groups who are physically distinct from the "white" (European) majority – an example of racist stereotyping' (Gillborn, 1990, p. 5). While 'biological race' was concerned with the nineteenth-century classification of physical differences such as skin colour, 'social race' applies to the social construction of people sharing common characteristics in which the physical plays a part. Groupings are not biological but 'defined into existence' (Gillborn, 1990, p. 4). It should be noted that racism is not necessarily deliberate. The inquiry into the murder of Stephen Lawrence defined institutional racism as

> the collective failure of an organisation to provide an appropriate and professional service to people because of their colour, culture, or ethnic origin. It can be seen or detected in processes, attitudes and behaviour which amount to discrimination through unwitting prejudice, ignorance, thoughtlessness and racist stereotyping which disadvantage minority ethnic people. (MacPherson, 1999, 6.34)

It is the outcomes and effects rather than the intentions that matter (Gillborn, 2006a). Following Erasmus (2010), I have 'placed the word "race" in quotation marks in this instance to remind us of its offensive and derogatory nature' (p. 387). In the interest of fluency I omit the inverted commas hereafter. I use the terms BGM by choice and BME where the literature does so and where I want to include White ethnic minority groups.

The 2011 UK census (ONS, 2011) asked the population to identify their country of birth as England, Wales, Scotland, Northern Ireland or the Republic of Ireland or to write in another country. Questions regarding arrival and length of proposed stay were asked of those born outside the United Kingdom. National identities were chosen from English, Scottish, Welsh, Northern Irish, British and Other. Ethnic groups were arranged under racialized headings as White; Mixed/multiple ethnic groups; Asian/Asian British; Black/African/Caribbean/ Black British; or Other ethnic group. Within each racialized section choices were based on a combination of national and racial identity. Religion choices included: No religion, Christian, Buddhist, Hindu, Jewish, Muslim, Sikh or Any other religion. The lists were ordered by expected proportion of the population from highest to lowest, emphasizing the dominance of English White secularism and English White Christianity. The only choice for main language was English with an opportunity to identify just one other main language. Competence in speaking English was graded from spoken 'very well' to 'not at all'. There were no opportunities to identify bilingualism/multilingualism or competence in languages additional to English. In 2009, in the local authority in question 68 per cent of the population was White; 3.1 per cent Mixed ethnic; 19.7 per cent Asian or Asian British; 6.6 per cent Black or Black British; 2.6 per cent Chinese or other ethnic group (ONS, 2012b).

BGM/BME leadership

A Critical Race Theory (CRT) perspective notes racism happens every day, it is 'ordinary, not aberrational – "normal science," the usual way society does business, the common, everyday experience of most people of color' (Delgado and Stefanic, 2001, p. 7). Racism is a central structure in society (Zamudio et al., 2011). Despite legislation, it occurs every day through the enactment of 'microaggression' or 'small acts of racism, consciously or unconsciously perpetrated' (Delgado and Stefanic, 2001, p. 2). It occurs as institutional racism endemic in education and wider society as the enactment of White supremacy in 'WhiteWorld' (Gillborn, 2006b, p. 318). Along with the ordinariness of racism is the 'theoretical eclecticism' (Gillborn, 2006a) that enables CRT to cross epistemological boundaries. It critiques the limitations of civil rights laws despite the recognition of the movement's historical value (Crenshaw et al., 1995); and liberalism (Zamudio et al., 2011) for its colour-blindness in the interest of an equality discourse. The 'call to context' recognizes (Tate, 1997, p. 235) 'the experiential knowledge of people of colour'.

Nevertheless, there is a relatively small literature about the experiences of BGM/BME school leaders working in English schools. Osler (1997) included school leaders in her exploration of the education and careers of Black teachers. Senior Black educators were more 'visible' than White colleagues; they incurred hostility for behaviours unnoticed among White leaders. Research into leadership development programmes also recounts BGM/BME leaders' experiences of disadvantage and discrimination (Bush et al., 2006; Coleman and Campbell-Stephens, 2010; Johnson and Campbell-Stephens, 2010; 2013; McKenley and Gordon, 2002). McKenley and Gordon (2002) cite the daily experience of one leader, 'To operate in two worlds, professional success and maintenance of our fragile acceptance in this "white" world, requires the internalisation or blocking of pain, anger and hurt experienced as we encounter discrimination day by day' (p. 45).

Examples of wide ranging discrimination and racism included the apparent alienation of White children excluded from ethnic achievement support; children of Mixed heritage being enrolled as White; White staff undermining the decisions of a Black headteacher; Black colleagues accusing a middle manager of 'selling out'; feelings of racism dissuading BME people from working in White-dominated schools; and racist name-calling from a parent (Bush et al., 2006). Further obstacles included discrimination in the recruitment and selection process (Bush et al., 2006; Campbell-Stephens, 2009; Coleman and Campbell-Stephens, 2010; McKenley and Gordon, 2002; McNamara et al., 2009). Examples of positive discrimination were seen largely as unhelpful (Bush et al., 2006; Coleman and Campbell-Stephens, 2010). Nevertheless, the report into the leadership aspirations of BME teachers recommended ethnic monitoring of the teaching workforce, monitoring of BME teachers' progression into leadership, further research into discrimination and the disproportionately high number of BME senior leaders in urban schools or schools with disproportionately high numbers of BME pupils (McNamara et al., 2009). It recommended 'systematic support' to mitigate the barriers to progression including 'workload, self-confidence, caring responsibilities and access to high quality leadership development opportunities' (McNamara et al., 2009, pp. 81–2). In the depiction of school leadership, BME role models should be used to 'create an image of an inclusive profession and to challenge the dominant cultural perceptions that BME teachers do not make good leaders' (McNamara et al., 2009, p. 82).

Although McNamara et al. (2009) recommend systematic support for BME teachers, the notion of customized leadership development has prompted positive and negative responses (Bush et al., 2006). The Investing in Diversity programme for aspiring BGM leaders in London was positively received (Campbell-Stevens, 2009; Coleman and Campbell-Stephens, 2010; Johnson and Campbell-Stevens, 2010, 2013); as was the nation-wide Equal Access to Promotion programme (Ogunbawo, 2012). One important benefit was to establish networks and identify BGM leaders as role models and mentors to benefit women and men. Despite being seen as better leaders than women (McNamara et al., 2009) BGM men leaders are now an under-represented group compared to women in both primary and secondary phases in England (DfE, 2012; Johnson and Campbell-Stevens, 2013). However, Bush et al. (2006) identified that the 'double bind' of racism and sexism was a particularly powerful obstacle for women. The intersection of gender and ethnicity is reported in the international literature (Battiste, 2005; Blackmore, 1999; Fitzgerald, 2006; Shah, 2006a). An increasingly diverse range of women leaders' voices force us to reconsider normative Whiteness (Asher, 2010; Benham and Murakami-Ramalho, 2010; Blackmore, 2010b; Fitzgerald, 2010; Shah, 2010; White, 2010). In so doing, Blackmore (2010b) draws on CRT to confront the invisibility of Whiteness among White women educational leaders.

Campbell-Stephens (2009) also writes about the joyous leadership and additionality that BGM leaders bring to schools (see also Coleman and Campbell-Stephens, 2010; Johnson and Campbell-Stevens, 2010). McKenley and Gordon (2002) note the strong desire of BME leaders to 'capture the joys of their leadership'; to 'add their rich cultural heritage to the common wealth of all schools' (p. 3). There was a sense of vocation to their communities. However, they cautioned against seeing BME leaders as a homogeneous group. There were many ways for BME leaders to lead. Campbell-Stephens (2009) notes the interconnectivity and social interdependence of *Ubuntu* rarely enters the literature on leadership. But such leadership practices (Campbell-Stephens, 2009) 'are intrinsic to the backgrounds of Black and global majority people' (p. 324). The social relationships that *Ubuntu* leadership fosters (see Bush, 2007; Msila, 2008) resonate with those that subvert hierarchy in Blackmore's (1989) feminist reconstruction of leadership. They resemble horizontal relationships referred to as relational leadership (Grogan and Shakeshaft, 2011).

Shah (2006a, 2010) notes the cultural and contextual factors, the beliefs and values that inform the construction of Islamic educational leadership by both the leader and the led. Each 'participate[s] in related activities informed by their ideological and cultural knowledge-transmitted from generation to generation and learned through living and sharing with a group or community as its member' (Shah, 2006a, p. 366). She explains the process using Bourdieu's notion of habitus (Bourdieu and Passeron, 2000). Leaders must become better informed to fill the 'awareness gap' (Shah, 2006a, p. 366) where it exists. Leading in Islam has connotations with leading towards knowledge and 'righteousness' as well as providing a role model (Shah, 2006a). The faith dimension of 'education for all' makes learning a religious obligation. Shah (2006a) identifies a three-dimensional model of leadership as: 'Teaching with knowledge and understanding as educator; Guiding with wisdom and values as prophet/ leader; Caring with responsibility and commitment as parent' (Shah, 2006a, p. 370). There are overlaps with notions of leadership for learning (Grogan and Shakeshaft, 2011; MacBeath, 2007); and ethical values informed leadership (Begley, 2006; Grace, 2000) based on the *ethic of care* (Begley, 2006). Shah (2006a) links the Islamic practices of meditation and reflection with the self-understanding identified here as spiritual leadership (Grogan and Shakeshaft, 2011). Further, Shah (2008) proposes *Adab* as a conceptual frame to enrich and develop existing concepts; as education to develop positive attitudes towards diversity; and as a practice contributing to social cohesion. Links between the features of *Adab* and good practice for managing ethnic diversity are made: '"Beautiful action" – respecting difference; "Sharing" – awareness of the learners' expectations; "Good manners" – attention to culture-appropriate behaviour/values; "Inviting" – developing inclusive attitudes/practices; "Giving happiness" – providing support and guidance; "Hospitality" – a deeper understanding of concepts such as *Adab, honour*, equality, and difference for responding to diversity' (Shah, 2008, p. 532).

Wong (1998) refers to eastern philosophies such as Buddhism that teach, 'the complementarity of human processes', that opens Easterners up to the possibility of 'reconciling alternate values' (p. 112). Wisdom-centred leadership is based on six Buddhist virtues of generosity (in giving openly), discipline (including self-discipline in helping others), patience (forbearance under threat), right effort (diligent perseverance, tireless and wise effort in helping others), meditation and concentration (mindfulness and being fully present to a situation to find the possibilities for the four previous virtues) and wisdom (uncommon common sense in seeing reality) (Ylimaki and McClain, 2009). Such leadership might ensure 'sustained equanimity, compassion and joy in the face of tremendous challenges' (Ylimaki and McClain, 2009, p. 30) of accountability and limited resources.

Ethnicity and education

In a critical review of research into racial/ethnic inequalities in English schools, Stevens (2007) identified five research traditions. The political arithmetic tradition described the relationship between educational inequality and race/ethnicity over time. It used large-scale data sets. The racism and racial discrimination in school tradition explored how school selection, the curriculum and White teachers' racist attitudes impacted on the education of racial/ethnic pupils. It used ethnographic and qualitative methods. The school effectiveness and school inclusion tradition investigated the characteristics of effective schools for all pupils, and specifically racial/ethnic groups. The culture and educational outcomes tradition looked at the importance of racial/ethnic cultures in influencing educational outcomes. The fifth tradition, educational markets and educational outcomes, explored the impact of policy changes since the Education Reform Act in 1988. The wide range of educational policy approaches towards diversity has included assimilation, integration, multicultural education, equal educational opportunities, anti-racist education, the new racist/cultural racisms, institutional racism and citizenship education (see Maylor et al., 2005). A dominant discourse has centred on the differential attainment of particular ethnic groups as a result of a conspiracy of 'White supremacy' in 'WhiteWorld' (Gillborn, 2006b, p. 318; see also Gillborn, 2008, 2010a,b). In particular, the media has misrepresented research findings (Gillborn, 2008). Analysis of the 'poor White' discourse demonstrates 'interest convergence' (Gillborn, 2010b, p. 3). As Bell (1980) argued, the 'principle of "interest convergence" provides: The interest of blacks in achieving racial equality will be accommodated only when it converges with the interests of whites' (p. 523). Interest convergence explains, 'the operation of these victim/degenerate discourses that seem at one level to split the White group and yet, ultimately, they help secure White supremacy overall' (Gillborn, 2010b, p. 21).

In the leadership literature there is a particular focus on Muslim pupils in British schools (Shah, 2006b, 2008, 2009; Shah and Conchar, 2009). Stevenson (2007) found that headteachers committed to a focus on social justice in multi-ethnic schools created space for their own personal and professional values. They developed policies for 'culturally sensitive teaching and learning; the promotion of inclusive organisational cultures; the nurturing and development of staff (especially minority ethnic staff); and the mobilisation of the wider community in support of school objectives' (Stevenson, 2007, p. 778).

The headteachers

In the following sections I refer to 18 headteachers' discourse about ethnicity. Their experiences of inequalities in ethnic relations impacted on their discourse about ethnicity differences among the school population. Experiences of ethnic inequalities in the fields of family, education and/or the workplace informed aspects of their headteacherly habitus and leadership discourse. First, I look at headteachers' recognition of their ethnic heritage. Secondly, I explore their recognition of differences among staff. Thirdly, I examine their recognition of differences among pupils. Headteachers talked about themselves, staff and pupils in relation to national identity, skin colour, language, cultural traditions and faith.

Headteachers' self-recognition

National identity

Three headteachers referred to their national heritage as other than British. Isabella described her mother as an Austrian immigrant; Muhsin referred to his Pakistani background; Sam had immigrated to the United Kingdom from Trinidad via France. He described himself as Black. Rosaline attended 19 schools worldwide as the daughter of a serviceman. East Africa was the location of one temporary stay. Tony married into 'Celtic culture', and identified an Irish role model. Three headteachers originated from specific English regions as the Midlands, London and Yorkshire. Two women were Welsh.

Faith

I have referred to headteachers' faith backgrounds in Chapter 3. However, it is worth recapping here that one headteacher was an atheist who traced her personal values to an Anglican upbringing; another described herself as not a 'churchgoer'. Eight headteachers presented as active believers if not practising worshippers. Six Christians represented a range of denominations. Another talked about his Buddhist beliefs. Muhsin's entire response was permeated with references to Islam. Three men had taken leadership roles in their respective places of worship (Muhsin, Robin, Sam).

Unequal ethnic/race relations

Based on headteachers' accounts of personal or witnessed experiences of ethnic and/or racial inequalities, I have grouped eight headteachers as *ethnicity aware* (Muhsin, Sam, Emily, Isabella, Rosaline, Rose, Robert and Tony). The remaining ten headteachers with no experience of unequal ethnic relations are grouped as *ethnicity unaware* (Diana, Katherine, Lucy, Silvia, Stephanie, Ben, Duncan, Gregory, Philip and Robin).

Emily grew up in 'White Britain'. Although not constructed as racist, she was aware of the dominance of Whiteness in her upbringing. Having married an Irish woman, Tony linked the assimilation of the Irish and Italian communities to a prediction about changing Pakistani cultural traditions. He outlined the historical context of migration in the authority.

The most powerful account of ethnic/racial inequality was Sam's. His migration to Europe was prompted by interest in foreign languages. A French government scholarship described as 'De Gaulle's way of spreading the French civilization throughout the world', facilitated the move. Sam's life was directly affected by European colonialism. Sam initially experienced no racism; with 'the only Black face in the streets ... [he] felt loved'. Desirous of making 'a meaningful contribution', he moved schools to work in an ethnically diverse region. He experienced racism for the first time, 'I felt animosity on the part of adults; the children were loving.' As a quasi advisor, he educated colleagues, including the headteacher, about Black children.

> Simple things like their body language, if they looked down it could be that they're not being rude, they're embarrassed, and things like that. Some of them were young Rastafarii (*sic*) as well. The headteacher didn't understand much about that. I wrote a few papers and things like what I call the Babylon Factor where they view any societal institution or the police as Babylon and systems contrary to their thinking about a utopia, a Zion and so on. I had to change attitudes among the staff even. (Sam)

Sam publically challenged misconceptions about children. Prevalent attitudes were racist, 'The whole system militated against student progress; because you came from a foreign country, India or the West Indies, you were deemed to be remedial.' He demonstrated that pupils with EAL were very able. Staff weren't very up-to-date with English as a second language, not realizing, the fact that these children could handle two or three different languages, showed they were clever. . . . I even went further and did A Level Spanish with some of them, to show that these children are not as thick as they think. I had to do that by my own practice to show them that these children are not compensatory [pupils with special educational needs]. (Sam)

He became a champion of, and for, the Welsh in voicing a minority perspective as member of a national advisory group. Selection for the work was partly because of his ethnicity, as a Black Asian modern linguist school leader. Sam rejected the term 'ethnicity' because of the word's earliest etymology, 'I don't like to use the word ethnic because it has heathen connotations.' He talked about 'friendship groups' that despite some commonalities remained heterogeneous.

[T]he friendship I come from and the friends' social groups, if you take one group for instance, let's take those of an Islamic background. Within that same culture you'd find different types of behaviour and different ambitions. So I don't like . . . to lump everybody in one category and to compartmentalize people because I treat each child as an individual. (Sam)

He developed 'milieu theory' with a doctoral student. It was based on observations while working with pupils in various schools and authorities. Young Black people belonged to a number of milieux such as,

the milieu that you inherit from say Jamaica, or whatever island your parents came from, and then you have the milieu of the part of England that you live for instance, there is a distinct difference in the milieu of Blacks in [one area compared to another]. Then you have the immigrant milieu from which you bring all sorts of norms into the food and all the arts and crafts and so on. Then you have the school milieu and the wider, in the case of [metropolitan district] and there are factors within all of that complex arena that affect the way you achieve things and then look at the home milieu. (Sam; from Fuller, 2012, p. 685)

A combination of factors influenced young people's achievement in school, not simply the colour of their skin.

Muhsin described no personal experience of racism or Islamophobia. However, as a 'Muslim minister of religion', he had worked with families frustrated by the treatment of children in English state schools. The drive to establish an Islamic school came from Muslim families' needs not being met in mainstream state schools. Muhsin described the concern of young people and their parents.

> They used to bring problems. Suppose when a youth would tease them or somebody used to say to me that 'when we go to state school, you have to do the mixed swimming where we are very shy, we are, we don't like doing it with the girls'. Girls used to also come to me . . . their parents used to come to me that, 'We don't feel actually that they should do this. Why should we do it? We have to send them to school. We cannot keep them at home'. (Muhsin)

Muhsin advised and represented families at meetings in state schools. Despite school cooperation, parents increasingly sent children to their countries of origin for the period of compulsory schooling prompted by activities associated with physical education (PE) such as compulsory swimming lessons, lack of privacy in the shower facilities and the nature of the PE kit. Muhsin's religious ethos pervaded his headship. It gave him self-control over emotions and desires 'for the sake of the peace, harmony, others' feelings'. He identified more commonality in Islam with the Abrahamic religions of Judaism and Christianity than Hinduism and Sikhism. Muhsin had organized interfaith debates between Christian and Muslim scholars attracting thousands of people. He worked to reconcile different Muslim groups. Differentiating between individuals and groups as 'this faith and this faith, this community and this community, this mosque and this mosque, this school and this school' (from Fuller, 2012, p. 684) was important in strengthening social cohesion. He learnt, 'from the practices and the experiences of the communities; how they actually act together; how they treat each other; how they should treat each other; for the sake of the harmony; for the sake of the peace and for the sake of the peace of the society'.

Robert described a formative experience as a young man visiting the American Deep South at the time of the Black Civil Rights movement. With Left-wing politics came the belief that, 'racism was wrong; you take people as you find them, all colours and creeds and so on'. Robert stayed with the political elite who as 'part of that southern liberal democrat spectrum' were in regular contact with President Johnson. He was introduced to the legal representative of Rosa Parks, who had refused to sit in the seat reserved for Black people on the bus. Meeting Black Civil Rights leaders was 'fantastic'. However, it is unclear whether he met Civil Rights leaders who were Black or other White liberals who supported their cause. He met the 'racist Governor Wallace' because his hosts wanted him to gain a balanced perspective. Robert attributed his 'multicultural bit, the liberal bit' in his headteacherly habitus partly to this experience.

Rose described a formative professional experience teaching at an inner city school during the 1980s riots. She did not construct the riots as racially motivated but described community tensions.

> [T]he school was on the knife edge for most of the five years that I was there. It was a very difficult school to teach in, especially because of the community outside and the tensions in the community which did spill over into the school on many occasions and it was really very volatile at times. (Rose)

She connected working at the school with her commitment to 'equality, gender and race, and . . . social background'. Subsequently reports identified the multiplicity and complexity of the causes of tension, but they have also been racialized by the media (BBC, 2005a,b). Rose was working with ethnically diverse pupils whose community was portrayed as one of racial tension and conflict.

In the sections that follow I examine headteachers' recognition of ethnic differences among the school population. I begin with staff.

Recognizing ethnic differences among staff

There were few references to ethnic differences among staff. Four *ethnicity aware* (Muhsin, Sam, Emily and Tony) and three *ethnicity unaware* headteachers (Rosaline, Robin and Diana) referred to national identity, skin colour, language or faith as markers of ethnic difference.

Ethnicity aware Muhsin identified all the staff except two as Muslim. In Chapter 3 I described how staff generally did not emulate Muhsin's tireless work to benefit the school and community. Sam described 'a multicultural staff'. He distinguished between teachers by national identity from Sierra Leone, Nigeria, Jamaica, Trinidad and St Kitts and Australia. Role models did not have to be the 'same culture'. Making a direct connection with the White role models who inspired him, Sam noted that a White Australian teacher provided an excellent role model for Black girls.

> [S]he was White and she was a proper role model. I don't believe in this sort of same culture only role model. Sometimes it works where you have the people of the same culture as your own, but anybody can be somebody's role model. Many of the teachers that inspired me were from England and others were West Indian as well. Anybody can be your role model. (Sam)

Opportunities were taken to persuade ethnically diverse adults to work with the children. School buildings were used as a church.

> Some of them are from South Africa. All I want from [them] is to teach my girls to sing the way [they] do, and they've already begun to do that. So I try to facilitate as many young people to be role models and if they can help the school and we can help them, I want it. (Sam)

Emily identified two teachers from ethnic minority backgrounds, but a higher proportion among non-teaching staff. Recent appointments included teachers she described by faith as Hindu and Muslim. She noted few applications from people of 'ethnic minority' backgrounds with a 'good degree from a good university'. Tony claimed teaching and non-teaching staff reflected the ethnic makeup of the pupils.

Ethnicity unaware Rosaline ensured that the full range of children's ethnicities was represented on the staff. In the event that two candidates were equally good, Rosaline selected the applicant with the ethnic background and language skills representative of pupils and families.

> [W]e've named certain languages that it would be desirable to talk, to speak. We've done that for care staff as well as teaching assistants. (Rosaline)

She hoped staff might provide role models for pupils but noted they might not relish that role. Isabella, Rose and Robert did not recognize ethnic differences among the staff at all. Robin's use of personal names of south Asian origin demonstrated BGM staff were encouraged to engage in CPD and took on leadership roles. Diana referred to a Sikh woman in her account of flexible working practices (see Chapter 4). She granted her two weeks of unpaid leave to get married following the religious traditions of her faith. The remaining seven *ethnicity unaware* headteachers made no reference to ethnic differences among staff.

Among those who identified ethnic differences in the staff body, Sam and Rosaline celebrated their ethnic diversity. Sam fully appreciated the additionality that exceptional people brought to the school for the benefit of pupils (Bush et al., 2006; Campbell-Stephens, 2009; Coleman and Campbell-Stephens, 2010; Johnson and Campbell-Stevens, 2010; McKenley and Gordon, 2002). Rosaline valued the language resources that the staff possessed. However, some might not want to be marginalized as role models for pupils (Johnson and Campbell-Stephens, 2010; Osler, 1997). Robin included teachers from a range of ethnic backgrounds in a staff development programme that afforded them leadership development opportunities. This was done as a matter of course, not because they were from BGM backgrounds. They would be good leaders able to lead in any institution because of their skills and talents (Bush et al., 2006). Diana demonstrated understanding of and respect for her colleague's cultural needs. Emily commented on the difficulties in recruiting BGM staff with 'good' degrees from 'good' universities. Her comment demonstrated the systemic nature of the problem. The recruitment of teachers from a range of ethnicities continues to be a priority (Wilkins and Lall, 2011). Muhsin complained that the Muslim staff did not share his Islamic educational values with respect to learning as a religious obligation that instils discipline (Shah, 2006a).

Eleven headteachers failed to recognize ethnic differences among staff. This non-recognition by White headteachers suggests lack of understanding regarding the experiences of BGM/BME teachers (Bush et al., 2006; Coleman and Campbell-Stephens, 2010; Johnson and Campbell-Stephens, 2010, 2013; McKenley and Gordon, 2002; Osler, 1997). Their needs might be overlooked as teaching and non-teaching staff and as aspiring leaders. When potentially marginalized members of staff are not recognized there is no redistribution of resources, nor is there representation with participatory parity (Fraser, 2000). There is no distributive, cultural or associational justice (Cribb and Gewirtz, 2003). Overall headteachers demonstrated that, 'relatively little attention has been paid to the ethnicity of educational staff' (Lumby with Coleman, 2007, p. 58).

Recognizing ethnic differences among pupils

Fourteen headteachers recognized ethnic differences among pupils, including all eight *ethnicity aware* and six *ethnicity unaware* headteachers (Diana, Lucy, Stephanie, Duncan, Philip and Robin). They used terms such as multicultural, multi-faith, multi-ethnicity, ethnicity differences, ethnic diversity, ethnic mix, ethnic makeup, ethnic grouping and ethnic minority. Headteachers referred to national identities, skin colour, languages, modes of dress, faith or cultural traditions.

National identities

All eight *ethnicity aware* headteachers referred to pupils' national identities as Pakistani, Indian, Somali, Iraqi, Jamaican, South Korean, West Indian and Mixed ethnic background as Ghanaian/Russian. Muhsin added pupils from Yemen, Bangladesh, Nepal, Bhutan and Afghanistan. Tony added Vietnamese,

Chinese and Arab pupils. While some pupils were described by their parents' or grandparents' nationality, in Sam's school others had newly arrived in the United Kingdom via countries such as Holland.

Ethnicity aware Muhsin was the only headteacher to identify British pupils who had relationships with their ancestors' countries of origin. Indeed he referred to Britishness many times, 'British born children'; British investment in children from birth through child benefit allowance; the British nation; being naturally British; British society; British community; British citizens; and the British education system. Other headteachers who recognized national heritage difference among pupils constructed it as something other than British. British or English children were assumed to be the dominant group. Three headteachers linked national identity to pupils' sex referring to 'Pakistani girls' (Tony); an 'Iraqi girl' (Emily); and 'West Indian girls' (Isabella). Two linked national identity with faith as 'Korean Christians' (Robert) and 'Pakistani Muslims' (Muhsin).

Ethnicity unaware Philip referred to the national heritage of pupils as 'non-English heritage, Asian Pakistani'. Twenty per cent of the school population was from this ethnic group.

Skin colour

Ethnicity aware Emily, Tony and Sam referred to skin colour. White middle-class families sent their children to ethnically diverse schools. Parents at Tony's school did not want their children to have a limited White, middle-class worldview. Emily was proud of the 'terrific ethnic diversity' appeal of the school population. She cited parents, who said elsewhere their daughter

> would be in a White school and I want her to be tolerant. I work in [City] myself (perhaps in a hospital or something like that), and it's not White and the world's not White. (Emily)

The largest 'ethnic minority' group in her school was Asian. Emily used faith to distinguish the dominant group within that as Sikh. Tony identified differences between children as their 'skin colour' as well as national identity (see above) and faith (see below). He distinguished between Black children as 'Black other, Black Caribbean, Black Africans' in a list of ethnic categories that did not include Black British.

Ethnicity aware Sam referred to Black children, Black girls distinguishing between the variety of Caribbean island origins and family dispositions towards education. The contrast between Black girls in his present and previous schools surprised him.

> [T]he animosity on the part of the girls and the confrontational attitude and the hatred that they had was totally alien to me. It was the first time I encountered this on the part of the students and I couldn't understand, and I still can't understand. (Sam)

Elsewhere he had taught colleagues about Black youths' resistance to authority. Here the resistance was against his authority. There was no common faith bond between him and pupils in this school as there had been previously. He linked this observation to the 'theory of milieu' (see above). He refuted the notion of Black children's underachievement, 'the Black children are the ones who achieve the highest grades in many cases'. When parents complained, Sam argued that the same teachers taught the Black children who achieved well.

> I don't believe that a group of children underachieve because they are a group of Black girls. When some parents come to me and say this school has failed their children, I tell them, because we have an honours list out there, you will see how many got five or more A*–Cs, and I show them all the Black girls. I say the same teachers that taught these Black girls who achieve, some of them sixteen starred A–Cs; they are the same teachers that taught your child. What's the difference? And I end it there. (Sam)

Sam challenged parents, who extolled the past virtues of the school as good discipline and smart uniform, about their own qualifications. He forced them to admit they were not entered for examinations

> because they were not even deemed fit enough to do O Levels. They used to do the old CSEs. I said 'How many CSEs – Grade 1s have you got?' And there is silence. (Sam)

Historically, the school had a reputation for strictness but not academic achievement. Some parents were favourably disposed towards education but children needed to want educational success too. There was an emphasis on treating individual children with respect to raise their self-esteem. Work to promote the achievement of Black children was ongoing and remained a priority for everyone.

> It's hard work. Everybody has a part to play. Not just the White population. The Blacks have got to take responsibility for their own lives as well. (Sam)

Sam wanted Black families to engage in an aspirational education discourse that would support pupils' educational outcomes. He constructed Black families as agential.

Ethnicity aware Isabella referred to West Indian girls (see below). *Ethnicity aware* Rose and *ethnicity unaware* Diana and Duncan referred to 'Afro-Caribbean' boys. Duncan described the school as 'monocultural' with 95 per cent described as 'indigenous White' and 85 per cent were from 'working-class' backgrounds.

Mixed heritage

Only *ethnicity aware* Emily and Robert referred to children as 'Mixed race' or of Mixed ethnic background. No *ethnicity unaware* headteachers referred to pupils of Mixed heritage.

Language

Ethnicity aware Rosaline recognized a range of language backgrounds. Asian and African languages and Spanish and Italian were spoken in pupils' homes. Cantonese- and French-speaking pupils were no longer in the school but had been catered for by staff in the past. Dutch, Portuguese, Urdu and Punjabi were spoken by pupils at Sam's school. He encouraged them to take examinations in their first languages to develop self-esteem on arrival at the school. If necessary, teaching expertise was brought into school. Arabic, Urdu and English were taught at Mushin's school.

> English as a medium and Arabic as a religious language for Muslim, in a Muslim faith school. Urdu because 80% community is from the [Indian] sub-continent. . . . They all speak Urdu, understand Urdu. (Muhsin)

Muhsin regretted not being able to do more to value the range of the pupils' home languages.

> [W]e will not be able to introduce all the languages of the community. It would be very difficult. So these two languages are more important ones to have. (Muhsin)

While Sam and Muhsin valued children's bilingualism/multilingualism, Tony was surprised by pupils' achievements, 'considering a lot come in with English as a second language, their success has been outstanding, in two languages in French and Spanish'. All children continued to learn at least one foreign language. He recognized their success and the importance of continuing language learning but did not understand the relationship between cognitive development and access to multiple linguistic resources.

No *ethnicity unaware* headteachers referred to pupils' additional linguistic resources.

Modes of dress

Pupils at *ethnicity aware* Muhsin's school wore a PE kit that covered them more fully than traditional PE kits in most state schools. Only he mentioned mode of dress.

Faith

Five ethnicity aware headteachers described pupils' faith backgrounds as Muslim (Muhsin, Sam, Robert), Sikh (Emily) and Catholic (Tony). Sam described the school's enjoyment of the Sikh celebration of Vaisakhi (see below). Emily saw Sikhs as dominant among the ethnic minority community. They were 'pretty cosmopolitan and tolerant of other people' which led to a high degree of tolerance among the diverse faith communities in the school. Her provision for faith groups extended to predominantly Christian assemblies that were given over to other faiths to celebrate festivals. She was sensitive about getting people's faith celebrations wrong so, 'I do try to get the girls when it is the festivals in different faiths to come and lead assembly for me and they can be very, very good at doing that.' The Iraq conflict prompted Emily to invite people to lead prayers, read or share their thoughts about what was happening. One girl, among thousands of school pupils locally and nationally, walked out of school in protest at the Iraq conflict. Although Emily was unhappy about the pupil's action at the time she subsequently invited her to speak in an assembly.

> I said 'Look, if you feel strongly about it come and tell the rest of us why you feel so strongly.' She held her own very nicely and we had television in fact came and did something. Uninvited by us, but they came. She held her own quite well there [expressing her views in the face of the publicity]. (Emily)

Emily was also very proud that an Iraqi girl, whose father was fighting, expressed her feelings publically. Similarly, assemblies at Tony's school were celebrations of not only Christian liturgy but also other faiths, 'even though we are in a Catholic school, by the very nature of where we are, we are about 48% Catholic, probably 10% practising'.

Robert identified the achievement of Muslim boys from less affluent backgrounds as 'one of the great delights of this school' and an example of social mobility. He gave two examples of Muslim boys in receipt of free school places reading medicine at Oxbridge as 'the most satisfying sort of success'. The school advertised in the Muslim community. Sam provided an interfaith prayer room,

> where there is peace and we respect everybody's religion. It's Ramadan now and behind you is a prayer mat where the girls kneel and pray. There is water in there. Mecca faces there and the girls respect the Prayer Room. It's a Prayer Room for everybody to come in not just the Muslims among us. Because I believe in prayer. (Sam)

Children from the same religious or cultural background might have totally different home circumstances necessitating the treatment of each child as an individual.

Muhsin established an Islamic school to prevent Muslim families from sending children out of the country for their compulsory schooling years. All British children should be well educated. Sending them away meant access to a good education was limited, particularly for girls.

> If we are British citizens we need to think about the welfare and strength of the future society's citizens. So I used to say that, in this way, you are encouraging to produce uneducated mothers of the future, and uneducated fathers of the future. . . . They are naturally British. So we are, we need to provide the facilities where they all have been taught in an environment which they like. (Muhsin)

The motivation was to 'save those girls from being sent out'. An Islamic school provided an Islamic religious ethos that could not be provided in a multi-faith school. It was too much to expect a state school to cater for the needs of the Muslim community.

> It's not practical because there are Hindu children, there are Sikh children, there are Catholic. . . . So we could not make a state school practise the Islamic faith. It's not practical. (Muhsin)

The religious ethos enabled resolution of conflict between boys through an appeal to shared beliefs and sense of brotherhood that was transferable between faiths.

> [T]his brotherhood which is between Muslim and Muslim, the same brotherhood could be transferred to the faith to faith, to all the people who believe in the faith. (Muhsin)

The school provided segregated education for boys and girls. Muhsin referred to a tendency among Muslim families to be concerned more with the education and upbringing of daughters. In his view, Muslim boys should also receive an Islamic education.

> We never thought, okay Muslim community is facing only problem with girls. No there's a lot of Muslims (*sic*) only care about girls and not about the boys. What I mean that they think that girls' honour, girls' dignity, girls' mannerism. They take care, a lot of care. But a boy could go how he wants to spend. That is also unbalanced. (Muhsin)

Muhsin noted the reported underachievement of Pakistani Muslims; the school bucked that trend. He celebrated the achievement of former pupils who completed higher education. Photographs depicted highly achieving boys, one of whom had learnt the whole of the Qur'an. However, there were no pictures of girls. There were no non-Muslim children in the school despite Muhsin's desire to be open to the wider community.

Two *ethnicity unaware* headteachers referred to pupils' faith backgrounds. Stephanie referred to a wide range in a city that was 'very, very multi-faith'. She associated education about diversity with religious studies as well as history, geography and mathematics. Staff were free to decide whether and how to teach a multicultural/intercultural curriculum. By contrast, Robin distinguished pupils very clearly by faith as Muslims, Sikhs, Hindus, those with no faith and Christians. He described his relationship with the Sikh community,

> being a person with a faith helps to attain, to get their respect. If I talk to people in the communities with faith, for instance the big gurdwara down the road. The big Sikh temple, I talk to the chairman who is kind of like, the spiritual leader who is a very wise guy, a very wise man. Enormously impressive guy. Having a faith, though even if it is not a common faith, but there is commonality at least in the perspective it gives, gave the point of contact. (Robin)

However, Robin's approach was not interfaith in the way Muhsin described (see above). He respected the right to hold different beliefs but thought they were 'wrong' and his evangelical Christianity was 'right'.

> They have the right to believe it. In a different context I might try to persuade them, but as a headteacher I couldn't possibly do it . . . Socially we could have a deep discussion about these things, which might be enlightening in the sense

that it would help each of us to understand how the other is thinking and why they're thinking as they are; probably not at all useful in terms of proselytizing one way or t'other. But in school that can't be done. They don't attempt it with people here and I wouldn't dream of attempting it. It would be an abuse of trust. (Robin)

Cultural traditions

Three *ethnicity aware* headteachers described cultural traditions in positive ways. Isabella illustrated different approaches two teachers might take to the behaviour of three 'West Indian' girls. Called to a music lesson because children were misbehaving, Isabella praised the girls for their singing. The teacher complained they were, 'just playing up, they're not singing' whereas Isabella invited the girls to sing for her in her office, '"Sing what you were singing," and the three West Indian girls came out with a couple of songs and it was absolutely fantastic.' The girls performed to parents then a wider audience at a public event. Isabella recounted the incident to demonstrate how easy it was for teachers to interpret children's behaviour in negative ways. She thought everybody's prejudices should be acknowledged.

> [T]he West Indian girls are loud, not all of them are, and those that are, you recognize that they are loud, they are not nastily loud, they are naturally loud and they are loud at home and they are loud in here etc and so you handle them a different way. But you recognize there are prejudices around and you deal with that. (Isabella)

Isabella valued the girls' same talents that the music teacher found challenging.

Tony described the recognition, celebration and value of ethnic differences. The school celebrated Africa week when two days were spent celebrating the culture and vitality of West Africa. He noted the cultural background of some Pakistani girls was more powerful than school culture.

> There are some that are more traditional. I wouldn't seek to influence that tradition. We would say how good they are if they are good and what they could do and what we hope they would do. But when they go to home it has far more influence than school ever has. (Tony)

Sam recounted several celebrations of diversity. Expressive arts enabled children 'to express their cultural values that they've picked up from their parents'. He described the variety of food, arts and crafts and celebrations of various ethnic groups. He pointed out artwork by children with SEN called

'Creating a real life identity'. The Sikh festival of Vaisakhi was celebrated by the whole community.

[W]e had Punjabi and drummers from India and so on, and everybody took part; the community, the parents, everybody. So we celebrate all this. So we don't attack things only on an individual basis, we have a collective sort of celebration as well. (Sam; from Fuller, 2012, p. 684)

One *ethnicity unaware* headteacher recounted an incident with Afro-Caribbean boys enacting masculinity in ways she found challenging.

[S]ome Afro-Caribbean boys, to look at a particular group, who find it very challenging to, for example, to look you in the eye and need to show off their maleness in other ways. But there are some things I won't backtrack on either. I do think when I'm talking to somebody they need to sit, they need to look at me and I'll look at them. So there are cultural differences that I would to some extent push to one side and say that the values that we bring as people are more important.

She did not see the boys' body language in the way Sam might. He had taught staff to recognize Black children's body language might mean something other than White teachers' interpretation of it. Where the White woman headteacher interpreted lack of eye contact as resistance of authority and disrespect, Sam interpreted it as a sign of embarrassment.

Integration

Community cohesion was important to *ethnicity aware* Emily and Muhsin. Muhsin advised children to go into careers that benefited the community as a whole, not just because they enjoyed the work or would be well paid. He countered the argument that faith schools isolated children from the rest of society with the view that integration was better done later when children had matured.

They need to be part of the community. They need to be part of the society. . . . But this state which is a schooling state it is not really beneficial mixing state. This mixing is childish mixing. 'Oh let's go to park.' Waste of time. 'Let's go to city centre.' That is not a useful mixing. The useful mixing start in the college when they are mature; so that we encourage. (Muhsin)

He did not value pupils' childhood social interactions with non-Muslims. Emily valued social integration between pupils.

[O]ne of the greatest things is when you see them walking about at lunchtime and they're arm in arm and they'll also be hugging. That friendship group contains people from, anything under the sun. I was out with Duke of Edinburgh expedition last week and I took the photo of one of the groups because you couldn't have had anything that was more multi-ethnic than that group of friends. (Emily)

She speculated mutual tolerance was established at home particularly among educated families who she constructed as open-minded about diversity.

Racism

Only two *ethnicity aware* headteachers referred to racism. Tony acknowledged racism was endemic in society and among some families but pupils did not bring it into school very often.

> [W]e don't have a place for racism in this school or bigotry or bullies. But there are racists, and there are bigots and there are bullies in the school because there are in every school. But they know the consequences if they bring that into the school. So most, I can guarantee 99% of it, they don't. They might go home to that but our school is a place where you don't bring that in. (Tony)

Similarly Robert was wholly intolerant of racism in school. Neither considered the possibility of a racist school structure or education system.

Attainment

Ethnicity aware Isabella and Rose monitored children's progress by ethnicity. Rose noted that despite low numbers, 'there is a pattern emerging that we are bucking the trend with our achievement with Afro-Caribbean boys with massively successful achievements among that group of kids, it is certainly quite small in numbers but for those youngsters the fact that they've achieved is really good and that pleases us greatly' (from Fuller, 2012, p. 679). There was no suggestion that a model minority group's achievement meant anything other than that they had individually achieved well. There was a sense that Rose knew the children personally and shared pride in their successes.

Ethnicity unaware Lucy carried out pupil book checks to monitor their school experience by ethnicity. Duncan was dismissive of using the data regarding ethnic minorities because there were so few pupils.

All eight *ethnicity aware* headteachers recognized pupils' national identities. Three referred to pupils' skin colour as White/Black. Two referred to pupils of Mixed heritage. Three recognized the multiplicity of linguistic resources among pupils. Five recognized pupils' faith backgrounds. Two acknowledged racism existed; two talked about integration. Two monitored pupils' attainment by ethnicity. Recognition and celebration of cultural differences was limited but there was evidence of awareness by some (Shah, 2006a).

Ethnicity unaware headteachers' recognition of ethnic differences was more limited. Four headteachers did not recognize ethnic differences at all. Robin's recognition of multiple faiths was linked with his own faith background. It was a discourse of tolerance and acceptance but not an inter-faith discourse like Muhsin's. Nevertheless, his respect for a religious leader implied parity of esteem (Fraser, 2007; Shields and Edwards, 2005). One headteacher's recognition of ethnic difference was wholly negative. She imposed her cultural values and behaviours on the pupils in a way that Tony and Robin would never consider doing (Begley, 2006; Cribb and Gewirtz, 2003). There was no recognition of White ethnic groups except possibly by implication at Rosaline's school where European languages were spoken. Sam noted Somali pupils arrived in the United Kingdom via Holland; the effects of European colonialism are widespread so I do not assume that European language speakers were White.

Non-recognition and misrecognition

Unequal ethnic/race relations among staff in the family and education

In the main very broad descriptions and outdated potentially offensive terminology were used by both *ethnicity aware* and *unaware* headteachers. There was very little recognition of BGM/BME staff at all and no recognition of their experiences of unequal relations in the family and education. Indeed, only one headteacher referred to the higher education of BGM/BME staff in a complaint that she could not appoint teachers with adequate qualifications.

Unequal ethnic/race relations among staff in the workplace

There was no recognition of unequal relations in the workplace. Sam had experienced racism from colleagues at a previous school but did not refer to any further discrimination or prejudice among staff. One woman accommodated a request for unpaid leave to meet a faith/family/cultural need. She anticipated it would strengthen personal and organizational loyalty.

Ethnic differences among pupils

Much of headteachers' discourse centred on the identification and labelling of pupils (Fuller, 2012; Gunter, 2006b). There was little recognition of pupils' cultural differences and needs by most headteachers though it was greater among *ethnicity aware* headteachers (Shah, 2006a). Indeed, the Islamic school had been established precisely because state schools did not meet Muslim pupils' needs (Shah, 2006a, 2009). However, Sam did celebrate pupils' diverse cultures (Fuller, 2012) with a discourse of interculturalism (Race, 2011). Muhsin was proud of pupils' achievements demonstrating their joyous leadership (Campbell-Stephens, 2009; Coleman and Campbell-Stephens, 2010; Johnson and Campbell-Stevens, 2010; McKenley and Gordon, 2002). Joyfulness was also apparent in relation to BGM pupils' social integration and achievements among *ethnicity aware* White headteachers; but not among the *ethnicity unaware*. Two White headteachers gave accounts of White families wanting their children to mix with ethnically diverse groups in ways resonant with contact theory (Erasmus, 2010). The additionality that BGM leaders brought to schools was evident (Coleman and Campbell-Stephens, 2010; Johnson and Campbell-Stevens, 2010). That was also evident in the mutual respect described by headteachers of faith. There was a sense of vocation to communities (Bush et al., 2006; McKenley and Gordon, 2002). Pupils of multiple ethnic backgrounds were barely mentioned at all even though this population in the United Kingdom is the fastest growing ethnic grouping (Rees et al., 2012). Some groups such as White minority ethnic groups were missing from every headteacher's account.

Misrecognition of unequal ethnic/race relations

In the main, where BGM staff were recognized at all, they provided role models or linguistic resources (Osler, 1997). There was no acknowledgement of discriminatory practices. The under-representation of the BGM population in the school workforce, as non-teaching staff, teachers, middle and senior leaders and headteachers suggests misrecognition of endemic racism in schools, the education system and wider society (Gillborn, 2005). The adoption of apparently colour blind, liberal approaches even though they might be founded on an understanding of historically important movements and events does not go far enough to improve BGM representation (Crenshaw et al., 1995; Zamudio et al., 2011). Only two headteachers acknowledged racism exists; one constructed it as external to the school. Neither connected it to the experience of staff.

To construct difference only as uniqueness and engage in a discourse that prioritizes the individual misrecognizes the racism widespread in broader structures of society. To see individuals and families as wholly agential is to misrecognize the impact of societal and institutional racism. Misrecognition was not confined to White headteachers. Few headteachers constructed a White world; none acknowledged their Whiteness. There is a possibility that headteachers have adopted the poor, White, working-class boys' narrative (Gillborn, 2010b). Certainly two emphasized the disproportionate school population of White, working-class boys.

There is also misrecognition of the intersection of gender, social class and ethnicity (Crenshaw, 1991). Black girls and Black boys were constructed as challenging and problematic by two headteachers; one a Black man, the other a White woman. It is possible that their apparently confrontational behaviour has developed as a response to generations of racism experienced by their families and communities. There was some evidence that families who lacked cultural capital with which to engage in dialogue about education were not enabled to speak. Headteachers might not be fully present in the dialogue to see the reality beneath the surface (Shields and Edwards, 2005; Ylimaki and McClain, 2009). There was no participatory parity or associational justice for these pupils and their families (Cribb and Gewirtz, 2003; Fraser, 2007). Indeed there was arguably cultural injustice in the lack of recognition and respect for multiple cultures, an ad hoc approach to multicultural/intercultural curriculum provision and imposition of White cultural norms (Cribb and Gewirtz, 2003; Gillborn, 2006b, 2008).

An Islamic school filled 'the vacuum left by mainstream education' (Shah, 2006b, 2009) for Muslims. Leadership for Muslim pupils resonated with Shah's (2006a, 2010) conceptualization. But the value of pupils' social integration with non-Muslim children was underestimated. Prevention of expatriation of pupils to families' countries of origin where they would receive an inferior or no education is an admirable aim. Nevertheless there might be misrecognition of the continued need. Segregated education might no longer be necessary or desirable. However, accounts by other headteachers revealed the extent of the 'awareness gap' (Shah, 2006a). Only one described an interfaith prayer room that Muslim pupils used. It was the only indication of sensitivity to religion and religion-related cultural differences (Shah, 2006a). It was confined to the level of religious practices and not necessarily extended to routine behaviour or social conduct (Shah, 2006a). Perhaps headteachers have *not* moved on from the

'1990s, when measures like language, dress, food, prayer-rooms, etc., were top priority to facilitate schooling for the Muslim children' (Shah, 2006a).

Summary

Ethnic headteacherly habitus

Staff and pupils are influenced by headteachers' performances of leadership. Some headteachers drew on personal or witnessed experiences of ethnic/race inequalities in the fields of family and education and in the professional field of teaching. Personal accounts of inequalities led to powerful emotions of personal and imagined injury causing headteachers to reflect on their own sense of injustice (Butler, 2004). Sam recognized racist attitudes among his former colleagues. Muhsin recognized the injury of sending children out of the country for the period of compulsory education. Experience of ethnic inequalities was not exclusive to BGM headteachers. Two White headteachers gave accounts of witnessing racism and racial tensions. Their feelings of injustice and frustration were powerful. Inequalities were endemic in social, political and legal structures with regard to civil rights in a segregated society in the United States. The tensions represented as racial by the media that Rose witnessed energized her to commit to comprehensive education. The BGM headteachers in this study overcame difficulties to acquire sufficient cultural capital to progress to headship. Their experiences informed their ethnic headteacherly habitus (Bush et al., 2006; McKenley and Gordon, 2002; McNamara et al., 2009).

It should be noted that witnessed racism did not translate into recognition of ethnic differences among staff. Many headteachers did not recognize ethnic inequalities in their backgrounds, in education and the workplace. Only six headteachers recognized ethnic differences among staff. There is a very real danger that headteachers' discourse of equality misrecognizes the experiences of discrimination and disadvantage described in the literature (Bush et al., 2006; Coleman and Campbell-Stephens, 2010; Johnson and Campbell-Stephens, 2010; 2013; McKenley and Gordon, 2002; McNamara et al., 2009).

Some headteachers did not fully understand the impact of ethnic differences on pupils. In many cases those who recognized differences merely labelled pupils by national heritage, skin colour or faith. There was little understanding and celebration of differences (Shah, 2006a). However, *ethnicity aware* headteachers were more likely to talk positively about pupils' differences than *ethnicity unaware* headteachers in ways that afforded cultural justice (Cribb and Gewirtz, 2003; Grogan and Shakeshaft, 2011).

Only by recognizing differences can headteachers hope to understand equality as located in difference, respect and celebrate difference (Fuller, 2012; Shah, 2008). As with gender relations in Chapter 4 and social class relations in Chapter 5, some headteachers connected their experiences of reduced status with those of pupils. Similarly, there were White headteachers with no experience of reduced status who recognized it among pupils. In particular, Muhsin was concerned with education as a route to knowledge for all pupils, the acquisition of discipline and behaviours associated with Islam (Shah, 2006a, 2010). His ethnic headteacherly habitus was informed by Islamic values (see Chapter 3). He valued the individual differences of pupils as a gift from God. It may be that Robin's ethnic headteacherly habitus was influenced by his professional work with BGM children. He was respectful of their various faiths; through his own securely held faith. With the exception of Muhsin, it is not clear how far headteachers engaged in dialogue with BGM families from a range of faith backgrounds (Shields and Edwards, 2005).

7

Conclusion

Introduction

In this concluding chapter I pull together thoughts from preceding chapters about the interactions between *gender, identity* and *educational leadership*. This chapter is structured in three main sections. First, I return to the notion of headteacherly habitus to explore the influence of gender, class and ethnic habitus formed and constantly modified in the fields of family, education and the workplace. Secondly, I return to headteachers' awareness of difference to explore how three particularly *aware* headteachers recognized and catered for gender, class or ethnicity differences. I take the opportunity to examine how one headteacher's leadership discourse was permeated by *faith values*. I consider the impact of the school on headteacherly habitus. I end the section by exploring the leadership discourse of three exceptional headteachers. Two were *gender, class* and *ethnicity* aware; one was *gender, class* and *ethnicity unaware*. In the third section I return to the concepts of non-recognition and misrecognition to discuss their importance in the light of dominant educational policy discourse. I identify nine misrecognitions and nine questions for teachers, aspiring headteachers and headteachers to reflect upon.

Headteacherly habitus

This research has afforded a glimpse into the headteacherly habitus and leadership discourse of 18 headteachers. I have drawn on four main aspects of habitus (Reay, 1995). I examined embodied habitus in terms of headteachers' emotions and thoughts. I looked at the dialectic interaction between a habitus and field to recognize that although choices might be limited some headteachers did exercise agency to achieve social mobility for example. Many overcame gender or class inequalities to access tertiary education. At least one overcame ethnicity/race inequalities to achieve headship. Thus I have explored the relationship between habitus and agency. The compilation of individual and collective trajectories has been examined in the sense of a collective understanding among a group of women headteachers as mothers, for example; or BGM headteachers as men of faith. There is danger in making assumptions and generalizations about the needs and motivations of apparently homogenous groups such as mothers, single women, Muslim men, or men of working-class origin for example. I have also explored at some length the complex interplay between past and present in headteachers' self-reported accounts of life experiences from childhood, adolescence and adulthood that impacted on their headship. Headteachers demonstrated the continuity and change that occurred as they crossed and re-crossed social and professional fields of family and the workplace (McLeod, 2005). Two women described the impact of fluid sociocultural roles on their professional roles.

Only two headteachers did not draw on their family backgrounds to construct a leadership discourse. For one woman there was deliberate division between her private and professional personae (Fuller, 2010). However, there was much reflection by others on the emotions provoked by unequal gender, class or ethnic relations by those who experienced or witnessed them. Headteachers felt the pain of symbolic violence. Many turned painful experiences into positive action (Butler, 2004). Affective responses impacted on cognitive responses (Fuller, 2012). However, there were other opportunities for reflection not prompted by such inequalities. One headteacher had faced a life-threatening illness. A hospital stay gave him much time for personal reflection and development of a personal philosophy, 'I now always measure things by what I would call life threateningness; so if it's not life threatening, it's not really serious.' His deep sense of powerlessness and vulnerability resulted in deep care for people. In some cases those with power had come 'from less powerful positions than those privileged by our society'; they 'reflected on the effects of their lack of access to power' (Gold, 1997; cited Reay and Ball, 2000, p. 149). Some did 'work differently with power when they had it from those who have never had to engage in such arguments' (Gold, 1997; cited Reay and Ball, 2000, p. 149). That was particularly clear in the comparison of *class aware* and *class unaware* headteachers.

Awareness of difference

In the case studies that follow I use three headteachers' accounts of intense multilayered experiences of unequal power relations that occurred over time in the fields of family, education and the workplace to show how successive layers modified their professional habitus with regard to gender, class or ethnicity awareness. In the fourth, I show how one headteacher's beliefs, developed following bereavement and depression, permeated his leadership discourse.

Gender awareness

Diana recounted multiple experiences of unequal gender relations in the fields of education and the workplace. First, she read a male-dominated subject at university; secondly, she engaged with feminist politics as a way to meet like-minded women; thirdly, she experienced overt sex discrimination in the selection process for a job in industry; and fourthly, she experienced the humiliation of being refused permission to miss an after-school meeting on returning to work following maternity leave. Diana's husband was equally committed to her career as his own; they split childcare evenly. Diana was well aware of the way her gender and sociocultural roles impacted on headship. She described how energy gained from her family was taken into school. Her children gave an additional perspective on her relationships with pupils.

Diana recognized and catered for the needs of women of various status as clerical and non-teaching staff, teachers and heads of department. She enabled women who had not achieved their potential at school to study for further qualifications and develop their skills. She automatically agreed to requests for part-time hours following maternity leave; the same flexibility was available to men. Her work in a male-dominated school led her to make tough decisions about senior male colleagues' leadership and junior male colleagues' teaching performance. She appointed women and men who enacted non-hegemonic masculinities to balance the school's gender regime (Connell, 2006). One appointment was deliberately made to 'get her out of a mindset'. Diana acknowledged the tendency for leaders to appoint people like themselves (Coleman, 2011). In her construction of gender among staff and pupils there was much evidence of her awareness of nuanced intersections of class, ethnicity and social skills (Connell, 2005). She engaged with feminist discourses of equality and difference as well as a post-structural gender discourse that does not link gender performance to the body (Francis, 2010). Diana's gender habitus impacted greatly on her headteacherly habitus.

Class awareness

Ben described his upbringing in 'quite a poor area'. Four older siblings left school aged 15 with no qualifications. They worked in shops and factories. Ben's education and career trajectory differed from theirs because of the social entrepreneurship of a local priest. He raised money for new school buildings to attract a new headteacher who developed an inclusive educational ethos. As a direct result Ben benefited from improved schooling. A teacher suggested he should aim for a career in teaching. Ben achieved social mobility (Lupton, 2006). He acknowledged his salary as headteacher was high but opened up his leadership priorities for scrutiny by the leadership team (Duffy, 1999; Grundy, 1993).

As headteacher, Ben was well aware of the importance of various forms of capital. He used social capital to secure resources from the local authority and multiple external agencies including local business people. They funded rewards with economic value otherwise inaccessible to pupils and their families. He was concerned with distributive justice in leadership for social justice (Cribb and Gewirtz, 2003; Grogan and Shakeshaft, 2011). The whole school population contributed to school and community vision building. Their voices were systematically represented in associational justice (Cribb and Gewirtz, 2003; Fraser, 2007). Ben's vision was to improve education for the whole community that he saw as interconnected and interdependent. Though he did not locate it as African, he referred to the proverb *it takes a whole village to raise a child* that conveys *Ubuntu* interconnectedness (Bidwell, 2010; Bush, 2007; Campbell-Stephens, 2009; Msila, 2008). Distributed leadership referred to emergent leadership from a wide range of people with formal and non-formal leadership roles depending on context, circumstances and expertise (Blackmore, 1989; Woods et al., 2004). Leadership development opportunities were systematically created to resonate with leadership for learning (Grogan and Shakeshaft, 2011; MacBeath, 2007). He worked with colleagues horizontally in relational leadership (Grogan and Shakeshaft, 2011). Ben described the lack of home resources available to pupils. He was the only headteacher who referred to the proportion of pupils eligible for FSM. He also recognized parental occupations, qualifications, housing tenure and household income. He worked with multiple agencies to support the pastoral needs of pupils and their families. A programme of extracurricular family learning opportunities was in place for adults. Ben engaged with academics and professionals to enhance his and others' understanding of community-based education. Ben's class habitus very much influenced his headteacherly habitus.

Ethnicity awareness

Sam migrated from Trinidad to France as a direct result of French colonialism. He moved to England where he experienced curiosity about his ethnicity; then racism from adults in his next school. He taught staff about ethnic differences. He demonstrated BGM pupils' ability by teaching them multiple languages. Sam challenged colleagues publically about their prejudices and discriminatory practices. He was persistent in his exercise of personal agency on behalf of BGM pupils in a racist school system (Gillborn, 2005). He wrote papers about multicultural education and engaged in research about the education of BGM pupils.

As headteacher Sam recognized and celebrated the contributions of a multicultural staff body. He identified the national heritage of many colleagues and recognized the role model a White Australian teacher had provided for Black girls. Sam actively sought intercultural activities for pupils to engage in. They expressed their cultural heritages through the visual and performing arts. Community events were highly valued. Sam was concerned with cultural justice in leadership for social justice (Cribb and Gewirtz, 2003; Grogan and Shakeshaft, 2011). Drawing on his Christian *faith values* Sam promoted an interfaith perspective in school by providing an interfaith prayer room that Muslim pupils used (Shah, 2006a). His account was of joyous leadership (Campbell-Stephens, 2009; McKenley and Gordon, 2002). Sam's ethnic habitus directed his headteacherly habitus.

Values awareness

When he was a teenager, a deputy headteacher gave Gregory money to buy a new shirt. His unkemptness was a symptom of depression following his parents' deaths. It was the first time he had been in receipt of a wholly non-altruistic act of kindness. Gregory went on to study forms of Buddhism and Buddhist psychology. Gregory began his responses in interview by noting the importance of his Buddhist beliefs and ended with a Buddhist saying.

Seen through the lens of wisdom-centred leadership based on six Buddhist virtues it is clear how Gregory found disrupting dominant educational policy discourses so apparently straightforward (Ylimaki and McClain, 2009). Each of the virtues was found in Gregory's account. There was *generosity* in providing refreshments on pupils' arrival at school and in times of distress, in resolving a transport difficulty for one pupil, and in supporting parents with school supervised sanctions. There was *discipline* in his self-discipline motivated by a desire to help others. Gregory saw himself as privileged to have a role whereby he could do so much for others. He demonstrated *patience* in his forbearance of abusive name calling from one pupil. He focused on her need rather than her behaviour. There was a sense of *right effort* in a tireless and wise approach to solving problems and resolving conflict. He was mindful of the impact of intense emotional labour on colleagues' health. Gregory's self-reflection is likely to have been partly exercised through *meditation and concentration*. His accounts of open dialogue with pupils demonstrated he was fully present to the situation and able to exercise *wisdom* or uncommon common sense in seeing reality (Ylimaki and McClain, 2009). What needed doing in some circumstances was seen as nothing 'very profound; it just needs noticing what people like'. Although Gregory's account did not appear to emphasize awareness of gender, class and ethnicity differences, indeed he also refused to distinguish between pupils and staff, his dialogue with others as pupils, parents and staff was entirely open. Gregory's faith habitus pervaded his headteacherly habitus.

Each of these headteachers described affective responses to their experiences and those of staff and pupils. There is much evidence in their accounts of feelings of injury, injustice, care, compassion, empathy) and joy (Fuller, 2012). Each engaged intellectually with these issues; Diana in feminist political debate; Ben in community-based education research; Sam in writing papers about multicultural education and collaborative research; Gregory in Buddhist studies. It is the engagement with both the affective and the cognitive that impacts so powerfully on headteacherly habitus. Each reflected on moments of vulnerability and powerlessness to be 'returned to a sense of human vulnerability, to our collective responsibility for the physical lives of one another' (Butler, 2004, p. 23). I have focused above on the impact of the social fields of family, education and faith communities on headteacherly habitus. However, the professional field of the school organization within the wider discourse of national educational policy also impacts on headteacherly habitus. In the following account I explore such impact.

School type – Comprehensive school

Philip was included in the *gender aware* group of headteachers because he gave an account of a former headteacher who made women uncomfortable by 'look[ing] them over'. It was his only reference to an awareness of gender, class or ethnicity inequalities. It occurred in the workplace. However, Philip worked in a mixed comprehensive school with a 'poor working class' population, a fifth of whom were Asian Pakistani. In his account, Philip enabled flexible working practices. A deputy headteacher had taken a six-week sabbatical, clerical staff were sent home early on Fridays and meetings were cancelled if there was nothing to discuss. He described 'a few [other] little tricks' he had learned over time that respected colleagues' professionalism and abilities. So although he did not demonstrate much explicit awareness of gender, class or ethnicity issues there was a sense of his personal relationships with colleagues. He talked to every member of staff personally at least once a week.

Philip identified pupils by sex, social class and ethnicity in broad descriptions of the population that resonated with sorting pupils (Gunter, 2006). However, he described at length two alternative curriculum pathways, as well as a traditional pathway, designed to meet particular pupils' needs. He noted that traditional approaches to education did not suit everyone. There was much evidence of his resistance of a 'blueprint' for good teaching. A new inexperienced colleague might solve a problem others had puzzled over for years. He was concerned with leadership for learning (Grogan and Shakeshaft, 2011; MacBeath, 2007). He ended his account by referring to Fullan's (2001) writing about emotional intelligence and change management. Like others, he engaged intellectually with what was also instinctive common sense practice. It may be that the school organization impacted on his headteacherly habitus more than his gender, class and ethnicity habitus.

Exceptional headteachers

Two headteachers were exceptional. They were included in each of the *gender, class* and *ethnicity aware* groups. They worked in mixed comprehensive schools where the school populations consisted of White and BGM girls and boys with variable access to forms of capital. Each talked about working collaboratively with senior leadership teams in ways that resonated with relational leadership (Grogan and Shakeshaft, 2011). Each sought opportunities to develop leadership capacity by affording development opportunities to colleagues (MacBeath, 2007). Isabella recounted opportunities for women; Rose offered opportunities in a systematic approach school-wide. Isabella described efforts to establish open dialogue between groups of colleagues and with her (Shields and Edwards, 2005). Rose described the shared development of a school-based conceptualization of good teaching and learning (MacBeath, 2007). Isabella supported teaching assistant staff to complete degrees and clerical staff with flexible working practices. Rose valued learning mentors supporting pupils with a range of needs.

However, each omitted to mention one sex or the other in the pupil population. Isabella talked about Black girls; Rose talked about Black boys. Rose also described meeting the needs of boys in a post-industrial society. She talked about academically able pupils. Each gave joyful accounts of BGM pupils' achievement demonstrating some White headteachers celebrated ethnic difference (Fuller, 2012). Those accounts were not as fulsome as those of BGM headteachers. Nevertheless, they demonstrated a sense of the intersectionality of gender, ethnicity and class (Connell, 2005; Crenshaw, 1991). They were very aware of individual differences and recounted many ways they tried to cater for them.

By contrast, Silvia was exceptional because she was not included in any of the *aware* headteacher groups. There were no accounts of direct or witnessed experiences of unequal gender, class or ethnicity relations. Like Gregory, she built her leadership discourse on a 'powerful values drive' articulated through a *rights values* discourse (see Chapter 3). I have discussed her engagement with feminist leadership discourse in Chapter 2. Although Silvia worked with individual pupils on the school council, she noted working mainly with 'mass groups' of pupils and that as a headteacher she was 'distanced from the individualities of the children'. Although she talked about boys and girls there was no mention of gender issues. Pupils were not identified in terms of socio-economic status or ability. The ethnicities of pupils were not identified. However, Silvia's leadership is particularly interesting in its disruption of the dominant educational policy discourse with regard to her refusal to narrow the curriculum to improve the school's performance. She critiqued local and national policy that damaged pupils and staff. Her headteacherly habitus was informed by her values habitus. Perhaps her sense of personal agency in disrupting the dominant discourse came from never having experienced powerlessness.

Non-recognition

There was uniform non-recognition of LGBTQ colleagues and pupils. The intersection of gender and sexuality was noted explicitly by one headteacher and indirectly by two. In each case it was a heteronormative discourse (Fuller, 2012; Sauntson and Simpson, 2011). In Chapter 2, I noted the lack of research on homosexuality and educational leadership. Rottmann (2006) offers a series of questions with which educational leaders should critically engage to expose homophobia, heterosexism and heterosexuality as a normative sexual identity. Queer theory has the potential to demystify leadership and open up critical dialogue. Queer communities might 'invest temporal and monetary resources into the development of new generations of lesbian, gay, bisexual, transgendered and transsexual-identified leaders and the infrastructure to support this work' (Rottmann, 2006, p. 16). Section 28 of the Local Government Act (1988) stated local authorities should not 'promote the teaching in any maintained school of the acceptability of homosexuality as a pretended family relationship' (p. 27). It was repealed in 2003 but its impact should not be underestimated. It might explain the absence of LGBTQ people in headteachers' accounts. Since 2005 the LGB charity Stonewall's *Education for All* campaign has tackled homophobia and homophobic bullying in schools (see Stonewall). In 2010 the Coalition government promised to help schools tackle homophobic bullying (HM Government, 2010). Another invisible group was that of White minority ethnicities. Headteachers' recognition of ethnicity was almost wholly located in BGM colleagues and pupils. Only two headteachers included European languages spoken by pupils. However, that need not suggest pupils were necessarily White. Somali pupils arrived in England via Holland for example. Mistry and Sood (2010) advocate that greater effort is needed by school leaders to dispel the negative assumptions of some teachers and teaching assistants with regard to pupils' abilities and needs as mass migration increases from Europe. Mixed heritage pupils were barely mentioned. At a time when the Mixed heritage population is the fastest growing ethnic group this is another clear concern (Rees et al., 2012). It might be an indication of Mixed pupils being enrolled as White (Bush et al., 2006). 'Looked after' children were not mentioned at all. Cheminais (2011) notes they are among the most vulnerable children. Their absence rates from school are significantly higher than other pupils (Reid, 2010). Nevertheless a nuanced approach is needed to avoid perpetuating stereotypes. Educational outcomes do not recognize the progress looked after children make in other ways, 'including major achievements such as getting back into education, furthering leisure interests and vocational skills, and, often for the first time, developing consistent, positive and trusting relationships with adults' (Frost and Stein, 2009, p. 317).

Key points for reflection

I end by identifying nine misrecognitions that lead to symbolic violence. Misrecognition occurs when social actors forget to contest the arbitrariness of what appears to be natural and obvious.

Nine misrecognitions

Concerning headteachers and aspiring headteachers

1. *Misrecognition of the reasons for women's under-representation in headship.* Further research is needed into nuanced accounts of which women and men achieve headship in relation to ethnicity, social class origins, sexuality and disability; reasons for some women and men's rejection of leadership roles need further investigation.
2. *Misrecognition in linking biological sex to gendered leadership performance.* Women are equally capable as men of using power to control and direct others; men are equally capable as women of using power to empower. Assumptions that women lead in particular ways are false. Men's gendered leadership performance needs further research. A discourse about men's gender awareness and their construction and performance of multiple masculinities might open up discussion about equal opportunities. How leadership is done in schools is an important focus for future research.
3. *Misrecognition that understandings about transrational values are shared understandings.* A discourse of equality, diversity and social justice does not mean the same to everyone. Dialogue that enables understanding of a variety of perspectives is necessary. This also applies to what is meant by ethical leadership.

Concerning staff

4. *Misrecognition of group desires, interests and needs.* Not all new mothers want to work part-time; new fathers might want flexible working practices. Single women and men might have care responsibilities. BGM teachers are not a homogenous group. There is a danger in focusing on collective trajectories that assumptions are made about individual members of groups.
5. *Misrecognition of an equality discourse that undermines divergent desires, interests and needs.* Attempts to see all staff as equal partners in the work of educating pupils might aim to secure mutual respect in the workplace.

However, an egalitarian discourse might hide deep inequalities in working practices.

Concerning pupils and families

6. *Misrecognition concerning gender relations among pupils.* There was no evidence of pupils being taught to deconstruct gender stereotypes though of course that might happen in some classrooms. Headteachers talked about girls and boys but there was little recognition of unequal gender relations or gender stereotyping.
7. *Misrecognition of some parents' lack of language with which to engage in discussion about their children's education.* The impact of some parents' lack of cultural capital was underestimated. Schools continue to be hard to reach for some families.
8. *Misrecognition of the impact of pupils' curriculum choices.* Headteachers might underestimate the reproduction of inequalities occurring from grouping arrangements based on 'ability' and the extent to which a variety of desires, interests and needs are met by providing alternative curricula. The aim of connecting pupils' existing knowledges with high status knowledges needs to be kept in focus.

Concerning everyone

9. *Misrecognition of endemic racism.* Where it was recognized at all racism was seen as external to schools and the school system. Headteachers' descriptions were often racialized. The desires, interests, needs and knowledges of BGM teachers and leaders barely featured; where pupils were recognized it was largely in the management of diversity rather than in affording cultural justice. Ethnicity equated with 'race'. White ethnic minorities were not recognized at all. Nor did headteachers acknowledge the impact of their Whiteness on headship. However, BGM headteachers did acknowledge the impact of Blackness and Muslimness.

Think about

1. Your *experiences of discrimination*, those you have witnessed, those you have heard about in school, outside school, in the family, in wider society. How will you make sure you do not misrecognize the reasons for a colleague's thwarted ambitions or another colleague's success?

2. Your *construction and performance of gender*, those of your family, your colleagues as leaders, teachers and non-teaching staff. How are multiple femininities and masculinities enacted in the school and family?

3. Your *personal values and their source*, those of your colleagues, those of pupils and their families. How do you know whether your understandings match those of others? How will you open up dialogue to find out?

4. Your *preconceptions about groups* of people as new mothers, Muslim men and working-class teachers. How will you ensure that you enable people to tell you about their particular desires, interests and needs?

5. Your *understanding of equal opportunities*. How might an equality discourse undermine the desires, interests and needs of some groups and individuals in your school? Whose different desires, interests and needs require a different approach?

6. Your *teaching and leadership of teaching about gender*. How do you and others teach pupils to identify and deconstruct stereotypes?

7. Your *relationships with families*. How do you encourage parents to engage with school life? How do you welcome families into school? Do you visit pupils' homes and communities?

8. Your *dialogue with pupils and families*. How do you help pupils and families to understand the school and education systems? The curriculum choices they have? Their implication on pupils' future pathways?

9. Your *understanding of racism*. Is there an intercultural curriculum in place? How do you know? Do you know about pupils' cultural heritages? Do you know about pupils' linguistic resources? How do you monitor pupils' curriculum choices? Examination entries? Grouping arrangements? How do you record racist incidents? How do you teach about racism?

Appendix

Table A1 Distribution of women secondary school headteachers by local authority in England in 2005 and 2010 ordered alphabetically

Local authority	No. of schools in 2010	Per cent women in 2005 (Fuller, 2009)	No. of women in 2010	Per cent women in 2010	Difference between 2005 and 2010
London boroughs					
Barking and Dagenham	9	11.1	1	11.1	0.0
Barnet	21	38.1	9	42.9	4.8
Bexley	16	37.5	5	31.3	−6.3
Brent	15	38.5	6	40.0	1.5
Bromley	18	38.9	7	38.9	0.0
Camden	10	55.6	6	60.0	4.4
Corporation of London					0.0
Croydon	21	30.4	4	19.0	−11.4
Ealing	13	53.8	6	46.2	−7.6
Enfield	18	50	9	50.0	0.0
Greenwich	13	38.5	5	38.5	0.0
Hackney	10	87.5	5	50.0	−37.5
Hammersmith and Fulham	8	25	4	50.0	25.0
Haringey	11	18.2	3	27.3	9.1
Harrow	10	45.5	5	50.0	4.5
Havering	18	33.3	8	44.4	11.1
Hillingdon	18	11.8	8	44.4	32.6
Hounslow	14	50	7	50.0	0.0
Islington	10	33.3	5	50.0	16.7
Kensington and Chelsea	4	25	1	25.0	0.0
Kingston-Upon-Thames	10	30	6	60.0	30.0
Lambeth	13	60	6	46.2	−13.8
Lewisham	14	53.8	8	57.1	3.3
Merton	8	37.5	3	37.5	0.0

Continued

Table A1 Continued

Local authority	No. of schools in 2010	Per cent women in 2005 (Fuller, 2009)	No. of women in 2010	Per cent women in 2010	Difference between 2005 and 2010
Newham	15	66.7	8	53.3	−13.4
Redbridge	17	29.4	3	17.6	−11.8
Richmond-Upon-Thames	8	50	5	62.5	12.5
Southwark	10	57.1	5	50.0	−7.1
Sutton	14	35.7	5	35.7	0.0
Tower Hamlets	15	50	7	46.7	-3.3
Waltham Forest	17	58.8	12	70.6	11.8
Wandsworth	11	27.3	4	36.4	9.1
Westminster	9	50	4	44.4	-5.6
Total London Boroughs	**418**	**41.1**	**180**	**43.1**	**2.0**
Greater metropolitan districts					
Tameside	17	33.3	3	17.6	−15.7
Bury	13	21.4	2	15.4	−6.0
Rochdale	13	28.6	4	30.8	2.2
Trafford	19	33.3	7	36.8	3.5
Wigan	20	25	6	30.0	5.0
Manchester	24	18.2	6	25.0	6.8
Bolton	17	25	6	35.3	10.3
Salford	15	21.4	6	40.0	18.6
Oldham	15	13.3	8	53.3	40.0
Stockport	14	21.4	9	64.3	42.9
Total Greater Manchester	**167**	**24.2**	**57**	**34.1**	**9.9**
Wirral	23	45.5	7	30.4	−15.1
Sefton	21	27.3	7	33.3	6.0
Liverpool	30	21.9	11	36.7	14.8
St Helens	10	18.2	4	40.0	21.8
Knowsley	9	45.5	7	77.8	32.3
Merseyside Total	93	30.6	36	38.7	8.1
Doncaster	17	5.9	3	17.6	11.7
Barnsley	14	35.7	5	35.7	0.0
Rotherham	16	56.3	7	43.8	−12.6
Sheffield	27	37	12	44.4	7.4
Total South Yorkshire	**74**	**33.8**	**27**	**36.5**	**2.7**

Continued

Table A1 Continued

Local authority	No. of schools in 2010	Per cent women in 2005 (Fuller, 2009)	No. of women in 2010	Per cent women in 2010	Difference between 2005 and 2010
Sunderland	17	27.8	3	17.6	−10.2
Gateshead	11	18.2	3	27.3	9.1
Newcastle-Upon-Tyne	14	9.1	4	28.6	19.5
North Tyneside	16	18.2	6	37.5	19.3
South Tyneside	9	27.3	4	44.4	17.1
Total **Tyne and Wear**	**67**	**21**	**20**	**29.9**	**8.9**
Sandwell	19	16.7	2	10.5	−6.2
Dudley	21	22.7	5	23.8	1.1
Wolverhampton	18	21.1	5	27.8	6.7
Coventry	19	31.6	8	42.1	10.5
Walsall	19	40	8	42.1	2.1
Birmingham	75	41	32	42.7	1.7
Solihull	14	46.2	7	50.0	3.8
Total **West Midlands**	**185**	**33.9**	**67**	**36.2**	**2.3**
Wakefield	18	16.7	4	22.2	5.5
Leeds	39	32.6	11	28.2	−4.4
Bradford	28	34.5	12	42.9	8.4
Calderdale	14	40	6	42.9	2.9
Kirklees	31	36	14	45.2	9.2
Total **West Yorkshire**	**130**	**32.3**	**47**	**36.2**	**3.9**
Total **metropolitan** **districts**	**716**	**29.8**	**254**	**35.5**	**5.7**
Non-metropolitan districts					
Bath and North East Somerset	13	46.2	7	53.8	7.6
Bedfordshire	49	11.8	15	30.6	18.8
Blackburn with Darwen	10	33.3	4	40.0	6.7
Blackpool	8	37.5	4	50.0	12.5
Bournemouth	9	40	2	22.2	−17.8
Bracknell Forest	6	33.3	1	16.7	−16.6
Brighton and Hove	8	20	3	37.5	17.5
Bristol	18	33.3	10	55.6	22.3

Continued

Table A1 Continued

Local authority	No. of schools in 2010	Per cent women in 2005 (Fuller, 2009)	No. of women in 2010	Per cent women in 2010	Difference between 2005 and 2010
Buckinghamshire	34	55.9	10	29.4	−26.5
Cambridgeshire	29	20	9	31.0	11.0
Cheshire East	18		4	22.2	
Cheshire West and Chester Council	19	20	4	21.1	No data
Cornwall	31	35.5	14	45.2	9.7
Cumbria	39	19	10	25.6	6.6
Darlington	7	14.3	3	42.9	28.6
Derby	14	28.6	3	21.4	−7.2
Derbyshire	47	23.9	12	25.5	1.6
Devon	37	18.9	10	27.0	8.1
Dorset	20	15	5	25.0	10.0
Durham	36	30.6	15	41.7	11.1
East Riding of Yorkshire	18	27.8	7	38.9	11.1
East Sussex	27	37	14	51.9	14.9
Essex	79	32.5	26	32.9	0.4
Gloucestershire	41	38.1	14	34.1	−4.0
Halton	8	37.5	3	37.5	0.0
Hampshire	71	28.2	30	42.3	14.1
Hartlepool	6	16.7	1	16.7	0.0
Herefordshire	15	21.4	2	13.3	−8.1
Hertfordshire	76	30.3	29	38.2	7.9
Isle of Wight	20	40	6	30.0	−10.0
Isles of Scilly	1	0	0	0.0	0.0
Kent	99	34.3	43	43.4	9.1
Kingston-Upon-Hull	14	26.7	6	42.9	16.2
Lancashire	80	22.7	20	25.0	2.3
Leicester	20	43.8	10	50.0	6.2
Leicestershire	54	38.9	20	37.0	−1.9
Lincolnshire	62	17.2	20	32.3	15.1
Luton	12	66.7	10	83.3	16.6
Medway Towns	20	42.1	7	35.0	−7.1
Middlesbrough Borough	9	11.1	1	11.1	0.0
Milton Keynes	12	40	4	33.3	−6.7

Continued

Table A1 Continued

Local authority	No. of schools in 2010	Per cent women in 2005 (Fuller, 2009)	No. of women in 2010	Per cent women in 2010	Difference between 2005 and 2010
Norfolk	52	21.2	14	26.9	5.7
North East Lincolnshire	11	41.7	4	36.4	−5.3
North Lincolnshire	12	35.7	6	50.0	14.3
North Somerset	10	20	2	20.0	0.0
North Yorkshire	47	26.7	8	17.0	−9.7
Northamptonshire	42	33.3	17	40.5	7.2
Northumberland	14	20	2	14.3	−5.7
Nottingham	15	27.8	5	33.3	5.5
Nottinghamshire	43	23.4	13	30.2	6.8
Oxfordshire	35	17.6	15	42.9	25.3
Peterborough	11	7.7	0	0.0	−7.7
Plymouth	16	41.2	5	31.3	−10.0
Poole	9	37.5	5	55.6	18.1
Portsmouth	10	50	4	40.0	−10.0
Reading	7	42.9	4	57.1	14.2
Redcar and Cleveland	11	33.3	4	36.4	3.1
Rutland	3	0	1	33.3	33.3
Shropshire	23	21.7	8	34.8	13.1
Slough	11	36.4	4	36.4	0.0
Somerset	37	20	8	21.6	1.6
South Gloucestershire	16	20	5	31.3	11.3
Southampton	12	50	8	66.7	16.7
Southend-On-Sea	12	33.3	4	33.3	0.0
Staffordshire	46	29.1	18	39.1	10.0
Stockton-On-Tees	14	14.3	3	21.4	7.1
Stoke-On-Trent	17	41.2	7	41.2	0.0
Suffolk	78	21.1	26	33.3	12.2
Surrey	53	30.2	20	37.7	7.5
Swindon	11	20	5	45.5	25.5
Telford and Wrekin	13	30.8	2	15.4	−15.4
Thurrock	10	30	3	30.0	0.0
Torbay	8	37.5	3	37.5	0.0

Continued

Table A1 Continued

Local authority	No. of schools in 2010	Per cent women in 2005 (Fuller, 2009)	No. of women in 2010	Per cent women in 2010	Difference between 2005 and 2010
Warrington	12	25	4	33.3	8.3
Warwickshire	36	26.3	9	25.0	−1.3
West Berkshire	10	40	4	40.0	0.0
West Sussex	39	36.1	14	35.9	−0.2
Wiltshire	28	27.6	6	21.4	−6.2
Windsor and Maidenhead	13	66.7	5	38.5	−28.2
Wokingham	9	33.3	3	33.3	0.0
Worcestershire	52	17.2	21	40.4	23.2
York	10	9.1	1	10.0	0.9
Total non-metropolitan districts	**2,114**	**28.9**	**718**	**34.0**	**5.1**
Total England	**3,248**	**30.1**	**1,152**	**35.5**	**5.4**

Table A2 Distribution of women secondary school headteachers by local authority in the Isles and Islands in 2005 and 2010 ordered alphabetically

Local authority	No. of schools in 2010	Per cent of women in 2005 (Fuller, 2009)	No. of women in 2010	Per cent of women in 2010	Difference between 2005 and 2010
Guernsey	5	33.3	2	40.0	6.7
Jersey	5	33.3	1	20.0	−13.3
Channel Islands	10	33.3	3	30.0	−3.3
Isle of Man	5	60	2	40.0	−20.0

Table A3 Distribution of women secondary school headteachers by local authority in Wales in 2005 and 2010 ordered alphabetically

Local authority	No. of schools in 2010	Per cent of women in 2005 (Fuller, 2009)	No. of women in 2010	Per cent of women in 2010	Difference between 2005 and 2010
Anglesey	5	20	1	20.0	0.0
Baenau Gwent	6	33.3	1	16.7	−16.6
Bridgend	10	11.1	3	30.0	18.9
Caerphilly	14	31.3	5	35.7	4.4
Cardiff	20	15	5	25.0	10.0
Carmarthenshire	14	6.7	4	28.6	21.9
Ceredigion	7	14.3	0	0.0	−14.3
Conwy	7	14.3	1	14.3	0.0
Denbighshire	8	50	6	75.0	25.0
Flintshire	14	16.7	2	14.3	−2.4
Gwynedd	14	7.1	3	21.4	14.3
Merthyr Tydfil	4	0	1	25.0	25.0
Monmouthshire	5	50	2	40.0	−10.0
Neath and Port Talbot	11	0	1	9.1	9.1
Newport	8	12.5	1	12.5	0.0
Pembrokeshire	8	25	4	50.0	25.0
Powys	14	15.4	5	35.7	20.3
Rhondda Cynon Taff	19	21.1	7	36.8	15.7
Swansea	15	13.3	3	20.0	6.7
Torfaen	8	12.5	1	12.5	0.0
Vale of Glamorgan	8	12.5	1	12.5	0.0
Wrexham	9	22.2	3	33.3	11.1
Total Wales	**211**	**17.2**	**56**	**26.5**	**9.3**

Table A4 Distribution of women secondary school headteachers by local authority in Scotland (2010) ordered alphabetically

Local authority	No. of schools	No. of women	No. unknown	Per cent of women	Per cent unknown
Aberdeen City	12	4	0	33.3	0
Aberdeenshire	17	4	0	23.5	0
Angus	9	0	0	0.0	0
Argyll and Bute	11	5	1	45.5	9.1
Clackmannanshire	3	0	1	0.0	33.3
Dumfries and Galloway	16	2	0	12.5	0
Dundee City	10	1	1	10.0	10
East Ayrshire	9	3	0	33.3	0
East Dunbartonshire	9	0	1	0.0	11.1
East Lothian	6	2	0	33.3	0
East Renfrewshire	7	2	2	28.6	28.6
Edinburgh City	23	9	0	39.1	0
Falkirk	8	3	0	37.5	0
Fife	20	2	2	10.0	10.0
Glasgow City	32	14	0	43.8	0
Highland	29	6	0	20.7	0
Inverclyde	7	2	0	28.6	0
Midlothian	6	2	0	33.3	0
Moray	8	3	0	37.5	0
North Ayrshire	9	2	0	22.2	0
North Lanarkshire	26	8	2	30.8	7.7
Orkney Islands	4	2	0	50.0	0
Perth and Kinross	10	5	0	50.0	0
Renfrewshire	13	4	2	30.8	15.4
Scottish Borders	9	2	0	22.2	0
Shetland Islands	7	3	0	42.9	0
South Ayrshire	8	3	0	37.5	0
South Lanarkshire	19	3	2	15.8	10.5
Stirling	7	3	0	42.9	0
West Dunbartonshire	6	1	1	16.7	16.7
West Lothian	11	2	0	18.2	0
Western Isles	11	1	0	9.1	0
Total Scotland	**382**	**103**	**15**	**27.0**	**3.9**

Table A5 Distribution of women secondary school headteachers by Education and Library Board (ELB) in Northern Ireland (2010) ordered alphabetically

Local authority	No. of schools	No. of women	Unknown	Per cent of women	Per cent unknown
Belfast	28	12	0	42.9	0.0
North-eastern ELB	50	14	0	28.0	0.0
South-eastern ELB	35	10	0	28.6	0.0
Southern ELB	51	12	0	23.5	0.0
Western ELB	44	14	0	31.8	0.0
Total Northern Ireland	**208**	**62**	**0**	**29.8**	**0.0**

References

Addi-Raccah, A. (2006), 'Women in the Israeli educational system', in I. Oplatka and R. Hertz-Lazarowitz (eds), *Women Principals in a Multicultural Society*. The Netherlands: Sense Publishers, pp. 49–70.

Adler, S., Laney, J. and Packer, M. (1993), *Managing Women: Feminism and Power in Educational Management*. Buckingham: Open University Press.

Apple, M. (1992), 'The text and cultural politics', *Educational Researcher*, 21(7), 4–11 and 19.

— (2009), 'Some ideas on interrupting the right: On doing critical educational work in conservative times', *Education, Citizenship and Social Justice*, 4(2), 87–101.

Asher, N. (2010), 'How does the postcolonial, feminist academic lead? A perspective from the US South', *International Journal of Leadership in Education*, 13(1), 63–76.

Bakhtin, M. (1981), *The Dialogic Imagination*, trans. M. Holquist and C. Emerson and ed. M. Holquist. Austin, TX: University of Texas Press, in P. Morris (ed.) (1994), *The Bakhtin Reader*. London: Arnold, pp. 74–80.

Ball, S. (2010), 'New class inequalities in education: Why education policy may be looking in the wrong place! Education policy, civil society and social class', *International Journal of Sociology and Social Policy*, 30(3/4), 155–66.

Battiste, M. (2005), 'Leadership and Aboriginal education in contemporary education: Narratives of cognitive imperialism reconciling with decolonization', in J. Collard and C. Reynolds (eds), *Leadership, Gender and Culture in Education. Male and Female Perspectives*. Buckingham: Open University Press, pp. 150–6.

Begley, P. (2003), 'In pursuit of authentic school leadership practices', in P. Begley and O. Johansson (eds), *The Ethical Dimensions of School Leadership*. Dordrecht: Kluwer, pp. 1–12.

— (2006), 'Self-knowledge, capacity and sensitivity: Prerequisites to authentic leadership by school principals', *Journal of Educational Administration*, 44(6), 570–89.

Begley, P. and Stefkovich, J. (2004), 'Introduction: Education, ethics, and the "cult of efficiency": implications for values and leadership', *Journal of Educational Administration*, 42(2), 132–6.

Begley, P. and Zaretsky, L. (2004), 'Democratic school leadership in Canada's public school systems: Professional value and social ethic', *Journal of Educational Administration*, 42(6), 640–55.

Belbin, R. (1981), *Management Teams: Why they Succeed or Fail*. London: Heinemann (reprinted by Oxford: Butterworth Heinemann).

— (1993), *Team Roles at Work: A Strategy for Human Resource Management*. Oxford: Butterworth Heinemann.

Bell, D. (1980), '*Brown v. Board of Education* and the interest-convergence dilemma', *Harvard Law Review*, 93, 518–33.

Benham, M. and Murakami-Ramalho, E. (2010), 'Engaging in educational leadership: The generosity of spirit', *International Journal of Leadership in Education*, 13(1), 77–91.

Bidwell, N. (2010), '*Ubuntu* in the Network: Humanness in Social Capital in Rural Africa', *Interactions*, 17(2), 68–71.

Blackmore, J. (1989), 'Educational leadership: A feminist critique and reconstruction', in J. Smyth (ed.), *Critical Perspectives on Educational Leadership*. London: Falmer, pp. 93–129.

— (1999), *Troubling Women*. Buckingham: Open University Press.

— (2010a), 'Policy, practice and purpose in the field of education: A critical review', *Critical Studies in Education*, 51(1), 101–11.

— (2010b), '"The Other Within": Race/gender disruptions to the professional learning of white educational leaders', *International Journal of Leadership in Education*, 13(1), 45–61.

Booth, T. (2005), 'Keeping the future alive: Putting inclusive values into action', *Forum*, 47(2/3), 151–8.

de Botton, A. (2012), *Religion for Atheists*, public lecture at London School of Economics and Political Science, 2 February 2012, available online at: www2.lse. ac.uk/newsAndMedia/videoAndAudio/channels/publicLecturesAndEvents/player. aspx?id=1335 [accessed 8 February 2013].

— (2013), 'Alain de Botton's 10 commandments for atheists', *The Telegraph*, 4 February 2013, available online at: www.telegraph.co.uk/culture/9843244/Alain-de-Bottons-10-Commandments-for-Atheists.html [accessed 8 February 2013].

Bourdieu, P. (1985), 'The social space and the genesis of groups', *Theory and Society*, 14(6), 723–44.

— (1986), 'The forms of capital', in J. G. Richardson (ed.), *Handbook of Theory and Research for the Sociology of Education*. New York: Greenwood Press, pp. 46–58.

— (2000), *Pascalian Meditations*. Cambridge: Polity Press.

— (2005), *Outline of a Theory of Practice*. Cambridge: Cambridge University Press.

Bourdieu, P. and Passeron, J. (2000), *Reproduction in Education, Society, and Culture*. London: Sage Publications.

Brighouse, T. (2008), 'The passionate teacher and the passionate leader in the passionate school', in B. Davies and T. Brighouse (eds), *Passionate Leadership in Education*. London: Sage, pp. 13–31.

British Broadcasting Corporation (2005a), 'Handsworth riots – Twenty years on', available online at: www.bbc.co.uk/birmingham/content/articles/2005/09/05/handsworth_riots_20years_feature.shtml [accessed 10 November 2012].

— (2005b), 'Fear and rumours grip Birmingham', available online at: http://news.bbc. co.uk/1/hi/uk/4373040.stm [accessed 10 November 2012].

— (2011), 'Secondary schools in England given new GCSE target', *BBC News Education and Family*, available online at: www.bbc.co.uk/news/education-13772923 [accessed 28 January 2013].

Brooks, A. and McKinnon, A. (2001), *Gender and the Re-structured University.* Buckingham: Open University Press.

Bush, T. (2007), 'Educational leadership and management: Theory, policy, and practice', *South African Journal of Education*, 27(3), 391–406.

Bush, T., Glover, D., Sood, K. and Cardno, C. (2006), 'Black and minority ethnic leaders in England: A portrait', *School Leadership and Management*, 26(3), 289–305.

Butler, J. (1990), *Gender Trouble.* London: Routledge.

— (2004), *Undoing Gender.* New York: Routledge.

Cairns, J. (2004), 'Morals, ethics and citizenship in contemporary teaching', in R. Gardner, J. Cairns and D. Lawton (eds), *Education for Values* (2nd edn). London: Kogan, pp. 6–24.

Campbell-Stephens, R. (2009), 'Investing in diversity: Changing the face (and heart) of educational leadership', *School Leadership and Management*, 29(3), 321–31.

Cheminais, R. (2011), 'Every child matters but not every child is heard', in G. Czerniawski and W. Kidd (eds), *The Student Voice Handbook.* Bingley: Emerald Group, pp. 45–55.

Cliffe, J. (2011), 'Emotional intelligence: A study of female secondary school headteachers', *Educational Management Administration and Leadership*, 39(2), 205–18.

Cockburn, C. (1985), *Machinery of Dominance: Women, Men and Technical Know-how.* London: Pluto.

Coleman, M. (1996a), 'Barriers to career progress for women in education: The perceptions of female headteachers', *Educational Research*, 38(3), 317–32.

— (1996b), 'The management style of female headteachers', *Educational Management and Administration*, 24(2), 163–74.

— (2000), 'The female secondary headteacher in England and Wales: Leadership and management styles', *Educational Research*, 42(1), 13–27.

— (2001), 'Achievement against the odds: The female secondary headteachers in England and Wales', *School Leadership and Management*, 21(1), 75–100.

— (2002), *Women as Headteachers: Striking the Balance.* Oakhill: Trentham Books Ltd.

— (2003a), 'Gender in educational leadership', in M. Brundrett, N. Burton and R. Smith (eds), *Leadership in Education.* London: Sage, pp. 36–51.

— (2003b), 'Gender and the orthodoxies of leadership', *School Leadership and Management*, 23(3), 325–39.

— (2005a), *Gender and Headship in the 21st Century.* Nottingham: National College for School Leadership.

— (2005b), 'Gender and secondary school leadership', *International Studies in Educational Administration*, 33(2), 3–20.

— (2011), *Women at the Top*. London: Palgrave MacMillan.

Coleman, M. and Campbell-Stevens, R. (2010), 'Perceptions of career progress: The experience of black and minority ethnic school leaders', *School Leadership and Management: Formerly School Organisation*, 30(1), 35–49.

Coleman, M. and Fitzgerald, T. (2008), *International Handbook on the Preparation and Development of School Leaders*, J. Lumby, G. Crow and P. Pashiardis (eds). Abingdon: Routledge, pp. 119–35.

Collard, J. (2001), 'Leadership and gender: An Australian perspective', *Educational Management Administration*, 29(3), 343–55.

Collinson, D. (1992), *Managing the Shop Floor: Subjectivity, Masculinity and Workplace Culture*. New York: W. de Gruyter.

Conley, H. and Jenkins, S. (2011), 'Still "a good job for a woman"? Women teachers' experiences of modernization in England and Wales', *Gender, Work and Organization*, 18(5), 488–507.

Connell, R. (2005), *Masculinities* (2nd edn). Los Angeles, CA: University of California Press.

— (2006), 'Glass ceilings or gendered institutions? Mapping the gender regimes of public sector worksites', *Public Administration Review*, November/December, 837–49.

Cowie, M. and Crawford, M. (2009), 'Headteacher preparation programmes in England and Scotland: Do they make a difference for the first-year head?', *School Leadership & Management*, 29(1), 5–21.

Crenshaw, K. (1991), 'Mapping the margins: Intersectionality, identity politics, and violence against women of color', *Stanford Law Review*, 43(6), 1241–99.

Crenshaw, K., Gotanda, N., Peller, G. and Thomas, K. (eds) (1995), *Critical Race Theory: The Key Writings that Formed the Movement*. New York: New Press.

Cribb, A. and Gewirtz, S. (2003), 'Towards a sociology of just practices', in C. Vincent (ed.), *Social Justice, Education and Identity*. London: RoutledgeFalmer, pp. 15–29.

Cubillo, L. and Brown, M. (2003), 'Women into educational leadership and management: International differences?', *Journal of Educational Administration*, 41(3), 278–91.

Davies, B. (2008), 'Introduction: Passionate leadership', in B. Davies and T. Brighouse (eds), *Passionate Leadership in Education*. London: Sage, pp. 1–9.

Delgado, R. and Stefanic, J. (2001), *Critical Race Theory: An Introduction*. New York: New York University Press.

Department for Children Schools and Families (2009a), *Gender and Education – Mythbusters*. Nottingham: DCSF.

— (2009b), *Gender Issues in School – What Works to Improve Achievement for Boys and Girls*. Nottingham: DCSF.

— (2009c), *Gender and Education: 'Gapbusters'*. Nottingham: DCSF.

— (2009d), *Breaking the Link between Disadvantage and Low Attainment*. Nottingham: DCSF.

Department for Education (2011), *Teachers' Standards*. London: DfE.

— (2012), *School Workforce in England: November 2011*, available online at: www.education.gov.uk/rsgateway/DB/SFR/s001062/index.shtml [accessed 27 April 2012).

Department for Education and Skills (2003a), *Every Child Matters*. Nottingham: DfES.

— (2003b), *Raising Standards and Tackling Workload: A National Agreement*. London: DfES.

— (2004a), *A National Conversation about Personalised Learning*. Nottingham: DfES.

— (2004b), *National Standards for Headteachers*. Nottingham: DfES.

— (2005), *Ethnicity and Education: The Evidence on Minority Ethnic Pupils*. Nottingham: DfES.

Drudy, S., Martin, M., Woods, M. and O'Flynn, J. (2005), *Men and the Classroom*. London: Routledge.

Duffy, E. (1999), 'Leading the creative school', in H. Tomlinson, H. Gunter and P. Smith (eds), *Living Headship: Voices, Values and Vision*. London: Paul Chapman Publishing Company, pp. 105–13.

Edwards, S. and Lyons, G. (1994), 'Female secondary headteachers – An endangered species?', *Management in Education*, 8(2), 7–10.

Erasmus, Z. (2010), 'Contact theory: Too timid for "Race" and racism', *Journal of Social Issues*, 66(2), 387–400.

Fitzgerald, T. (2006), 'Walking between two worlds: Indigenous women and educational leadership', *Educational Management, Administration and Leadership*, 34(2), 201–14.

— (2010), 'Spaces in-between: Indigenous women leaders speak back to dominant discourses and practices in educational leadership', *International Journal of Leadership in Education*, 13(1), 93–105.

Flintham, A. (2008), '"Reservoirs of hope": Sustaining passion in leadership', in B. Davies and T. Brighouse (eds), *Passionate Leadership in Education*. London: Sage, pp. 57–72.

Francis, B. (1999), 'Modernist reductionism or post-structuralist relativism: Can we move on? An evaluation of the arguments in relation to feminist educational research', *Gender and Education*, 11(4), 381–93.

— (2010), 'Re/theorising gender: Female masculinity and male femininity in the classroom?' *Gender and Education*, 22(5), 477–90.

Fraser, N. (2000), 'Rethinking recognition', *New Left Review*, 3, May/June.

— (2007), 'Re-framing justice in a globalising world', in T. Lovell (ed.), *(Mis)recognition, Social Inequality and Social Justice*. Abingdon: Routledge, pp. 17–35.

Frost, N. and Stein, M. (2009), 'Editorial: Outcomes of integrated working with children and young people', *Children and Society*, 23, 315–19.

Fullan, M. (2001), *Leading in a Culture of Change*. San Francisco, CA: Jossey-Bass.

Fuller, K. (2009), 'Women secondary head teachers: Alive and well in Birmingham at the beginning of the twenty-first century', *Management in Education*, 23(1), 19–31.

— (2010), 'Talking about gendered headship: How do women and men working in schools conceive and articulate notions of gender?', *Journal of Educational Administration and History*, 42(4), 363–82.

— (2012), 'Leading with emancipatory intent: Headteachers' approaches to pupil diversity', *Educational Management Administration and Leadership*, 40(6), 672–89.

Fuller, K., Parsons, S., MacNab, N. and Thomas, H. (2013), 'How far is leadership distributed in extended services provision?', *Educational Management Administration and Leadership* (in press).

Gemmill, G. and Oakley, J. (1992), 'Leadership: An alienating social myth?', *Human Relations*, 45(2), 113–29.

General Teaching Council (2004), *The GTC Statement: The Statement of Professional Values and Practice for Teachers*. Birmingham: GTC.

Giddens, A. (1989), *Sociology*. Cambridge: Polity Press.

Gillborn, D. (1990), '*Race*', *Ethnicity and Education*. London: Unwin Hyman Ltd.

— (2005), 'Education policy as an act of white supremacy: Whiteness, critical race theory and education reform', *Journal of Education Policy*, 20(4), 485–505.

— (2006a), 'Critical race theory and education: Racism and anti-racism in educational theory and praxis', *Discourse: Studies in the Cultural Politics of Education*, 27(1), 11–32.

— (2006b), 'Rethinking white supremacy: Who counts in "WhiteWorld"', *Ethnicities*, 6(3), 318–40.

— (2008), 'Coincidence or conspiracy? Whiteness, policy and the persistence of the black/white achievement gap', *Educational Review*, 60(3), 229–48.

— (2010a), 'The colour of numbers: Surveys, statistics and deficit-Thinking about race and class', *Journal of Education Policy*, 25(2), 253–76.

— (2010b), 'The white working class, racism and respectability: Victims, degenerates and interest-convergence', *British Journal of Educational Studies*, 58(1), 3–25.

Gold, A. (1997), '"Power to" or "Power over": Reflections on issues of power raised in development courses for educational managers', paper presented at the *Conference for the European Network for Improving Research and Development in Educational Management*, Orebro, Sweden, 18–21 September.

Gold, A., Evans, J., Earley, P., Halpin, D. and Collarbone, P. (2003), 'Principled principals? Values-driven leadership: Evidence from ten case-studies of "outstanding" school leaders', *Educational Management and Administration*, 31(2), 127–37.

Gorard, S. (2012), 'Who is eligible for free school meals? Characterising free school meals as a measure of disadvantage in England', *British Educational Research Journal*, 38(6), 1003–17.

Grace, G. (1995), *School Leadership*. London: The Falmer Press.

— (2000), 'Research and the challenges of contemporary school leadership: The contribution of critical scholarship', *British Journal of Educational Studies*, 48(3), 231–47.

Gray, H. (1989), 'Gender considerations in school management: Masculine and feminine leadership styles', in C. Riches and C. Morgan (eds), *Human Resource Management*. Milton Keynes: Open University Press, pp. 110–23.

— (1993), 'Gender issues in management training', in J. Ozga (ed.), *Women in Educational Management*. Buckingham: Open University Press, pp. 106–15.

Greenfield, T. (1993), 'The decline and fall of science in educational administration', in T. Greenfield and P. Ribbins (eds), *Greenfield on Educational Administration: Towards a Humane Science*. London: Routledge, pp. 134–61.

Grogan, M. and Shakeshaft, C. (2011), *Women and Educational Leadership*. San Francisco, CA: Jossey-Boss.

Gronn, P. (2007), 'Interviewing leaders: Penetrating the romance', in A. Briggs and M. Coleman (eds), *Research Methods in Educational Leadership and Management*. London: Sage, pp. 189–204.

Grosvenor, I. and Myers, K. (2006), 'Progressivism, control and correction: Local education authorities and educational policy in twentieth-century England', *Paedagogica Historica: International Journal of the History of Education*, 42(1/2), 225–47.

Grundy, S. (1993), 'Educational leadership as emancipatory praxis', in J. Blackmore and J. Kenway (eds), *Gender Matters in Educational Administration and Policy*. London: The Falmer Press, pp. 165–77.

Gunter, H. (2002), 'Purposes and positions in the field of education management: Putting Bourdieu to work', *Educational Management & Administration*, 30(2), 7–26.

— (2003), 'Intellectual histories in the field of education management in the UK', *International Journal of Leadership in Education: Theory and Practice*, 6(4), 335–49.

— (2006a), 'Knowledge production in the field of educational leadership: A place for intellectual histories', *Journal of Educational Administration and History*, 38(2), 201–15.

— (2006b), 'Educational leadership and the challenge of diversity', *Educational Administration and Leadership*, 34(2), 257–68.

Gunter, H. and Rayner, S. (2007), 'Modernizing the school workforce in England: Challenging transformation and leadership', *Leadership*, 3, 47–64.

Gunter, H. and Ribbins, P. (2003), 'Challenging orthodoxy in school leadership studies: Knowers, knowing and knowledge?', *School Leadership & Management: Formerly School Organisation*, 23(2), 129–47.

Habermas, J. (1974), *Theory and Practice*. Boston: Beacon.

Hall, V. (1996), *Dancing on the Ceiling*. London: Paul Chapman Publishing Ltd.

— (1997), 'Dusting off the phoenix. Gender and educational leadership revisited', *Educational Management and Administration*, 25(3), 309–24.

— (1999), 'Gender and education management: Duel or dialogue?' in T. Bush, L. Bell, R. Bolam, R. Glatter and P. Ribbins (eds), *Educational Management: Redefining Theory, Policy, and Practice*. London: Paul Chapman Publishing Ltd, pp. 155–65.

Halliday-Bell, D., Jennings, D., Kennard, M., McKay, J., Reid, H. and Walter, N. (2008), *Mission Possible: Strategies for Managing Headship*. Nottingham: National College for School Leadership, pp. 1–30.

Hanchard, M. (2003), 'Acts of misrecognition: Transnational black politics, anti-imperialism and the ethnocentrisms of Pierre Bourdieu and Loïc Wacquant', *Theory, Culture & Society*, 20(5), 5–29.

Hatcher, R. (2005), 'The distribution of leadership and power in schools', *British Journal of Sociology of Education*, 26(2), 253–68.

Haydon, G. (2007), *Values for Educational Leadership*. London: Sage.

Haywood, C. and Mac an Ghaill, M. (2003), *Men and Masculinities*. Buckingham: Open University Press.

Heck, R. and Hallinger, P. (2005), 'The study of educational leadership and management: Where does the field stand today?', *Educational Management Administration & Leadership*, 33(2), 229–44.

HM Government (2010a), *The Equality Act*, available online at: www.legislation.gov.uk/ukpga/2010/15/part/1 [accessed 13 January 2013].

— (2010b), *The Coalition: Our Programme for Government*. London: Crown Copyright.

— (2011), *Prevent Strategy*. Crown Copyright, The Stationery Office, available at: www.homeoffice.gov.uk/publications/counter-terrorism/prevent/prevent-strategy/prevent-strategy-review?view=Binary [accessed 9 May 2012].

Hobbs, G. and Vignoles, A. (2010), 'Is children's free school meal "eligibility" a good proxy for family income', *British Educational Research Journal*, 36(4), 673–90.

Hodgkinson, C . (1983), *The Philosophy of Leadership*. Oxford: Basil Blackwell.

— (1991), *Educational Leadership: The Moral Art*. Albany, NY: Suny Press.

Hustler, D., Brighouse, T. and Ruddock, J. (eds) (1995), *Heeding Heads: Secondary Heads and Commentators in Dialogue*. London: David Fulton.

Jackson, S. and Scott, S. (eds) (2002) *Gender: A Sociological Reader*. London: Routledge.

Jirasinghe, D. and Lyons, G. (1996), *The Competent Head*. London: The Falmer Press.

Johnson, L. and Campbell-Stephens, R. (2010), 'Investing in diversity in London schools: Leadership preparation for black and global majority educators', *Urban Education*, 45(6), 840–70.

— (2013), 'Developing the next generation of black and global majority leaders for London schools', *Journal of Educational Administration*, 51(1), 24–39.

Kingdon, G. and Cassen, R. (2010), 'Ethnicity and low achievement in English schools', *British Educational Research Journal*, 36(3), 403–31.

Lingard, B. and Christie, P. (2003), 'Leading theory: Bourdieu and the field of educational leadership. An introduction and overview to this special issue', *International Journal of Leadership in Education: Theory and Practice*, 6(4), 317–33.

Lingard, B. and Douglas, P. (1999), *Men Engaging Feminisms: Pro-feminism, Backlashes and Schooling*. Buckingham: Open university Press.

Local Government Act (1988), c. 9, Part IV, Miscellaneous, Section 28, available online at: www.legislation.gov.uk/ukpga/1988/9/section/28 [accessed 13 February 2013].

Lovell, T. (ed.) (2007), *(Mis)recognition, Social Inequality and Social Justice*. Abingdon: Routledge.

Lumby, J. with Coleman, M. (2007), *Leadership and Diversity*. London: Sage.

Lupton, B. (2006), 'Explaining men's entry into female-concentrated occupations: Issues of masculinity and social class', *Gender, Work and Organization*, 13(2), 103–28.

Lupton, R. (2011), '"No change there then!"(?): The onward march of school markets and competition', *Journal of Educational Administration and History*, 43(4), 309–23.

Lyman, L., Strachan, J. and Lazaridou, A. (eds) (2012), *Shaping Social Justice Leadership*. Lanham: Rowman and Littlefield.

Mac an Ghaill, M. (1994), *The Making of Men*. Buckingham: Open University Press.

MacBeath, J. (2007), 'Leadership as a subversive activity', *Journal of Educational Administration*, 45(3), 242–64.

Macpherson, W. (1999), *The Stephen Lawrence Inquiry*, CM 4262-I. London: The Stationery Office.

Maguire, M. (2005), '"Not footprints behind but footsteps forward": Working class women who teach', *Gender and Education*, 17(1), 3–18.

Marshall, C. (2004), 'Social justice challenges to educational administration: Introduction to a special issue', *Educational Administration Quarterly*, 40(1), 5–15.

Martino, W. (2008), 'Male teachers as role models: Addressing issues of masculinity, pedagogy and the re-masculinization of schooling', *Curriculum Inquiry*, 38(2), 189–223.

Maylor, U., Ross, A. and Hutchings, M. (2005), 'National policy and practitioner practice in the UK', in A. Ross (ed.), *Teaching Citizenship*. London: Children's Identity and Citizenship in Europe, pp. 59–66, available online at: http://learning.londonmet.ac.uk/cice/docs/2005-59.pdf [accessed 16 June 2013].

McKenley, J. and Gordon, G. (2002), *Challenge Plus: The Experience of Black and Minority Ethnic School Leaders*. Nottingham: National College for School Leadership.

McKnight, D. and Chandler, P. (2012), 'The complicated conversation of class and race in social and curricular analysis: An examination of Pierre Bourdieu's interpretative framework in relation to race', *Educational Philosophy and Theory*, 44(S1), 74–97.

McLay, M. and Brown, M. (2000), 'The under-representation of women in senior management in UK independent secondary schools', *The International Journal of Educational Management*, 14(3), 101–8.

McLean, C., Lewis, S., Copeland, J., Lintern, S. and O'Neill, B. (1997), 'Masculinity and the culture of engineering', *Australian Journal of Engineering Education*, 7(2), 143–56.

McLeod, J. (2005), 'Feminists re-reading Bourdieu: Old debates and new questions about gender habitus and gender change', *Theory and Research in Education*, 3(11), 11–30.

McNamara, O., Howson, J., Gunter, H. and Fryers, A. (2009), *The Leadership Aspirations and Careers of Black and Minority Ethnic Teachers*. Birmingham: NASUWT.

— (2010), *No Job for a Woman? The Impact of Gender in School Leadership*. Birmingham: NASUWT.

McNamara, O., Howson, J., Gunter, H., Sprigade, A. and Onat-Stelma, Z. (2008), *Women Teachers' Careers*. Birmingham: NASUWT.

Mensah, K. and Kiernan, K. (2010), 'Gender differences in educational attainment: Influences of the family environment', *British Educational Research Journal*, 36(2), 239–60.

Mistry, M. and Sood, K. (2010), 'English as an additional language: Assumptions and challenges', *Management in Education*, 24(3), 111–14.

Moore, A., George, R. and Halpin, D. (2002), 'The developing role of the headteacher in English schools', *Educational Management and Administration*, 30(2), 175–88.

Moreau, M.-P., Osgood, J. and Halsall, A. (2007), 'Making sense of the glass ceiling in schools: An exploration of women teachers' discourses', *Gender and Education*, 19(2), 237–53.

— (2008), 'Equal opportunities policies in English schools: Towards greater gender equality in the teaching workforce?', *Gender, Work and Organization*, 15(6), 553–78.

Msila, V. (2008), '*Ubuntu* and school leadership', *Journal of Education*, 44, 67–84.

National College for School Leadership (2008), *Female Heads at All Time High*, available online at: www.ncsl.org.uk [accessed April 2008].

National Joint Council for Local Government Services (NJC), *Pay Scales (England and Wales) 2008–2009*, available online at: *NASUWT,* www.nasuwt.org. uk/TrainingEventsandPublications/NASUWTPublications/Publications/ NJCforlocalgovernmentservices2007–20089/index.htm [accessed 28 January 2013].

National Union of Teachers (2012), 'Pay calculator', available online at: *NUT,* www. teachers.org.uk/pay-calculator/leadership [accessed 20 December 2012].

Office for National Statistics (2011), *Household Questionnaire,* available online at: www. ons.gov.uk/ons/guide-method/census/2011/how-our-census-works/how-we-took-the-2011-census/how-we-collected-the-information/questionnaires--delivery--completion-and-return/2011-census-questions/index.html [accessed 16 June 2013].

— (2012a), *Statistical Bulletin: 2011 Annual Survey of Hours and Earnings (SOC 2000)*, available online at: www.ons.gov.uk/ons/rel/ashe/annual-survey-of-hours-and-earnings/ashe-results-2011/ashe-statistical-bulletin-2011.html [accessed 11 December 2012].

— (2012b), *Neighbourhood Statistics*, available online at: www.neighbourhood.statistics. gov.uk [accessed 3 February 2013].

Office for Standards in Education (2013), *The Framework for School Inspection*. Manchester: Ofsted.

Ogunbawo, D. (2012), 'Developing black and minority ethnic leaders: The case for customized programmes', *Educational Management Administration and Leadership*, 40(2), 158–74.

Osler, A. (1997), *The Education and Careers of Black Teachers: Changing Identities, Changing Lives*. Open University Press: Buckingham.

Ouston, J. (1993), *Women in Education Management*. Harlow: Longman.

Oxford Dictionaries. Available online at: http://oxforddictionaries.com/definition/english/ethnicity [accessed 15 November 2012].

Oxford English Dictionary (OED). Available online at: www.oed.com/view/Entry/64791?redirectedFrom=ethnicity& [accessed 15 November 2012].

Ozga, J. (ed.) (1993), *Women in Educational Management*. Buckingham: Open University Press.

Paton, G. (2010), 'A-level results: Gender gap narrowing', *The Telegraph*, available online at: www.telegraph.co.uk/education/educationnews/7954079/A-level-results-gender-gap-narrowing.html [accessed 22 December 2012].

— (2011), 'Teachers must "uphold British values" to work in schools', *The Telegraph*, available online at: www.telegraph.co.uk/education/educationnews/8638501/Teachers-must-uphold-British-values-to-work-in-schools.html [accessed 19 January 2013].

Qualifications and Curriculum Authority (QCA) (2007), *The National Curriculum*. London: QCA.

Race, R. (2011), *Multiculturalism and Education*. London: Continuum.

Raffo, C. (2011), 'Barker's ecology of disadvantage and educational equity: Issues of redistribution and recognition', *Journal of Educational Administration and History*, 43(4), 325–43.

Raphael Reed, L. (2001), '"Re-searching, re-finding, re-making": Exploring the unconscious as a pedagogic and research practice', in B. Francis and C. Skelton (eds), *Investigating Gender: Contemporary Perspectives in Education*. Buckingham: Open University Press, pp. 77–90.

Ratcliffe, R. (2012), 'Gender gap in university applications widens further after fees rise', *The Guardian*, available online at: www.guardian.co.uk/education/2012/dec/13/gender-gap-university-applications-widens [accessed 22 December 2012].

Reay, D. (1995), '"They employ cleaners to do that": Habitus in the primary classroom', *British Journal of Sociology of Education*, 16(3), 353–71.

— (1997), 'Feminist theory, habitus, and social class: Disrupting notions of classlessness', *Women's Studies International Forum*, 20(2), 225–33.

— (2000), 'A useful extension of Bourdieu's conceptual framework?: Emotional capital as a way of understanding mothers' involvement in their children's education', *The Sociological Review*, 48(4), 568–85.

— (2004), '"It's all becoming a habitus": Beyond the habitual use of habitus in educational research', *British Journal of Sociology of Education*, 25(4), 431–44.

Reay, D. and Ball, S. (2000), 'Essentials of female management', *Educational Management Administration and Leadership*, 28(2), 145–59.

Rees, P., Wohland, P., Norman, P. and Boden, P. (2012), 'Ethnic population projections for the UK, 2001–2051', *Journal of Population Research*, 29, 45–89.

Regan, H. (1990), 'Not for women only: School administration as a feminist activity', *Teachers College Record*, 91(4), 565–77.

Reid, K. (2010), 'Management of school attendance in the UK: A strategic analysis',
    Educational Management Administration & Leadership, 38(1), 88–106.

Ribbins, P. (2007), 'Interviews in educational research: Conversations with a purpose',
    in A. Briggs and M. Coleman (eds), *Research Methods in Educational Leadership and
    Management*. London: Sage, pp. 207–23.

Ribbins, P. and Marland, M. (1994), *Headship Matters*. Harlow: Longman.

Richardson, H. (2011), 'Why boys trail further behind girls at GCSE top grades',
    British Broadcasting Corporation, available online at: www.bbc.co.uk/news/
    education-14664916 [accessed 22 December 2012].

Roper, M. (1994), *Masculinity and the British Organisation Man since 1945*. Oxford:
    Oxford University Press.

Rottmann, C. (2006), 'Queering educational leadership from the inside out',
    International Journal of Leadership in Education: Theory and Practice, 9(1), 1–20.

Russell, H. (1999), 'Friends in low places: Gender, unemployment, and sociability',
    Work, Employment and Society, 13(2), 205–25.

Sargent, P. (2001), *Real Men or Real Teachers? Contradictions in the Lives of Men
    Elementary School Teachers*. Harriman: Men's Studies Press.

Sauntson, H. and Simpson, K. (2011), 'Investigating sexuality discourses in the UK
    secondary English curriculum', *Journal of Homosexuality*, 58(6–7), 953–73.

Scott, J. (1988), 'Deconstructing equality-versus-difference: Or, the uses of
    poststructuralist theory for feminism', *Feminist Studies*, 14(1), 32–50.

Sergiovanni, T. (1992), *Moral Leadership: Getting to the Heart of School Improvement*.
    San Francisco, CA: Jossey-Bass.

Shah, S. (2006a), 'Educational leadership: An Islamic perspective', *British Educational
    Research Journal*, 32(3), 347–63.

— (2006b), 'Leading multiethnic schools: A new understanding of Muslim youth
    identity', *Educational Management Administration and Leadership*, 34(2), 215–37.

— (2008), 'Leading multi-ethnic schools: Adjustments in concepts and practices for
    engaging with diversity', *British Journal of Sociology of Education*, 29(5), 523–36.

— (2009), 'Muslim learners in English schools: A challenge for school leaders', *Oxford
    Review of Education*, 35(4), 523–40.

— (2010), 'Re-thinking educational leadership: Exploring the impact of cultural and
    belief systems', *International Journal of Leadership in Education*, 13(1), 27–44.

Shah, S. and Conchar, C. (2009), 'Why single-sex schools? Discourses of culture/faith
    and achievement', *Cambridge Journal of Education*, 39(2), 191–204.

Shain, F. (2000), 'Managing to lead: Women managers in the further education sector',
    Journal of Further and Higher Education, 24(2), 217–30.

Shakeshaft, C. (1987), *Women in Education Administration*. New York: Sage.

Shields, C. and Edwards, M. (2005), *Dialogue is Not Just Talk*. New York: Peter Lang.

Skelton, C. (2002), 'The "feminisation of schooling" or "re-masculinising" primary
    education?', *International Studies in Sociology of Education*, 12(1), 77–96.

Skelton, C. and Francis, B. (2009), *Feminism and 'The Schooling Scandal'*. Abingdon:
    Routledge.

Skelton, C., Francis, B. and Valkanova, Y. (2007), *Breaking Down the Stereotypes: Gender and Achievement in Schools*. Manchester: Equal Opportunities Commission.

Smith, E. (2003). 'Understanding underachievement: An investigation into the differential attainment of secondary school pupils', *British Journal of Sociology of Education*, 24(5), 575–86.

Smith, J. (2011), 'Agency and female teachers' career decisions: A life history study of 40 women', *Educational Management Administration and Leadership*, 39(1), 7–24.

Sobehart, H. (ed.) (2009), *Women Leading Education across the Continents: Sharing the Spirit, Fanning the Flame*. Lanham, MD: Rowman and Littlefield with the American Association of School Administrators.

Stevens, P. (2007), 'Researching race/ethnicity and educational inequality in English secondary schools: A critical review of the research literature between1980 and 2005', *Review of Educational Research*, 77(2), 147–85.

Stevenson, H. (2007), 'A case study in leading schools for social justice: When morals and markets collide', *Journal of Educational Administration*, 45(6), 769–81.

Stonewall. *Education for All*, available online at: www.stonewall.org.uk/about_us/2532. asp [accessed 13 February 2012].

Strain, M. (2009), 'Some ethical and cultural implications of the leadership "turn" in education: On the distinction between performance and performativity', *Educational Management Administration and Leadership*, 37(1), 67–84.

Strand, S. (2011), 'The limits of social class in explaining ethnic gaps in educational attainment', *British Educational Research Journal*, 37(2), 197–229.

Tate, W. F. (1997). 'Critical race theory and education: History, theory, and implications', in M. W. Apple (ed.), *Review of Research in Education*, 22. Washington, DC: American Educational Research Association, pp. 195–247.

Taylor, C. (1994), *Multiculturalism*. Princeton, NJ: Princeton University Press.

Thomson, P. (2005), 'Bringing Bourdieu to policy sociology: Codification, misrecognition and exchange value in the UK context', *Journal of Education Policy*, 20(6), 741–58.

— (2010), 'Headteacher autonomy: A sketch of a Bourdieuian field analysis of position and practice', *Critical Studies in Education*, 51(1), 5–20.

Thornton, M. and Bricheno, P. (2000), 'Primary school teachers' careers in England and Wales: The relationship between gender, role, position and promotion aspirations', *Pedagogy, Culture & Society*, 8(2), 187–206.

— (2006), *Missing Men in Education*. Stoke-on-Trent: Trentham Books.

Tolson, A. (1977), *The Limits of Masculinity*. London: Tavistock.

Tomlinson, H., Gunter, H. and Smith, P. (eds) (1999), *Living Headship: Voices, Values and Vision*. London: Paul Chapman Publishing Company.

United Nations (1948), *The Universal Declaration of Human Rights*, available online at: www.un.org/en/documents/udhr/index.shtml [accessed 8 February 2013].

Vincent, C. (2003), *Social Justice, Education and Identity*. London: RoutledgeFalmer.

Watts, R. (1998), 'From lady teacher to professional: A case study of some of the first headteachers of girls' secondary school in England', *Educational Management Administration and Leadership*, 26(4), 339–51.

Webster, R., Blatchford, P., Bassett, P., Brown, P., Martin, C. and Russell, A. (2010), 'Double standards and first principles: Framing teaching assistant support for pupils with special educational needs', *European Journal of Special Needs Education*, 25(4), 319–36.

White, N. (2010), 'Indigenous Australian women's leadership: Stayin' strong against the post-colonial tide', *International Journal of Leadership in Education*, 13(1), 7–25.

Whitehead, S. (2001), 'The invisible gendered subject: Men in education management', *Journal of Gender Studies*, 10(1), 67–82.

Whitehead, S. and Barrett, F. (eds) (2001), *The Masculinities Reader*. Cambridge: Polity Press.

Wilkins, C. and Lall, R. (2011), '"You've got to be tough and I'm trying": Black and minority ethnic student teachers' experiences of initial teacher education', *Race, Ethnicity and Education*, 14(3), 365–86.

Willis, P. (1979), 'Shop-floor culture, masculinity and the wage form', in J. Clarke, C. Critcher and R. Johnson (eds), *Working Class Culture: Studies in History and Theory*. London: Hutchinson, in association with the CCCS, University of Birmingham.

Wilson, M. (ed.) (1997), *Women in Educational Management: A European Perspective*. London: Paul Chapman Publishing Ltd.

Wong, K. (1998), 'Leading schools in a global era: A cultural perspective', *Peabody Journal of Education*, 73(2), 106–25.

Woods, P. (2005), *Democratic Leadership in Education*. London: Paul Chapman.

Woods, P., Bennett N., Harvey, J. and Wise, C. (2004), 'Variabilities and dualities in distributed leadership: Findings from a systematic literature review', *Educational Management Administration & Leadership*, 32(4), 439–57.

Wright, N. (2003), 'Principled "bastard leadership"? A rejoinder to Gold, Evans, Earley, Halpin and Collarbone', *Educational Management and Administration*, 31(2), 139–44.

Wrigley, T., Lingard, B. and Thomson, P. (2012), 'Pedagogies of transformation: Keeping hope alive in troubled times', *Critical Studies in Education*, 53(1), 95–108.

Ylimaki, R. and McClain, L. (2009), 'Wisdom-centred educational leadership', *International Journal of Leadership in Education: Theory and Practice*, 12(1), 13–33.

Zamudio, M., Russell, C., Rios, F. and Bridgeman, J. (2011), *Critical Race Theory Matters: Education and Ideology*. New York: Routledge.

Index